Persuading Judges

ALSO BY C.J. WILLIAMS
AND FROM MCFARLAND

Sentencing Advocacy: Principles and Strategy (2022)

How Not to Rob a Bank: And Other Stories from 20 Years as a Federal Prosecutor (Exposit, 2022)

Persuading Judges

*Principles and Strategies
for Effective Advocacy
in Trial Courts*

C.J. WILLIAMS
and LEONARD T. STRAND

McFarland & Company, Inc., Publishers
Jefferson, North Carolina

LIBRARY OF CONGRESS CATALOGING-IN-PUBLICATION DATA

Names: Williams, C.J., 1963– author | Strand, Leonard T., 1965– author
Title: Persuading judges : principles and strategies for effective advocacy
   in trial courts / C.J. Williams and Leonard T. Strand.
Description: Jefferson : McFarland & Company, Inc., Publishers, 2026. |
   Includes bibliographical references and index.
Identifiers: LCCN 2026001735 | ISBN 9781476699806 paperback ∞
   ISBN 9781476658261 ebook
Subjects: LCSH: Trial practice—United States | Judges—United States |
   Practice of law—United States
Classification: LCC KF8915 .W55 2026
LC record available at https://lccn.loc.gov/2026001735

ISBN (print) 978-1-4766-9980-6
ISBN (ebook) 978-1-4766-5826-1

© 2026 C.J. Williiams and Leonard T. Strand. All rights reserved

No part of this book may be reproduced or transmitted in any form
or by any means, electronic or mechanical, including photocopying
or recording, or by any information storage and retrieval system,
without permission in writing from the publisher.

Front cover image: © Gorodenkoff/Shutterstock.

Printed in the United States of America

McFarland & Company, Inc., Publishers
   Box 611, Jefferson, North Carolina 28640
      www.mcfarlandpub.com

Table of Contents

Preface	1
Introduction	3
ONE. The Evolving Trend of Litigation	11
A. Vanishing Jury Trials	12
B. Increasingly Rare Appellate Oral Arguments	14
C. Increase in Motions Practice	15
D. The Relative Finality of District Court Judge Decisions	16
E. Conclusion	17
TWO. The History of Legal Advocacy Pedagogy	18
A. Development of Appellate Advocacy Programs	19
B. Development of Trial Advocacy Programs	20
C. Advocacy Courses in Law School	21
D. Conflicting Timelines	22
E. The Absence of Programs and Education for Persuading Judges	22
THREE. How Judges, Jurors, and Appellate Panels Differ	25
A. Differences in Context	27
B. The Decision-Maker	49
C. Conclusion	57

Table of Contents

FOUR. The Art of Advocacy	58
A. Methods of Advocacy	58
B. Means of Advocacy	60
C. Conclusion	61
FIVE. Methods and Means of Persuading Judges	63
A. Methods of Effectively Persuading Judges	63
B. Means of Effectively Persuading Judges	70
C. Ten Practice Pointers	81
SIX. Persuading Judges in Different Settings	86
Part One: The Settings	87
A. Motions and Hearings	87
B. Bench Trials (and Quasi Bench Trials)	90
C. Jury Trials	91
D. Quasi Appellate Review Proceedings	92
E. Conclusion	92
Part Two: Effective Advocacy to Judges in Detail	93
A. Advocacy to Judges in Motions Practice	93
B. Advocacy to Judges in Bench Trials	118
C. Advocacy to Judges in Jury Trials	135
SEVEN. Teaching Integrated Legal Advocacy	151
A. Rethinking Legal Advocacy Training	152
B. A Proposal for an Integrated Legal Advocacy Program	153
Conclusion	157
Chapter Notes	159
Bibliography	179
Index	185

Preface

This book addresses effective advocacy to trial court judges and explains how such advocacy differs from advocacy to a jury or to a panel of appellate judges. As federal district court judges who spent many years as trial attorneys, we had a general understanding that trying a case or arguing a motion to a judge is not the same as trying a case to a group of jurors (or presenting an appellate argument to a panel of judges). We have both presided over bench trials in which it was obvious that the attorneys did not know how to adjust their presentations to account for the fact that the jury box was empty. Similarly, we have regularly observed oral and written advocacy during motion practice that reflects a limited understanding of the trial judge's experience, time demands, and preexisting knowledge of the facts and law.

After discussing our common experiences and doing some investigation, we discovered a likely cause of this problem: Most lawyers have received little or no training about effective advocacy to a trial court judge. As we will discuss in this book, law schools provide training in appellate advocacy and offer trial advocacy programs that focus on jury trials. Organizations that provide trial advocacy courses for practicing attorneys focus on jury trials. Books and articles about effective legal advocacy tend to address either appellate practice or jury trials.

We dug deeper by exploring the many books, articles, courses, and other training aids available to law students and practicing attorneys. We were surprised to discover that very few resources exist to educate attorneys about the specific skills and tactics necessary for effective advocacy to trial court judges. While some trial advocacy texts address the topic of bench trials, for example, they tend to do so in a cursory fashion.[1] We were unable to locate a single, authoritative source that focuses on effective advocacy to trial court judges. We found this to be surprising, as it is a crucial skill. The number of jury trials have plummeted in the last 100 years, and there has been a steady decrease in appellate courts granting

Preface

oral arguments. Indeed, most trial attorneys will spend much more time during their careers attempting to persuade trial court judges, whether through motion practice or bench trials, than attempting to persuade jurors or appellate court judges.

We were not the first to notice this gap in the resources available to trial attorneys.[2] In deciding to address this topic, it is our hope that readers will benefit from our perspectives as trial court judges and former trial attorneys. As we will attempt to explain, there are significant differences between presenting a case or motion to a trial court judge and presenting a case to a jury or an argument to appellate judges. We are convinced that attorneys who understand those differences, and adjust for them, will be in a better position to advocate effectively on behalf of their clients.

Introduction

We begin this book with the premise that the skills involved in effectively persuading a judge are fundamentally and materially different from those involved in persuading either a jury or a panel of appellate judges. The context in which attorneys engage in advocacy before judges, juries, and appellate panels are significantly dissimilar in many ways. Likewise, judges, jurors, and appellate judges differ as decision-makers in a myriad of ways. In practice, though, most attorneys argue to judges as they would to juries, or as they would before an appellate panel. And more often than not, they do so unpersuasively.

Practices and methods that may constitute effective advocacy before a jury are not always effective with a judge, sometimes can be quite ineffective, and indeed, in some instances may be counterproductive. What could be very persuasive when arguing to a judge, on the other hand, may constitute impermissible argument before a jury. Similarly, the style of advocacy effective in a formal, timed legal argument before a panel of appellate judges on a cold record may not be as effective before a district court judge in a more informal setting where facts are in dispute and there exists an opportunity to engage in a conversation with the judge. In contrast, an attorney's more informal and free-flowing verbal engagement with a district judge may appear improper or incongruent in the more formal and structured setting of an appellate courtroom.

The skills lawyers use to persuade jurors are only marginally transferable and effective with district judges. Likewise, the skills that make for effective appellate advocacy, while similar, still differ in many material ways from those that are the most effective for persuading judges. Effective advocacy to judges involves and requires its own discipline and skill set.

There are fundamental reasons for why advocacy skills effective with jurors and appellate panels are not directly transferable to persuading judges. Judges differ from jurors in education, training, and reasoning.

Introduction

Judges have access to facts jurors often lack due to evidence rules. Through their training and experiences, judges have knowledge of the law most jurors lack. Judges also arrive at their decisions differently because they make their decisions alone and not as part of a group decision-making process. Lawyers talk at jurors; they can talk with judges.

Similarly, judges sitting alone at the district court level differ from their counterparts on the appellate bench in many material ways. District judges deal with evolving and developing facts, while appellate judges work off a cold record. District judges reach their decisions alone and write their opinions by themselves (perhaps aided by law clerks), while appellate judges reach their decisions through a group decision-making process and their written opinions are the results of a collaborative process among a panel of appellate judges. Lawyers appearing in appellate courtrooms are on the clock, their time to talk dictated by yellow and red lights, while lawyers appearing in trial courtrooms are limited only by the judge's busy schedule. And so on.

Unfortunately, there has been little thought given to the differences between effective advocacy before judges as opposed to before a jury or a panel of appellate judges. Law school pedagogy has historically been, and continues to be, devoted to teaching budding lawyers the skills of appellate advocacy and, to some extent, jury trial advocacy. For reasons that will be explained in this book, law schools have placed an emphasis on teaching appellate advocacy as a core part of law students' first- or second-year curriculum. Appellate advocacy has been a required course used by law schools to teach students both written and oral advocacy skills. Appellate advocacy programs are focused on teaching students the skills of appellate brief writing and persuading a panel of judges in a timed and structured oral argument setting. Trial advocacy, in contrast, is an elective course most law schools offer for those students who want to become litigators. These trial advocacy programs are almost entirely focused on teaching the skills involved in persuading jurors.[1] In short, law schools primarily provide opportunities for students to learn the art of legal persuasion through appellate advocacy classes in the first instance, and secondarily through jury trial advocacy programs.

Similarly, professional advocacy programs for practicing attorneys focus on teaching students the skills of presenting evidence to and persuading juries. Several organizations, such as the National Institute for Trial Advocacy and the United States Department of Justice, offer practicing attorneys the opportunity to hone their trial advocacy skills, and a few offer similar classes on appellate advocacy. Books abound providing

Introduction

advice and inside tips to lawyers on the secrets of persuading jurors through effective advocacy skills.

In stark contrast, few law schools or professional organizations exert any effort in teaching students how to effectively advocate to district judges. This oversight is astounding, given that the vast majority of daily in-court litigation involves lawyers speaking in front of, and trying to persuade, individual district judges. Fewer and fewer cases are resolved through jury trials these days. And fewer still are the lawyers who regularly appear before appellate panels. Very little time or attention is devoted, however, to teaching the skills involved with advocacy to a district judge—judge advocacy, if you will. And there is a difference. As we will discuss, the skills taught in trial advocacy and appellate advocacy courses have limited application to advocating to a district court judge, particularly when that judge is serving in a fact-finding capacity.

In addition to an absence of courses teaching the skills involved in persuading judges, there is also an absence of written material. There are legions of books and articles about trial advocacy, but they all focus almost exclusively on advocating to juries.[2] They seldom mention bench trials or explore how advocacy skills might need to be modified when trying to persuade a judge instead of a jury. There is also a plethora of books and articles on appellate advocacy, that is, advocating to appellate judges. Unlike jury trial advocacy and appellate advocacy, there is a dearth of anything written on the topic of persuading judges.

Even a book promisingly titled MAKING YOUR CASE: THE ART OF PERSUADING JUDGES, by Antonin Scalia and Bryan A. Garner (Thompson/West 2008), is almost exclusively focused on persuading appellate judges. Though there are passing references in a half dozen places to district court judges, the book overwhelmingly discusses advocacy in the context of appellate litigation. Given the lead author was a justice of the United States Supreme Court and never served as a district court judge, that focus is understandable, of course.

In short, both academia and professional organizations have focused on teaching and developing the skills of advocating to juries and to appellate panels, with little or no emphasis placed on advocating to trial judges. Yet, the ability to effectively advocate to a judge has never been more important than it is today. In the last century, the number of jury trials has plummeted. Similarly, during this same time period appellate courts have cut in half the number of times they grant oral argument. Meanwhile, the number of hearings before lower-court judges, and the number of cases

Introduction

resolved through motions practice before these judges, has increased substantially. Increasingly, especially in civil matters but also in criminal prosecutions, cases are decided by judges ruling on a wide variety of motions. Judges dispose of criminal cases when ruling on motions to suppress evidence and to dismiss indictments, while in civil cases judges grant dispositive motions to dismiss or for summary judgment. Importantly, attorneys also frequently advocate to judges in connection with a wide variety of non-dispositive motions and other proceedings. Judges often hold hearings on motions, while in other instances they rule on the pleadings. Some hearings involve the presentation of evidence and judicial factfinding, such as with motions to suppress evidence or sentencing hearings in criminal cases. Other hearings may involve purely legal arguments. The reality, then, is that attorneys spend much more time advocating to judges than they ever do advocating to jurors or appellate judges. The day-to-day, practical experience of litigation involves frequently attempting to persuade a judge, not a jury and not an appellate panel.

Also of importance is the fact that, as a practical matter, a district judge's decision on a disputed matter is very likely to be the final answer. Although litigants have the right to seek review by appellate courts, parties can rarely appeal a judge's decision until final judgment. Moreover, because of the discretion afforded judges, parties rarely prevail on appeal, as we will discuss in more detail in the next chapter. The point here is that because most decisions judges make are the final word on the matter, knowing how to effectively persuade judges is critical.

This book seeks to fill the gap and address the overlooked topic of effective legal advocacy to judges. When we first wrote on this topic in a law review article,[3] we found there wasn't even a term in academia or the literature to describe the act of advocating to lower-court judges. In the absence of a term, in that article we coined the term "judicial advocacy" to describe the skill and practice of advocating before such judges. Upon further reflection, however, we tried to simplify the term to "judge advocacy." The term more precisely describes the concept of persuading a single judge, whereas the term "judicial advocacy" could seemingly encompass persuading a group of appellate judges as well. The proper term remains elusive, however, as both judicial advocacy and judge advocacy suggests advocacy by judges as opposed to advocacy to judges. So, we will avoid trying to label the skill and instead refer generally to persuading judges.

In this book, we have generally used the titles "district court judge," "district judge," or simply "judge" instead of "trial judge" to recognize one of the premises of this book—that the decreasing number of trials and

Introduction

appellate arguments mandate a greater emphasis on persuading judges—but also to emphasize that a large part of advocacy occurs before judges outside trial settings. Indeed, we hesitate to label judges at the district court level, like ourselves, as "trial judges" or "trial-level judges" when the reality is that we preside over a decreasing number of trials each year. It is akin to the change in terminology adopted by many attorneys by moving away from calling themselves "trial attorneys," and instead using the broader term "litigators."[4]

Hence, we have chosen to refer from now on in this book to judges below the appellate level simply as "judges" and to include within the definition of this term all judicial officers below the appellate court level who decide matters, whether they are motions or bench trials, on their own and not as a member of a panel with other judges. In the federal system, United States magistrate judges preside over a large number of proceedings, including bench trials in civil cases when the parties consent. Also, the federal judicial system includes bankruptcy courts, presided over by bankruptcy judges. Both magistrate judges and bankruptcy judges are appointed under Article I of the United States Constitution, whereas district court judges and appellate judges are appointed under Article III. In state courts, judicial officers carry other titles, such as magistrates and commissioners. In many agencies, federal and state, administrative law judges preside over matters, at times and in various settings making findings of facts and conclusions of law. We believe the general observations we have about persuading judges apply to judicial officers in all these various settings, at all these levels, by whatever title they are known. Thus, unless otherwise noted, when we refer to a judge in this book we are referring to a district court judge, a magistrate judge, or any other judge sitting below the appellate level.

Litigation involves persuasion through written and oral advocacy. The role of advocacy in the American justice system is pivotal. Ours is an adversarial system that relies on opposing parties using effective advocacy to advance the interests of their clients. We trust the adversarial system to ferret out the factual truth and to fully vet the opposing legal theories, so as to provide the decision-maker with all the material facts and controlling law necessary to make an informed and wise decision. It is through this form of adversarial litigation that we endeavor to peacefully resolve legal disputes and establish the rule of law to prosper as a country and a society.

As this book will explain and explore in much more detail, effective advocacy to a judge is different from effective advocacy before a jury, as it is different from persuading a panel of judges on an appellate court.

Introduction

The skills needed in one arena are not always transferrable to another. The setting, the stresses, the interaction between the advocate and the decision-maker is fundamentally different. Attorneys who approach argument before a district judge using the same techniques and practices that they exercise before a jury or even a panel of appellate judges will find their advocacy striking a discordant tone more often than not.

We came to fully appreciate the need for effective advocacy to judges only after we became judges. Before we ascended to the bench, we were trial lawyers ourselves. We frequently advocated for our clients from the well of the courtrooms. We tried many jury trials and a few bench trials, and we argued many cases on appeal. The reality, though, was that we tried to persuade judges far more often. We argued to judges in hearings almost every day, and certainly every week, in hundreds of hearings and almost daily filed motions and responses. And we likely did so poorly and ineffectively.

We, like other trial attorneys, had never been taught that there might be differences in advocacy when trying to persuade a judge versus a jury versus a panel of appellate judges. We had not thought of it any more than most other lawyers. Once we became judges—and the target of attorney advocacy—we came to recognize what we had never seen before. We came to observe advocacy techniques that failed to move us as judges. We became aware of gaps between what we as decision-makers needed and what advocates were providing us. As we look back over our years as practicing attorneys now, knowing what we know from this side of the bench, we recognize in our own performances how we fell short of effectively persuading judges.

Our goal in this book, then, is to use our own past mistakes and misperceptions, together with our observations gained from our positions as district court judges, to impart our insight and share our views about what we believe is effective in persuading judges. It is our modest hope with this book that law students and lawyers alike can benefit from our words to become better advocates for their clients, and through that improve our adversarial system of justice. Our more ambitious hope is that this book influences both law schools and lawyers to shift their thinking to embrace a new focus on developing skills with persuading judges in mind.

We organized this book in the following manner. The first chapter, "The Evolving Trend of Litigation," is intended to explain why there is an increased need for focusing on persuading judges. In that chapter, we describe how jury trials have disappeared, appellate oral arguments are increasingly rare, and motions practice before judges has grown in number and importance.

Introduction

In Chapter Two, we explore the history of legal advocacy pedagogy. The purpose of this chapter is to explain how our focus in the legal profession, particularly in law schools, has been on preparing lawyers to persuade jurors and appellate panels of judges, but not judges. Given the decrease in jury trials and appellate oral arguments, this emphasizes why attorneys need to be trained in effectively persuading judges.

Chapter Three is the key chapter explaining why and how advocacy before judges, jurors, and appellate panels are materially different. We point out that the context in which legal advocacy occurs is significantly different between judges, jurors, and appellate panels. We also identify and explain the difference between judges, jurors, and appellate judges as decision-makers, differences that call for modification of methods for advocacy to be effective.

In Chapter Four, we explore the classic study of rhetoric and advocacy as the art of persuasion. Here, we discuss how the core principles methods of persuasion—logos, pathos, and ethos—are employed in advocacy in general and legal advocacy in particular. Here, too, we also explore how other theories of persuasion, such as identifying and addressing the listener's motives, concerns, and principles, can increase the effectiveness of persuasion.

Having identified the need for learning how to persuade judges, explaining why there has been so little attention devoted to the subject, and explored the general methods of persuading judges, we discuss in general terms in Chapter Five how to persuade judges. Here, we explain in broad brushstrokes the skills and tactics necessary for effectively persuading judges. This includes both written and oral advocacy.

In Chapter Six, we drill down into greater detail, addressing the art of persuading judges in a myriad of specific settings in which advocacy occurs before judges. The first part of Chapter Six is devoted to identifying the primary settings for advocating to judges. The second part discusses each setting and provides detailed advice on effectively persuading judges in each setting given the unique opportunities and challenges each of them pose.

In Chapter Seven, we discuss a proposal for transforming the way law schools teach legal advocacy. Here, we suggest that law schools place more emphasis on, and begin with, training law students to advocate before judges, not appellate panels and not jury trial advocacy. Then we propose an integrated curriculum in which teaching advocacy to judges is followed by classes on jury trial advocacy, followed by classes on appellate advocacy. Through these integrated classes, using a single case problem, students

Introduction

would be provided an opportunity to follow litigation from district court, through jury trial, and on to appeal, just as attorneys do in real life.

Lastly, we wrap up our discussion of persuading judges with some parting thoughts and conclusions.

ONE

The Evolving Trend of Litigation

To persuade readers that our book is worth a read, we first must establish there is a need to learn the skill of effectively persuading judges. To support our premise is a three-part endeavor. We will show in this chapter that the trend line of litigation in America is away from jury trials and appellate oral arguments and toward an increase in motions practice before judges. In the next chapter we will show that training in advocating to judges is lacking and why that is so. In Chapter Three, we will seek to persuade the reader that there is a difference in persuading judges, jurors, and appellate panels of judges. So, let's start with the trend line of litigation.

"For the first one hundred years following the invention of the modern American law school in 1870, trials were common occurrences and were generally accepted as a primary method of resolving legal disputes in this country."[1] No longer is this the case. Much has been written already about vanishing jury trials,[2] and at least some has been written, in passing, about the decrease in appellate oral arguments.[3] This book does not intend to add any new data or insight into the causes for the marked decline. Rather, the point here is to take a more careful look at that data in relation to when law schools began providing trial and appellate advocacy classes. Here, our goal is to summarize the findings regarding the significant decrease in jury trials and appellate oral arguments and increase in motions practice. In the next chapter, we will contrast the trend line of these events with the timeline of law schools offering courses on jury trial advocacy and appellate advocacy. Through this analysis we hope to explain why advocacy pedagogy has historically emphasized appellate and trial advocacy and spotlight the need to focus on persuading judges.

A. *Vanishing Jury Trials*

Resolving disputes—both civil and criminal—through jury trial is a fundamental part of our justice system and a core component of our democratic foundations. Among other grievances, the Declaration of Independence identified King George's attempt to deprive the colonies of a trial by jury as one of the primary abuses of power that compelled the colonies to declare their independence from England.[4] The Founding Fathers believed the right to a jury trial so important that they included it in three places in the Bill of Rights: the Fifth, Sixth, and Seventh amendments to the Constitution. As John Adams wrote, "representative government and trial by jury are the heart and lungs of liberty. Without them we have no fortification against being ridden like horses, fleeced like sheep, worked like cattle, and fed and clothed like swine and hogs."[5]

But, today, trial by jury is an increasingly rare method of resolving disputes.[6] Although litigation has increased in absolute numbers over the course of American history, with the number of lawsuits filed each year constantly trending upward, fewer and fewer of those lawsuits are resolved by jurors. This holds true for both civil and criminal cases.

In the 1930s, a fifth of all civil cases filed in federal courts were resolved at trial.[7] In a very real sense, "[c]ivil practice was still [then] in significant measure a trial practice."[8] By 1962, this number had fallen to the point that only 11.5 percent of civil cases proceeded to trial.[9] In 1972, around the time law schools started offering jury trial advocacy courses,[10] about 9 percent of federal civil cases went to trial.[11] By 2002, the number of federal civil cases proceeding to trial crashed to 1.8 percent.[12] By 2016, a mere 1 percent of federal civil cases were resolved at trial.[13] Two years later, that number even slipped below 1 percent.[14]

There is reason to believe that even these numbers overstate the percentage of federal civil cases that actually go to trial in the common understanding of that term when either a judge or a jury renders a verdict after presentation of evidence. That is because the Administrative Office of the United States Courts counts as "trials" "all contested proceeding[s] at which evidence is introduced."[15] In federal court, judges preside over many contested sentencing hearings and revocation of supervised release hearings in which the parties offer evidence and call witnesses. For statistical purposes, the Administrative Office count these as "trials." And appropriately so, in the sense that many of these hearings take on the appearance of mini-trials. But what's important for purposes of this discussion is that all of those hearings are before judges, not juries.

One. *The Evolving Trend of Litigation*

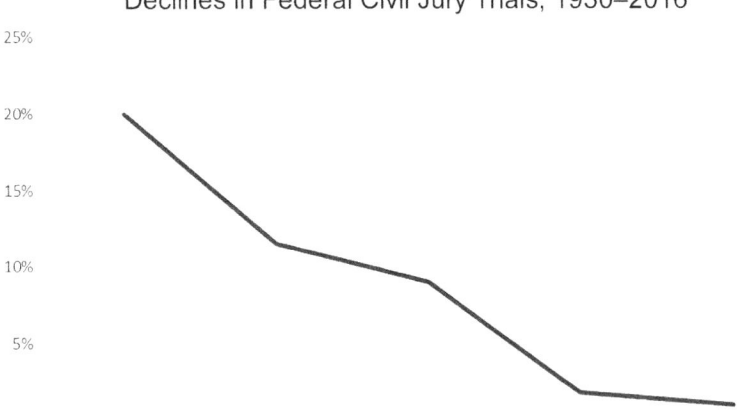

Declines in Federal Civil Jury Trials, 1930–2016

To the extent they resemble trials, they resemble bench trials. Those contested hearings provide a venue for advocating to judges, not jury trial advocacy.

In state courts, where most cases in America are filed,[16] the trend lines are the same. The number of civil cases proceeding to trial in state courts has also dropped precipitously. Between 1976 and 2002, the percentage of state civil cases proceeding to jury trial plummeted from 1.8 percent to .06 percent, and the number of civil cases proceeding to bench trials more than halved from 34.3 percent to 15.2 percent.[17] It is important to note, however, that from 1976 to 2002, far more state cases were resolved by bench trial than by jury trial.[18] From 1992 to 2002, there was an even more pronounced 44 percent drop of the number of state civil cases proceeding to jury trial, and bench trials decreased by 21 percent.[19]

The number of criminal cases proceeding to jury trial has also fell precipitously. In 1962, again shortly before law schools began teaching jury trial advocacy, approximately 15 percent of federal criminal cases went to trial.[20] By 2002, that number had diminished to under 5 percent.[21] By 2018, the number of defendants tried by a jury fell to 2 percent.[22] The decrease was similar in state criminal cases, slipping from 8.5 percent proceeding to trial in 1976 to 3.3 percent proceeding to trial in 2002.[23]

In short, "we have gone from a legal world in which trials, typically jury trials, were routine, to a world in which trials have become 'vanishingly rare.'"[24] It is also interesting, and relevant to the importance of effective advocacy to judges as opposed to jury trial advocacy, that the

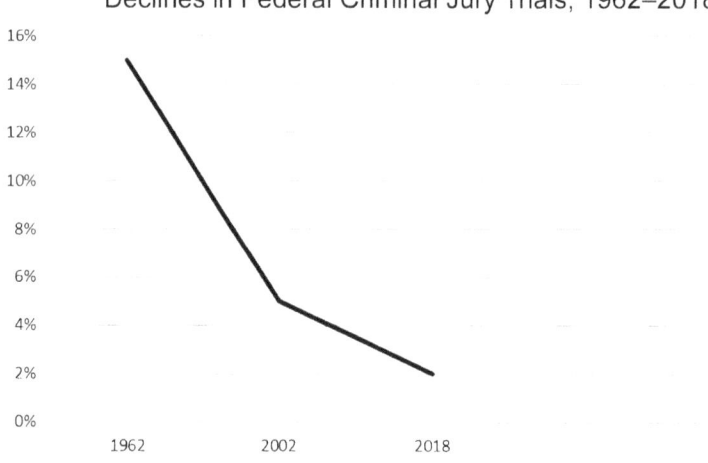

Declines in Federal Criminal Jury Trials, 1962–2018

few trials which do occur each year are also getting shorter.[25] Likewise, another important takeaway from these statistics is the number of bench trials, though decreasing over time, have decreased at a slower rate.

Finally, and as we will discuss in detail in Chapter Six, even when a jury trial does happen, the ability to advocate effectively to a judge is nonetheless important. Before, during and after a jury trial, the judge will be called upon to make numerous decisions that may have a substantial impact on the trial and the ultimate outcome of the case. The advocacy skills addressed in this book don't become irrelevant simply because the disputed factual questions will be resolved by a jury.

B. *Increasingly Rare Appellate Oral Arguments*

The number of cases proceeding to appeal and oral argument has also declined significantly in the last century. As would be expected, with the decline in cases going to trial, there is a corresponding decline in the number of cases appealed because many of those cases were resolved by settlement or guilty plea. Federal cases resolved through trial are appealed four times more often than cases terminated without trials, "[a]nd as the proportion of tried cases falls, the portion of concluded appeals that are from trials falls and so does the absolute number of appellate decisions in tried cases."[26] More importantly, fewer appeals are resulting in oral arguments. Between 1997 and 2007, federal appeals courts went from hearing oral arguments in 40 percent of all cases to 27 percent, on average, a stark 33 percent decline.[27] For the fiscal year ending September 2018, data from the United States Courts reflected that oral arguments were granted in only slightly more than 20 percent of all appeals terminated on the merits.[28] By 2020, that number fell to 19.3 percent.[29] And the drop hasn't stopped. By 2021, the number had plunged to 18.9 percent.[30]

C. Increase in Motions Practice

Unlike the sharp decline in jury trials and appellate oral arguments, there has been an increase in the number of motions judges preside over and resolve.[31] In civil cases, judges can enter orders that are dispositive as to all or some of a party's claims in ruling on motions to dismiss or motions for summary judgment.[32] In federal courts, the development of civil discovery, combined with the adoption of the summary judgment rule (Federal Rule of Civil Procedure 56) in 1937, together with the Supreme Court's broad interpretation of Rule 56 in a trilogy of cases in 1986,[33] has led to an increase in the number of cases disposed of by district judges.[34] Although reliable empirical evidence on the percentage increase in cases disposed of by summary judgment as a result of these developments is lacking,[35] the evidence is clear that the numbers have increased by as little as 6 percent to as much as 73 percent in some types of cases.[36] In short, "we have moved from a world in which dispositions by summary judgment were equal to a small fraction of dispositions by trial into a new era in which dispositions by summary judgment are a magnitude several times greater than the number of trials."[37] Regardless of the number of times district judges disposed of cases on summary judgment, the important point is that they have the power to do so. And increasingly, parties are filing motions for summary judgment where persuading a judge is crucial to whether the case survives for jury trial. Similarly, in criminal cases district judges can make dispositive rulings on motions to dismiss and to suppress.[38]

Filing, resisting, and arguing motions before judges is what most litigators do most of the time. Attorneys engage in advocacy to judges quite frequently—far more frequently than they engage in jury trial or appellate advocacy—and these efforts at persuading judges often make the difference between winning and losing a case. Lawyers, particularly young lawyers, are far more likely to appear before judges arguing motions and the like than they are to appear before juries or appellate panels.[39] Appearing before and advocating to judges has been described as "the blue-collar, day-in-day-out thing lawyers do routinely—and sometimes not very well."[40]

D. The Relative Finality of District Court Judge Decisions

When assessing the importance of effective advocating to judges, it bears considering the fact that the decisions judges make are, for all intents and purposes, final decisions. To be sure, litigants can always appeal a judge's decision to a higher court. But let's look realistically at this option.

First, the vast majority of decisions judges make are on preliminary litigation matters, such as resolving discovery dispute, ruling on motions in limine, and even more routine matters such as whether to grant a continuance. As a practical matter, parties very rarely appeal these routine judicial rulings. Although litigants have the right to seek review by appellate courts, this right typically arises only after a final judgment has been entered.[41] Most cannot be appealed interlocutory. By the time for an appeal arises, many have been rendered moot or are no longer important enough to appeal.

Second, when parties do appeal, appellate advocacy wisdom tells lawyers to choose only a few of the most important issues to appeal. Attorneys can't and won't raise on appeal all the judge's decisions. Thus, although the parties may believe the judge made scores of erroneous decisions, realistically the parties are not going to appeal them all.

Finally, when parties do appeal a judge's decision, they usually lose. Courts of appeal afford judges varying degrees of discretion. So, even when a judgment is appealed, the dozens (or even hundreds) of decisions the district judge made during the lower court proceedings rarely result in reversal. For example, appellate judges may reject a district judge's findings of fact only if those findings are clearly erroneous.[42] This is a "deferential standard."[43] A wide range of other decisions, including rulings as to the admissibility of evidence, may be reviewed under the similarly deferential abuse of discretion standard.[44] Even when appellate judges conclude that a district judge made an erroneous decision on a particular issue, reversal is not warranted if the error was harmless.[45] Perhaps it is not surprising, then, that historical reversal rates by federal courts of appeal have been 9 percent or less for all cases (and even lower for criminal cases).[46] As district judges, we take comfort in the fact that appellate courts are available to review our decisions and correct them when necessary. However, when preparing to advocate to a district judge, an attorney should assume that the judge's decision is going to be the last word on the issue.

E. Conclusion

In short, jury trials have nearly disappeared and appellate oral arguments are becoming rarer, while the number of pretrial motions has increased significantly. Realistically, appealing a judge's decisions cannot substitute for effectively persuading the judge to rule in your favor in the first instance. Thus, the focus of litigation has shifted to the pretrial stage. It has shifted from juries and appellate panels to judges.

In one sense, vanishing jury trials and the decrease in appellate oral arguments makes it all that much more important that attorneys hone their skills in those areas. On the other hand, when attorneys are more likely, day in and day out, to file motions with and present oral arguments to district court judges, it would strongly suggest that greater effort should be placed on teaching attorneys the skills of effectively persuading judge. Each set of skills is important, and neither should be ignored. But if, as we assert, the skill sets are different between the two, then it begs asking why so many resources are devoted to jury trial advocacy and appellate advocacy when attorneys are decreasingly given an opportunity to exercise those skills.

All this shows that the importance of effectively advocate to juries, and even to appellate panels, pales in comparison to the importance of effectively persuading judges. Being skilled at the art of persuading judges has never been more important. Nevertheless, law schools keep producing graduates who have been prepared to try jury trials and argue appellate arguments, but few emerge from law school having learned anything about motion practice or how to effectively argue a hearing before district judges. So, why, then, has our educational system churned out, and continues to churn out, lawyers who have been taught the skills of appellate advocacy and, to a lesser extent jury trial advocacy, but few with the skills of persuading judges? That is the subject of our next chapter.

Two

The History of Legal Advocacy Pedagogy

In the early stages of American history, most lawyers learned the craft and entered the profession through an apprenticeship. Men, and we use the word here intentionally because in the beginning almost all lawyers were men,[1] would "read the law" by working for a practicing lawyer.[2] The apprentice lawyer learned by watching and doing. The apprentice developed advocacy skills by emulating those of his mentoring attorney, or perhaps on occasion the advocacy skills of opposing lawyers who bested his mentor. Other men practiced law without even the benefit of an apprenticeship. In truth, before the American Civil War few states required even an apprenticeship, let alone any formal legal education, to practice law.[3] Back then, one could simply declare oneself a lawyer, hang a shingle, and sue away. Abraham Lincoln, for example, never apprenticed under another attorney nor received any formal legal education, but instead read law books on his own, obtained a county certificate attesting to his good moral character, and started practicing law.

Formal legal education—law schools as we know them in the modern sense—grew out of the apprenticeship system. At first, law schools offered the same type of hands-on training, only in group settings larger than could be provided in law firms of the time.[4] Think of the first law schools like you would think now of a legal clinic in a law school. Law schools had their origins in the late 1700s, but began in earnest in the early 1800s, at first through independent schools focused on providing practical training and skills, including sometimes optional and sometimes required moot court courses.[5] But by 1900, legal education became dominated by universities and colleges which provided more formal legal education and had the authority to confer degrees.[6] As with the early independent law schools, university-based law schools offered moot court training largely

Two. The History of Legal Advocacy Pedagogy

as a supplement to classes focused on learning the law, as opposed to learning advocacy skills.

Today, law schools primarily educate students about effective legal advocacy in two litigation settings: jury trials and appeals. The focus on teaching students how to advocate to juries and appellate courts appears to be the product of two developments in the history of legal education. Appellate advocacy training developed first as a result of the focus in modern legal education on appellate cases. A jury trial advocacy organization, on the other hand, spearheaded the start of jury trial advocacy programs that law schools later incorporated into their curriculum.

A. Development of Appellate Advocacy Programs

The adoption of moot court programs as part of the curriculum in American law schools began in the early 1800s. Harvard Law School started its moot court program in 1820, and the University of Virginia School of Law followed a couple decades later.[7] This was a natural extension of the apprentice-based system of legal education, with a focus on learning by doing.

All that changed in the late 1800s with a shift away from practical skills and toward a more scientific, intellectual approach to legal education. The modern legal pedagogy's use of the case method of legal education became the dominant form of American legal education after Professor Christopher Columbus Langdell introduced the practice at Harvard Law School in 1870.[8] This method focuses on the examination of appellate court decisions as a means of understanding the purpose, development, and meaning of the law.[9] This was a quasi-scientific approach to the law that diverted attention away from the development of more practical advocacy skills that practicing lawyers used every day. Thus, "Langdell's new teaching method came with a price—its 'scientific' approach to the law and its exclusive focus on appellate court decisions caused legal education to become divorced of nearly all skills training except legal analysis, research, and writing."[10] Only later did law schools recognize the need to supplement the case method with skills-based training. Appellate moot court programs were the result.

Law school moot court complemented and really became an extension of the case method of teaching in law school because both methods focused on appellate courts.[11] Moot court programs can also accurately be described as appellate advocacy programs because they invariably are set in a mock appellate court.[12] That means, of course, that the focus is on legal issues, and not factual disputes, which are almost always the actual focus of a district court's ruling.[13] Today, most, if not all, law schools have moot court programs as part of their curriculum.[14] These moot court programs, and the national and international competitions that have arisen from them, involve students writing appellate briefs and making oral arguments in a mock appellate court setting.[15] It is often one of the few law school courses that teach students anything about oral advocacy.[16]

Law schools generally require students to take an appellate advocacy class, which involves writing an appellate brief and making a corresponding oral argument.[17] The course is intended to provide basic research, writing, and oral advocacy skills thought to be of aid to every law student, even if they later chose not to enter the litigation field. Law schools use the appellate advocacy class as a means of teaching law students the fundamentals of how to write and argue like lawyers. It is assumed that these skills are directly transferrable to any context involving written or oral advocacy. Thus, students are generally required to successfully complete at least one appellate advocacy class as part of their first or second-year schedule. Students interested in becoming litigators can thereafter pursue advanced appellate advocacy classes or participate in appellate advocacy competition programs. And since the 1970s, students can also seek out elective trial advocacy training.

B. Development of Trial Advocacy Programs

Jury trial advocacy courses are a more recent development, although they are now a half-century old. The first jury trial advocacy courses were offered in law schools in the 1970s.[18] There were, to be sure, earlier versions of skills-based advocacy courses offered in the mid-century, but they largely focused on legal analysis and the drafting of legal documents related to trial practice and bore little resemblance to the modern jury trial advocacy course.[19]

Jury trial advocacy courses were the direct result of the founding of the National Institute for Trial Advocacy (NITA) in 1971.[20] NITA offered its first jury trial advocacy course in the summer of 1972.[21] Soon thereafter, law schools began somewhat reluctantly offering jury trial advocacy classes as elective courses.[22] Nevertheless, the NITA methodology, which focused on jury trial advocacy, eventually became the model upon which all law school jury trial advocacy programs were based.[23] Today, "every law school in the country offers a course focused on building trial advocacy skills."[24]

It may seem ironic at first that law schools began offering courses focused on jury trial advocacy as the number of jury trials was plummeting. But, perhaps, it reflected the recognition that something had to be done to develop and maintain skills that attorneys would have less opportunity to develop on the job. As the number of jury trials decreased, so, too, did the ability of attorneys to develop effective trial advocacy skills through practice, literally through trial and error. To fill the gap, skills-based training was needed.

C. Advocacy Courses in Law School

Trial advocacy and advanced appellate advocacy courses, which feed into competitions, are typically elective upper-level law school courses. The courses are not interconnected, meaning the factual record and legal issues in the trial advocacy and appellate advocacy courses are not the same. In other words, the appellate advocacy course does not involve an appeal of the case problem that was the subject of the trial advocacy course.

Indeed, law schools teach advocacy backwards. Appeals proceed from trials. But law schools teach second-year students the art of appellate advocacy and only in later elective classes do they offer students the opportunity to examine trial advocacy. Little effort is undertaken to help students understand the chronology of litigation and show them in practical exercises how what happens at earlier stages of litigation, like trials, affects the nature and scope of issues on appeal.

In recent decades, law schools have made some pedagogical changes in response to the increasing use of alternative dispute resolution (ADR) instead of trials to resolve legal disputes. Scores of law schools now offer classes on mediation or other forms of ADR, and law school ADR competitions have arisen as well.[25] NITA has also broadened its publication offerings in response to an increase in ADR use to include numerous volumes on mediation, arbitration, and litigation before administrative agencies.[26]

Missing from the advocacy curriculum in law schools today are courses focused on teaching students the skills they are most likely to exercise in practice, such as persuading a judicial officer occupying the role of decision-maker. NITA offers courses on many topics, but only two courses (one online, the other in-person) for "motions skills" appears on its 2025 calendar of courses.[27] As we have shown in the preceding chapter, this is a skill of increasing importance given the precipitous drop in the number of jury trials and the dramatic decline of appellate oral arguments, while the number of motions before judges has continued to climb.

D. Conflicting Timelines

Tracing and comparing the timeline of the history of legal advocacy education and the trend lines of jury trials and appellate oral arguments reveals how they were once more closely matched and today no longer are. In summary, when appellate advocacy programs were adopted in law schools, approximately 20 percent of civil cases proceeded to trial, many of which led to appellate oral arguments. Today, less than 1 percent of all federal civil cases proceed to trial, resulting in far fewer appeals, and when cases are appealed, oral argument is granted in less than 20 percent of the cases. Similarly, when jury trial advocacy courses were introduced into American law schools in the 1970s, approximately one in ten civil cases still proceeded to jury trial. Today less than one in a hundred federal civil cases proceed to jury trial. The numbers are not significantly better for criminal jury trials and appellate arguments, or in state courts.

In the meantime, the number of motions filed and decided by district judges have increased significantly since law schools began teaching jury trial advocacy. And in particular, this includes the number of cases in which judges make dispositive decisions affecting the survival of claims that could end up before a jury. In short, to the extent American law schools are teaching legal advocacy skills today, they are teaching skills that were in dominant use in a bygone litigation era and are failing to teach the skills litigators increasingly use every day in courtrooms across America: advocating to judges. It is akin to military academies training cadets to fight the last war, not the next one.

E. The Absence of Programs and Education for Persuading Judges

This survey of the history of legal advocacy pedagogy reflects a focus on trial and appellate advocacy. Conspicuous by its absence is any real attention paid to teaching the skills of advocating to judges. It is true that some law schools have offered classes that encompass aspects of persuading judges. Typically, these classes are labeled "pretrial practice." Other classes are structured around administrative law practice, which involves advocacy before administrative law judges. From a perusal of the curriculum for these classes, however, it appears that the emphasis is on process and procedures, and not on developing written and oral advocacy skills unique to persuading judges, be they district judges or administrative law judges.

For example, the John Marshall Law School recently described its pretrial practice class as follows:

> A study of the pretrial process in civil litigation. Students will represent a client beginning with an intake interview through cross-motions for summary judgment. Students will draft pleadings, discovery requests, and pretrial motions. Students will engage in simulated exercises including interviewing and counseling a client, arguing motions, negotiating settlements, and taking or defending depositions.[28]

The University of Chicago College of Law has described its Pretrial Litigation: Strategy and Advocacy course as follows: "Students will learn how to evaluate and develop fact and legal theories; develop themes; take and defend fact and expert witness depositions; draft pretrial motions; and use various tactics to prepare a case for trial," and offered conducting a deposition as the practical exercise.[29] A 2016 syllabus from the U.C. Berkeley School of Law devoted one of 14 classes to the skills of persuasion, with the vast majority of classes devoted to discovery litigation.[30] The 2021 Washington Law School syllabus for its pretrial litigation course described the skills it would teach as "focus[ing] on include interviewing, counseling, negotiation, plea bargaining, drafting pleadings, discovery and pretrial motion briefs."[31] Professional programs for practicing attorneys similarly focus on procedures and not advocacy skills before judges. For example, the 2024 description of the Practicing Law Institute's class on pretrial practice states that its students will learn how to: "Plan the litigation; Investigate the facts and the law; Plead their case; Conduct pretrial motions; [and] Master settlement strategies."[32]

In short, there appears to have been no recognition or acknowledgment that persuading judges could be different from persuading juries or appellate panels. As a result, legal advocacy pedagogy has completely neglected teaching law students and practicing lawyers the skills needed to be effective judge advocates. It is as if those responsible for designing advocacy curriculum seem to discount the importance of persuading judges. Rather, a judge's decisions in pretrial litigation are seen as merely a backdrop against which the real focus of advocacy matters: jury trials and appeals. In reality, what a judge decides in pretrial litigation controls and shapes what happens at trial—if there even is one—and on appeal. Winning before the judge, persuading the judge to rule in the attorney's favor on motions, is the key today to litigation success. In some ways, trials and appeals mark failures in pretrial litigation. Success before a judge may result in the case being dismissed, entry of summary judgment in a civil case, or suppression of critical evidence in criminal case. Only when attorneys lose those motions do they find themselves going to trial.

We recognize that our argument that there is a need for greater emphasis on persuading judges in legal pedagogy is premised on our assertion that there is a fundamental and material difference in effective advocacy to judges than to juries or appellate panels. If the skills and methods of effective jury trial advocacy and appellate advocacy were identical to the skills and methods of effective advocating to judges, then there would be no problem. But they are not. There are many material differences between judges and jurors, judges and juries, and judges and appellate panels. The dissimilarities in who these decision-makers are, what their decision-making process is, and the context in which these diverse decision-makers operate, highlights the need for advocacy skills to be more specifically tailored with the decision-maker in mind.

It is to that topic that we turn in the next chapter.

Three

How Judges, Jurors, and Appellate Panels Differ

To appreciate the need to develop skills for persuading judges as a separate skill set from jury trial advocacy or appellate advocacy skills, one has first to recognize there are significant differences between jurors, juries, judges, and panels of judges, as decision-makers, and in their decision-making process. There are differences in the nature of the decision-maker, the context in which the decision-maker makes decisions, the information the decision-maker uses to arrive at decisions, the pressures on the decision-makers, and the methods of decision-making, among other things. Effectively persuading judges requires the advocate to identify and lean into these differences, adjusting advocacy skills in a manner designed to respond to and exploit the differences.

Some supporters of jury trial advocacy and appellate advocacy programs argue that they prepare students to argue in any type of legal setting.[1] That assumption may be true, to a limited degree. Unfortunately, there has been little thought given to the extent to which there are also significant differences between arguing to a jury or appellate panel in comparison to arguing to a district judge. There is very little in the literature on advocacy to district judges and how it differs from arguing to a jury or an appellate panel. In FUNDAMENTALS OF PRETRIAL LITIGATION, the authors devote a chapter to courtroom advocacy.[2] The focus in that chapter, however, is largely on written advocacy. Although the book identifies some differences between arguing to a judge and arguing to an appellate panel of judges, it does not contrast these differences to arguing to a jury. In his book on pretrial litigation, Professor Mauet, the director of trial advocacy at the University of Arizona Law School, makes only passing references to, and provides little advice for, advocating to judges during hearings.[3]

As it turns out, there are significant differences in the context in which the argument is made and the nature of the decision-maker whom

Persuading Judges

the advocate is attempting to persuade. Thus, neither the skills learned in jury trial advocacy, which focus on persuading a jury, nor the skills in appellate advocacy, which focus on persuading an appellate panel of judges, are wholly transferable to persuading a district judge. Indeed, as we will discuss, some jury advocacy methods may not only be inappropriate or inapplicable but may also be ineffective or counterproductive when trying to advocate to a judge.

There are many differences in advocating to juries, to a panel of appellate judges, and to judges, but such advocacy generally falls into two broad categories: context and the decision-maker. Within the context category, there are differences in whether: (1) there is two-way communication; (2) advocacy is linear; (3) advocacy is written and oral, or only oral; (4) facts are in dispute; (5) evidence rules apply; (6) advocates are likely to reappear before the decision-maker; (7) there is group decision-making; (8) the collateral pressures on the decision-makers; (9) time and space limits, and (10) the power the decision maker has over the advocate. Within the decision-maker category, there are differences in whether the decision-maker: (1) is legally trained; (2) is knowable; (3) impacts others with their decisions; and (4) explains their decisions. Charting out these differences helps illustrate where they occur.

Factor	Jury	*Appeals Court*	*District Judge*
Two-way communication	No	Yes	Yes
Linear and dynamic communication	No	Yes	Yes
Written and oral communication	No	Yes	Yes
Facts in dispute	Yes	No	Often
Evidence rules apply	Yes	No	Sometimes
Reappear before decision-maker	No	Maybe	Often
Group decision-making	Yes	Yes	No
Time and Space Limits	Yes	Yes	Some
Collateral pressures on decision-maker	No	No	Yes
Decision-maker has power over advocate	No	Yes	Yes
Decision-maker legally trained	No	Yes	Yes
Decision-maker knowable	Limited	Yes	Yes
Decision-maker impacts others	No	Yes	No
Decision-maker explains decisions	No	Yes	Yes

We will discuss each of these differences in more detail below.

Three. How Judges, Jurors, and Appellate Panels Differ

A. Differences in Context

1. One-Way or Two-Way Communication

The ability to persuade another person is affected by the means of communication. In some instances, a speaker can only send a message to the listener and hope it is heard, is understood, and has resonance. In other instances, a speaker can receive a response from the listener that informs the speaker whether the listener is hearing, understanding, and receptive to the intended message. Feedback from the listener can be critical in tailoring arguments in a manner that can respond to the listener's questions or concerns, doubts, presumptions, and misunderstandings. In the practice of law, there are significant differences in the ability to communicate with decision-makers, depending on who the decision-maker is.

Jury trial advocacy involves one-sided communication in which attorneys talk at jurors, hoping the message gets through. Attorneys can't ask jurors if they understand an argument, if they have questions, or what they are thinking. At most, attorneys may attempt to assess whether they are getting through to and persuading jurors by reading jurors' body language and demeanors. And generally jurors cannot ask questions of attorneys. In most cases, jurors remain mute observers.[4] Some judges do permit jurors to ask questions of witnesses, at least after the questions are screened by the judge. Our former colleague, Judge Mark W. Bennett, a true judicial innovator, was among those who experimented with the practice and advocated in favor of it. But it remains an uncommon practice. And even then, the communication between advocate and decision-maker is not direct. A juror-posed question directed to a witness may give an attorney a clue as to what the jurors are hearing, understanding, and focused on, but juror questions posed to witnesses don't involve a two-way exchange between attorneys and jurors.

When attorneys are advocating to either trial or appellate judges, however, communication can be two-way. Judges can engage with the advocate by asking questions, and, though seldom done, advocates are able to ask questions of judges. Even when communication is two-sided with judges, however, the nature of that communication is different before judges than it is before appellate panels.[5]

Judges differ significantly from juries as decision-makers because judges have the ability to, and often do, ask questions of witnesses and attorneys. This difference significantly alters how attorneys advocate to jurors versus how they advocate to judges. Attorneys and judges can have a conversation and through that conversation achieve a level of understanding that cannot occur when attorneys are limited to only talking at jurors. Attorneys can ask judges if their arguments are understood and inquire of judges about what questions or concerns judges have about the evidence or argument. Judge questions of attorneys convey, either explicitly or implicitly, the extent to which the judges is hearing, understanding, and being persuaded by the attorney's argument. Although a judge may ultimately disagree with an attorney's position, through conversation it can at least be certain that the judge understands the attorney's position.

But, the opportunity for a true conversation is greater with district judges that it is in an appellate setting. Appellate arguments are rigid and timed with even the longest of them seldom exceeding a half-hour per side (and many appellate arguments are limited to ten or fifteen minutes per side). Further, appellate arguments have the tone and appearance of formal debates. Questioning is also one-sided. To the extent there is a verbal exchange, it resembles much more an interrogation than a conversation, with only one side asking questions.[6]

In contrast, although district judges generally have more time pressures than appellate judges, most district judges don't impose arbitrary and short deadlines to arguments. District judges are much more flexible in the amount of time the allow attorneys to argue. Because the setting before a district judge is less formal, the prohibition against attorneys asking substantive questions of the judge generally don't exist (depending on the receptivity of individual judges, of course) like it does in the formal setting of an appellate tribunal. Thus, with district judges there is a real opportunity for a more informal exchange to take place. There is a greater opportunity for attorneys to fully air their views and concerns without the artificial time limits and formality of appellate court. Advocacy to a district judge, then, assumes a very different tone and can become much more of a conversation than a formal appellate presentation.

2. Linear or Dynamic Communication

Somewhat related to whether communication with the decision-maker is one- or two-sided is whether the advocacy is presented in linear form. When advocating to jurors, attorneys have complete control over the order of presentation. The attorney decides where to start, the structure of the presentation, and how to end. They march through in linear fashion without interruption from the listener. There's no back and forth, no interruptions, no redirection. This can be a disadvantage, though, because the

Three. How Judges, Jurors, and Appellate Panels Differ

lack of two-way communication prevents advocates from adjusting their presentations to suit the order in which the listener wants to hear things. The decision-makers—the jurors—are passive and must accept the attorney's presentation in the order the attorney chose. The attorney is left to hope that the organization the attorney chose is the most persuasive one.

The presentation of evidence, whether to jury or judge, is linear in nature, and within the control of the attorney to a large degree. An attorney wanting to persuade a jury or judge to give weight to a particular witness' recollection of events may do so by surrounding that witness' recollection with other facts that tend to corroborate the witness. An attorney wanting to minimize the impact of an unfavorable fact may choose to bury the fact in the midst of contrary or more favorable evidence.

When arguing to judges, both district and appellate judges, attorneys advocate in both linear and non-linear forms. In written advocacy, the attorney is in control of the order of communication. The attorney structures written briefs and motions in the manner the attorney believes is most persuasive. When providing the court with a factual summary, attorneys can order the facts in any manner they want. Written advocacy is linear in nature. When attorneys have several grounds to support their positions, they can raise those grounds in writing in the order that they believe is most persuasive. It is true that statutes and court decisions sometimes set out factors courts are to consider in resolving certain legal issues and it is common for attorneys to address the factors in the order set out by statute or court decision. But, they are not bound to do so, and good attorneys will address such factors in an order that is most persuasive to their client's position.

Oral arguments before judges, on the other hand, are dynamic in nature. In making oral arguments, attorneys are no longer in control of the presentation. Judges will often interrupt with questions. On other occasions, judges will ask attorneys to address particular issues in an order the judge is interested in, which may be different from the advocate's choice. Judges can easily derail attorneys' linear approach to their arguments. This requires a different skill set for attorneys. When the presentation is not linear, when the listener is suddenly in control of the order of the presentation, it requires attorneys to develop flexibility. Good oral advocacy before judges, whether at the district court or appellate court level, involves learning to welcome interruptions and changes in topics. It requires attorneys to develop skills of reading into judges' questions to discern the judges' focus and concerns. It necessitates attorneys developing the ability to pivot when subject to re-direction through judge-posed questions. Attorneys should react to the fact or issue the judge believes is important and to directly address the judges' concerns. Good oral advocates also learn the skill of shifting the interrupted argument back around to the linear presentation the attorney prepared, to address the issues in the order the attorney believes is most persuasive for the client's position.

3. Written or Oral Communication

There are generally two forms of legal advocacy: written and oral. There are significant differences, and advantages and disadvantages, of each form of persuasion. Written advocacy can often be a more certain form of communication because the author can carefully craft the message. The advocate can take the time needed to write the most persuasive argument. In contrast oral advocacy is often less precise and thought out. Oral advocacy requires attorneys often to think on their feet, to speak extemporaneously, which can lead to inarticulate responses and even misstatements. Written advocacy also provides the decision-maker with a document to which the decision-maker can return as many times as necessary to read and reread so as to fully comprehend the message. Oral advocacy, on the other hand, is fleeting and the degree to which it has lasting impact depends on the ability of the listener to retain the words in their minds or accurately translate and record them in written notes. The written word, however, can be misunderstood or misinterpreted, while oral communication can sometimes provide an opportunity for the advocate to clarify or correct misunderstandings.[7] Written communication also lacks the immediacy and emotion of oral communication. It is sometimes more difficult to further the method of pathos through the written word than it is through an oral presentation. The tone and emphasis the writer has in mind when typing the words on paper may not be the tone and emphasis the reader applies to the same words. Absent the use of italics, bold, underlining, or some other such use of fonts, a writer cannot necessarily be sure that the emphasis the writer has in mind is the emphasis the reader will absorb. Thus, whether advocacy can be presented in written form, oral form, or both makes a dramatic difference in the nature and effectiveness of advocacy presented.

When attorneys advocate to judges, they can, and often do so, use both written and oral advocacy. Unlike jurors, judges make decisions based not just on what is presented in the courtroom, in evidence, or during oral argument, but also based on the written submissions of the parties in the form of motions, responses, proposed findings of fact and

Three. How Judges, Jurors, and Appellate Panels Differ

conclusions of law, and a myriad of other pleadings. Attorneys file briefs or memoranda summarizing the relevant facts, setting out the legal standards, and arguing why their clients should prevail. When attorneys advocate to appellate courts, they always do so in writing, and sometimes (but as we have seen, decreasingly) also advocate orally before an appellate panel. Frequently, if not always, both district judges and appellate judges have reviewed the attorneys' briefs before oral argument, and if they have not, they do so after oral argument. Thus, unlike jurors, judges begin to form their views and opinions about cases as a result of reading written submissions by the parties before the attorneys make any courtroom presentation. Indeed, when judges read the briefs in advance of argument, they may enter the hearings or oral arguments already having a fair idea of how they will likely rule.[8] Thus, in advocating to judges, persuasion begins, and sometimes ends, in writing.

Compare this practice to jury trials. Jurors don't have the benefit of written briefs discussing the facts, stating the law, or summarizing the parties' arguments. Jurors learn everything they know about the facts of a case only through oral presentation and exhibits. Trial attorneys explain their theory of the case, their chain of logical reasoning from the facts they believe show their clients should prevail, solely through oral advocacy in opening statements and closing arguments. The ability of attorneys to persuade the factfinder through the written word is wholly absent in trial advocacy. Likewise, although judges provide written instructions on the law to jurors, the instructions are presented in a neutral manner.[9] Court jury instructions are not a form of advocacy. Attorneys are unable to use jury instructions to meld the law to the facts in a persuasive way like they can and do when trying to persuade a judge through a written motion or brief. Thus, in advocating to juries, persuasion begins and ends in the spoken word.

Consider, then, how these differences can affect legal advocacy. It is well-known that people, including judges, comprehend and remember things better when provided with both written and oral explanations.[10] Because jurors learn the facts of the case, and the parties' theories, exclusively through oral presentation of testimony and argument, this places jurors at a distinct disadvantage for comprehending and recalling what is often complex and confusing information. Those who teach trial advocacy recognize this limitation and emphasize means of addressing this weakness. This includes instructing students to use repetition as a means of enhancing comprehension and reinforcing memory.[11] It is common, then, for attorneys to have witnesses repeat statements in various ways, and to often call multiple witnesses in part to repeat key testimony, so as to enhance juror comprehension and memory. Likewise, in argument attorneys will often repeat important points as a means of ensuring the jurors, or at least one of the jurors, will absorb and remember the points the attorney believes are important. Trial advocacy books, articles, and courses also urge attorneys to use charts, diagrams, and other demonstrative and pedagogical tools to help enhance jurors' comprehension and retention.[12]

When, however, a judge is the factfinder, attorneys can use both written and oral advocacy to aid the judge's comprehension and memory. Unlike jurors, judges will have the benefit of having read the parties' motions and briefs, greatly aiding in the judge's ability to understand and remember the key facts. Unlike jurors, judges can refer to the written materials when necessary to seek out the facts, to compare and contrast recitations of facts, to fully comprehend the material. Oral presentation by the attorneys, instead of being the only method of persuasion as it is with juries, becomes a supplemental method of persuasion. The role of oral argument before a judge who has the benefit of the parties' written briefs is materially different than it is before a jury. Likewise, whereas repetition is an important means of enhancing comprehension and retention of information in jury trial advocacy, repetition is much less necessary when judges are the decision-makers and have access to the parties' written materials. Indeed, unnecessary repetition by attorneys when advocating to judges may be counterproductive. When attorneys advocate both in writing and orally to judges, it requires them to determine the best way to weave those methods together. Attorneys who merely repeat in oral argument what they wrote in their briefs are ineffective.[13]

It is also important to consider when and how decision-makers arrive at conclusions. Jurors are instructed to keep an open mind and not to begin to make up their mind until the end of trial when they are back in the jury room during deliberations. Although there is some indication jurors begin to make up their minds early in trials, sometimes as early as opening statements, the reality is that it is very difficult for jurors to reach definitive conclusions because of the fractured manner in which they necessarily receive information. Jurors are fed the facts witness by witness. It is often the case that because individual witnesses have limited personal knowledge about the material facts, each witness provides jurors with only a partial picture of the case. Often, those pictures conflict because of natural differences in witnesses' perception, knowledge, and memory. To fully comprehend the facts and understand what happened and then fit those facts into the burden of proof and elements provided by the judge in jury instructions, it requires jurors to wait until all the evidence is in, and until they have the chance to discuss the evidence in deliberations to attempt to make sense of it all. As some attorneys explain it to jurors, the evidence presented in a jury trial is like so many odd-shaped pieces of puzzles that the jurors must arrange and fit together during deliberations. As a direct result of the staccato manner in which jurors receive the information they need to reach their decisions, jurors are seldom able to reach definitive conclusions until they have received all the evidence, heard oral argument by the lawyers, and are instructed on the law by the judge.

When, however, a judge is the decision-maker and has been provided written briefs by the parties, the timeline of decision-making shifts. Assuming that judges read the written materials before the proceeding—whether it is a hearing or a bench trial—the judge already knows through the written advocacy the essential material facts of the case and the legal and logical theories of the attorneys. Judges already know the law. So unlike jurors who must await the presentation of evidence, oral argument, and legal instructions before they can begin to engage in decision-making, judges have already begun that decision-making upon reading the attorneys' written materials. Of course, in evidentiary hearings and bench trials judges, like jurors, must await testimony and other evidence to fully comprehend the facts. But, unlike jurors who have no access to written advocacy in advance, judges have at least begun to arrive at possible solutions even before presentation of live evidence. In short, attorneys should consider the possibility that the judges may have already partially made up their minds from the written briefs about the way they may rule long before the presentation of evidence and oral argument.

To be effective advocates before judges as decision-makers, then, it requires attorneys to learn and embrace different skill sets. Effectively persuading judges requires attorneys to develop methods of communicating with judges to discern what judges are thinking, how they might be leaning, as a result of having read the written advocacy of the parties. As we discussed, unlike with jury trials in which attorneys can only talk at jurors, when judges are decision-makers there is an opportunity to engage in a two-way conversation, opening up a method of persuasion unavailable to attorneys in jury trials. Also, much more than with jurors as decision-makers, when judges are the decision-makers it requires attorneys to develop stronger skills in persuading judges to change their minds, to shift their preconceived notions derived from the written advocacy. It is one thing to shape an opinion through oral advocacy. It is another thing altogether to change an opinion through oral advocacy.

4. Facts in Dispute

The content and nature of an attorney's advocacy depend significantly on whether the decision-maker is also a factfinder. Juries are always factfinders. District judges often occupy the factfinder role as well, but not always. District judges frequently preside over evidentiary hearings in various forms. In criminal cases, judged preside over detention hearings and suppression hearings which almost invariably involve the presentation of evidence and fact-finding by the judge. In civil cases, judges preside over many types of hearings involving some form of factfinding, such as motions for summary judgment, in which the parties provide the court with supposedly uncontested facts, or motions for preliminary injunctions or other injunctive relief. Likewise, district judges will serve as the factfinders, of course, in bench trials. Still, in some cases, a district judge may preside over hearings that don't involve any fact-finding. An example of such hearings are motions to dismiss, when the judge is bound by the four corners of the complaint or the indictment and makes no factual conclusions, assuming for the sake of ruling on the motion that the facts alleged in the complaint or indictment are true.

Unlike both juries and district judges, appellate court judges don't act as factfinders.[14] The facts come to appellate judges having already been decided. Appellate judges are presented the facts on a cold and established record. Appellate judges decide the legal question, typically accepting the facts as established in the lower courts.[15]

There is a fundamental difference in advocacy when facts are in dispute versus when the facts are not in dispute or exist on a cold record. When attorneys are advocating that a decision-maker find certain facts, it calls upon all the skills of rhetoric using pathos, ethos, and logos.[16] Effective advocates either intentionally or intuitively incorporate all three elements into their arguments to some degree when striving to persuade a factfinder.[17] The most talented attorneys, however, recognize that the focus and emphasis on the elements should vary, depending on the nature of the case. In some cases, logic is the most compelling aspect of the argument, while in others, an appeal to emotion is more likely to succeed. Attorneys must persuade the factfinder to find the facts favorable to their parties and then explain how those facts support their legal positions. Sometimes an attorney must use rhetorical and reasoning skills to persuade a factfinder that their client should prevail even when the factfinder does not find the facts to be as claimed.

On the other hand, attorneys argue to a court of appeals on a cold record; this calls upon very different advocacy skills.[18] Sometimes attorneys use their rhetorical skills to bring the cold record to life. Usually, though, appellate attorneys focus on the logos part of rhetoric to persuade appellate courts as a matter of legal reasoning based on the facts developed below.[19] In appellate advocacy, the emphasis is on legal persuasion, not factual persuasion. The appellate advocate, in written and oral advocacy, is focused on the law. The skill there is to accept the facts as established in the lower court and then apply the law comparing the facts of the case on appeal with precedent. The appellant is often tasked with using persuasive skills to distinguish the facts of adverse precedent from the facts of the case on appeal, while the appellee seeks to persuade the appellate judges that the facts of the case on appeal are materially similar to favorable precedent.

When the facts are in dispute before district judges in bench trials or evidentiary hearings, attorneys often rely on trial advocacy skills they learned in persuading jurors to decide the facts. On other occasions, attorneys must use their appellate advocacy skills to persuade the judge that the facts—either those found by the judge or assumed from the pleadings—are similar or dissimilar to precedent. But again, the skills used to persuade jurors as factfinders are not directly transferrable to those used to persuade judges as factfinders. To be effective advocates when persuading jurors, attorneys often lean more into pathos and emotional appeals, whereas with judges logic is often more persuasive, as we will explain in later chapters.

5. Evidence Rules Apply

Evidence rules control the flow of information to factfinders. As we noted, appellate judges are not factfinders. Although both jurors and judges serve as factfinders, evidence rules don't apply to them equally. That practical reality implicates the need for attorneys to modify their advocacy skills depending on whether and to what extent evidence rules constrain their persuasive efforts.

When jurors serve as factfinders, the rules of evidence apply. Indeed, the primary purpose of evidence rules is to protect jurors from unreliable evidence.[20] As Professor Wigmore, a famous expert on the rules of evidence, once explained, the rules of evidence are "based on the purpose of saving the jurors from being misled" due to jurors' "inexperience in analyzing evidence, and their unfamiliarity with the chicanery of counsel."[21] This purpose is reflected in Federal Rule of Evidence 104(c), which requires judges to conduct hearings regarding the admissibility of evidence "so that the jury cannot hear it" under certain circumstances or when "justice so requires."[22] Consequently, effective advocacy to juries involves presenting evidence that is admissible under the evidence rules and objecting to inadmissible evidence. Understandably then, a significant amount of time in trial advocacy courses is spent working on skills tied to getting exhibits admitted into evidence under the rules of evidence, and using the evidence rules to prevent the opponent's evidence from reaching the jury.

In stark contrast, when judges serve as factfinders, the rules of evidence often don't apply at all, and even when they do apply, they apply in a "relaxed" manner.[23] Because it is understood that the Federal Rules of Evidence were designed to protect unsophisticated jurors from unreliable evidence and the chicanery of clever counsel, it is not surprising that the Federal Rules of Evidence would generally not apply when judges serve as factfinders. In theory, trained judges are experienced in analyzing evidence and are familiar with the chicanery of counsel; therefore, they don't need the protection that evidence rules provide to laypersons. Thus, it makes sense, for instance, that in making evidentiary rulings, judges are not bound by any of the Federal Rules of Evidence "except those on privilege."[24] Similarly, Rule 1101(d) states that the Federal Rules are inapplicable in many proceedings when judges act as factfinders, particularly in criminal cases.[25] These miscellaneous proceedings include: (1) extradition or rendition; (2) issuing an arrest warrant, criminal summons, or search warrant; (3) preliminary examination in a criminal case; (4) sentencing hearings; (5) probation and revocation hearings; and (6) detention hearings.[26] The Federal Rules of Evidence don't apply in detention hearings,[27] suppression hearings,[28] or sentencing hearings,[29] for example.

Thus, attorneys advocating to judges in hearings where the rules of evidence don't apply should consider the implications. Evidence that wouldn't be admissible under the rules is admissible when the rules are inapplicable. Attorneys cannot object to the admission of evidence by invoking evidence rules that don't apply. That is not to say, however, that evidence rules are irrelevant even in hearings when they don't apply. Judges are trained in the rules of evidence and will be more skeptical of and give less weight to evidence that wouldn't be admissible under the applicable evidence rules, even when the rules don't apply. Knowing this, effective attorneys should still strive to present evidence that would be admissible under the rules. Alternatively, attorneys should present evidence in a way that would bolster the reliability of the evidence, even if the evidence wouldn't comply with the rules of evidence. Also, in argument, attorneys should acknowledge evidence that would be inadmissible under the rules, understand the reasons for the various rules, and use these reasons to persuade the judge about what weight to give the evidence.

For instance, Federal Rule of Evidence 404(a) prohibits admission of character evidence to prove a person acted in conformity with that character because the rule drafters believed a person's character is a poor predictor of behavior.[30] On the other hand, Rule 406 permits admission of habit evidence for the purpose of showing a person acted on a particular occasion consistent with that habit because of the belief that a habit is a good predictor of behavior.[31] In other instances, the Federal Rules of Evidence prohibit admission of evidence for policy reasons. For example, Federal Rule of Evidence 407 bars admission of evidence of subsequent remedial measures because we, as a society, want people or companies to take remedial measures to prevent future harms.[32] The point is that attorneys need to understand the reasoning underlying each rule to effectively advocate to a judge even when the rules of evidence are inapplicable.

The Federal Rules of Evidence do apply in some settings, such as in all bench trials, when judges serve as factfinders.[33] Even then, though, not all Federal Rules of Evidence apply when a judge is a factfinder in a bench trial, or at least don't apply to the same degree as they do when a jury is the factfinder. For example, Rule 403 provides that "[t]he court may exclude relevant evidence if its probative value is substantially outweighed by a danger of one or more of the following: unfair prejudice, confusing the issues, misleading the jury, undue delay, wasting time, or needlessly presenting cumulative evidence."[34] Courts have held, however, that Rule 403 is "relaxed significantly" or even unnecessary when a judge is the factfinder.[35] The same is true of Rule 404(b).[36] Courts reason that a judge "can hear relevant evidence, weigh its probative value and reject any improper inferences."[37] Similarly, there is little need in bench trials for so-called *Daubert* motions to bar admission of expert testimony because "[t]he main purpose of *Daubert* exclusion is to protect juries from being swayed by dubious scientific testimony."[38]

Indeed, courts have held that all evidence rules are generally relaxed when a judge is the factfinder.[39] For that reason, judges are "entitled to greater latitude in evidentiary rulings," when they are factfinders and will be reversed "only where they affect a substantial right of the complaining party."[40] Thus, judges often prefer to err on the side of caution by admitting evidence when they serve as factfinders, even if the evidence may be inadmissible under a strict adherence to the Federal Rules of Evidence, because judges are able to afford the evidence appropriate weight.[41]

Persuading Judges

In general, then, judges are generally expected to apply the rules of evidence in bench trials and bar inadmissible evidence. In ruling on the admissibility of the evidence, however, judges must necessarily see or hear the evidence to rule on its admissibility. This conundrum requires judges to exercise mental discipline to disregard and ignore evidence they just saw, and that may be very difficult to do in some instances.[42] Judges are assumed to have the mental acuity to disregard inadmissible evidence. Nevertheless, attorneys must recognize the conundrum and address this issue if they want to effectively advocate to a judge as factfinder.

Attorneys can raise evidentiary issues before trial by filing a motion in limine, or during the trial by objecting.[43] The purpose of a motion in limine is to allow a judge to rule in advance of trial on the admissibility and relevance of certain forecasted evidence so as to prevent a jury from being exposed to unreliable evidence.[44] Thus, motions in limine further a judge's gatekeeping responsibility to eliminate from consideration evidence that shouldn't be presented to the jury because it wouldn't be admissible for any purpose.[45] When a judge is the factfinder, though, motions in limine are generally inappropriate.[46] An exception to this general rule might be when an order granting a motion in limine would significantly impact the trial, such as by eliminating a witness or the ability of a party to prove a claim or item of damages.[47]

In short, the way attorneys advocate is greatly impacted by whether evidence rules apply, and whether and how they apply depends on whether the factfinder is a jury or a judge.

6. Advocate Will Reappear Before Decision-Maker

Juries are comprised of individuals randomly gathered together and selected through an empanelment process that results in each jury being unique from every other jury. Thus, attorneys will never appear again before the same jury. Indeed, most courts excuse jurors from further service for some extended period of time once they have served on a jury, so it is highly likely that attorneys will never again see even an individual juror again.

Appellate panels are somewhat similar to juries in that, except for supreme courts, appellate panels are typically comprised of three appellate judges randomly assigned to the case. It follows, then, that attorneys usually don't appear before the same panel of judges. It is possible, of course, depending on the nature of an attorney's practice and the frequency of appearing in the court of appeals, that an attorney could appear before

Three. How Judges, Jurors, and Appellate Panels Differ

the same panel more than once in different cases. It is likely that any attorney with a regular appellate practice will appear before the same appellate judges repeatedly, albeit on different panels.

In contrast, attorneys will regularly appear before the same district judges over and over again. It is quite common for attorneys to appear before the same judges repeatedly, to the point that judges and attorneys come to know each other well. This is particularly so in smaller districts where there are fewer judges, and especially in criminal practice when there are many more hearings and trials than in civil cases and a smaller cadre of prosecutors and defense attorneys. The only exception to this is, perhaps, in very large metropolitan areas where scores of judges have chambers in a courthouse. In those circumstances, it is possible for attorneys to practice for many years and perhaps never appear before the same judge very often. Even when attorneys may not reappear before the same judge in different cases, they may very well appear before the same judge repeatedly in the same case. Attorneys may advocate before the judge in multiple pretrial motions, with or without oral argument, and then also appear before the same judge in a bench or jury trial. Thus, whenever an attorney is engaged in persuading a judge, in whatever district and however many judges there may be, in most cases they have to consider the very real possibility that they will be seeing that judge again. So what they say and how they handle themselves before him may influence the judge's later perception of them.

Whether an attorney will reappear before a decision-maker can affect advocacy. Attorneys need not worry about future consequences with juries. Attorneys can take inconsistent positions from one jury to the next. They can engage in sharp practices before a jury without worrying about how it may affect them in the future on other cases. They can exaggerate and bluff without being concerned that it could affect their future credibility in the next trial before a different jury. Not so with judges, whether they be district or appellate judges. Attorneys must always consider the reputation they form with judges before whom they may or will reappear.[48] The reputation of a speaker—part of the ethos of persuasion—affects the decision-maker's receptivity of the message. Reputation for credibility is earned over time by attorneys who demonstrate they are trustworthy through their honest, candid, and reliable representations. To be persuasive judge advocates, attorneys must be ever vigilant in maintaining their credibility for though it takes time and effort to establish a reputation for credibility, it can be lost in an instant by a misrepresentation or tantrum.

7. Group or Individual Decision-Making

There are significant differences as decision-makers between jurors, judges, and appellate panels when it comes to the decision-making process. Those differences can have an impact on how decision-makers process information to arrive at decisions. That, in turn, may influence how attorneys advocate to the decision-makers.

JURIES AND JURORS

Juries reach decisions as a result of a collaborative process. Courts regularly instruct jurors that each juror must make up their own mind, but only after fully discussing the evidence with fellow jurors.[49] Thus, though each juror must arrive at their own decision and vote accordingly, they arrive at their decision through a group decision-making process.

There are many benefits from this group-decision-making process. The saying "two heads are better than one" is premised on the belief that when more than one person is involved in solving a problem, there is an increased benefit from the collaborative process over having a single person making the decision. This applies equally in juries, when there are not just two heads, but up to 12 heads making a group decision. In jury group decision-making, the jurors benefit from hearing differing and conflicting points of view. Some jurors may have heard evidence missed by other jurors, or some jurors may comprehend some difficult or confusing evidence or argument and be able to explain it to other jurors who struggled with it. A group of jurors contains individuals with differing levels of intelligence, education, experience, and background. The jurors bring to the group decision-making process their varied attributes and contribute to the group decision-making process in different ways and to different degrees.

Yet, a jury must reach a single decision, despite consisting of a group of individuals. Juries must reach unanimous decisions. If they fail to do so, then it results in a hung jury and a mistrial. Unlike appellate panels, there is no opportunity for dissenting opinions. The jury as a decision-making body must reach a consensus decision, or there is no decision at all.

APPELLATE JUDGES AND APPELLATE PANELS

Like juries, appellate judges engage in a form of group decision-making. Like individual jurors, each judge on an appellate panel must reach their own decision, but they do so as part of a group. Appellate

Three. How Judges, Jurors, and Appellate Panels Differ

judges on a panel discuss and debate cases before them and are influenced both positively[50] and negatively[51] by the input of their fellow judges.

> One of the more troubling aspects of a career judiciary ... is that experience can degenerate into routine, so that panels of judges feel no need to explain to each other what the strength or weakness of the case are as all will understand them, and that in general a process of group-think governs deliberations.[52]

When oral argument is granted in appellate cases, the group decision-making process begins during the give and take of oral argument. It is not uncommon that the questions appellate judges pose to advocates are designed more to convey a message to and persuade a fellow judge on the panel than they are to obtain an answer to the question. After oral arguments, appellate judges meet in conference and discuss the cases before them, coming to some preliminary positions, resulting in the presiding judge assigning to one of the judges on the panel the duty of writing the panel's decision on the case.

The group decision-making process continues in the course of writing the court's decision. Drafts of the court's opinion are exchanged among the judges on the panel. Judges propose edits, additions, and deletions from the written draft in an effort to reach consensus. Through this group-effort opinion-writing process, judges attempt to persuade other judges through the logic and reasoning of their written draft opinions. Sometimes this results in a shift in the outcome of the case when a dissenting judge or group of judges persuades one or more judges formerly constituting the majority to change positions.

Unlike juries as group decision-makers, appellate panels need not reach unanimous decisions. Like district judges, but unlike juries, appellate judges ultimately reach individual decisions and are not bound to agree with their fellow appellate judges. And even when appellate judges may agree with the outcome of the appellate panel's decision, they don't have to agree with its reasoning. Appellate judges may issue concurring or dissenting opinions; jurors cannot. And neither can district court judges.

DISTRICT COURT JUDGES

District judges arrive at their decisions alone. They don't engage in group decision-making. And they don't dissent with themselves.

As decision-makers, individual judges differ much more significantly from juries than they do from individual jurors. Likewise, district judges differ from appellate panels more than they do from appellate judges. Judges, both on the district and appellate benches, comprehend and retain information in the same manner as jurors. They learn from hearing and seeing, in response to aural and visual stimuli. In short, judges employ similar cognitive processes, subject to the same limitations, as any other human.[53]

In hearings and bench trials, though, district judges are juries of one. They are panels of one. Gone are both the negative and positive attributes of group decision-making.[54] The danger of groupthink is absent. Judges don't face peer pressure influencing their decisions during the judges' internal mental deliberations. Also missing, however, are the advantages of the exchange of multiple points of view and different perspectives and the pooling of memories, dynamics that occur in group decision-making.[55] The benefits of sounding out ideas, bouncing around possible solutions, debating points, and brainstorming are not available when a judge alone must reach a decision.[56]

True, most district judges have staff members who assist them. In particular, federal judges have one or more law clerks who are bright, often young lawyers. In some instances, judges may talk out decisions with these law clerks.[57] Indeed, a law clerk may have been present during the hearing or trial and may have seen the same evidence the judge saw. Judges often have law clerks take the laboring oar of drafting a written order reflecting the judge's decision, or review and edit the judge's draft order.

But unlike appellate panels, district judges don't always issue written decisions. Indeed, in many hearings district judges pronounce oral decisions during or at the conclusion of the hearing without any written decision to follow. This is particularly so in criminal proceedings. When magistrate judges decide whether to release or detain an offender pending trial, the judge almost always reaches that decision at the hearing, pronouncing the decision orally. Though there may be a written order following the hearing, they are often form documents reflecting judges' oral decision justifying detention or setting conditions of pretrial release. Similarly, at sentencing hearings judges pronounce decisions on contested sentencing issues orally and pronounce sentences orally. The written judgments that follow are form documents reflecting the judges' oral pronouncements. Only occasionally will judges issue written sentencing rulings. The same is true in civil cases, such as in making rulings on evidentiary disputes, although it is more common for judges to issue written orders reflecting their decisions in civil cases.

Even when judges employ their staff to assist them in their work, it is not the same group decision-making process as exists either with juries or even with appellate panels. The group dynamic is significantly different not only because of the fewer number of people involved but also because of the disparate power relationship between a judge and a law clerk. The judge is the law clerk's boss. The judge and law clerk are not on equal footing, like jurors with other jurors, or like appellate judges are with each other. A discussion a judge may have with law clerks is fundamentally and qualitatively different from the discussion lay people serving on a jury would have with each other in reaching a decision. Likewise, a discussion about a decision between a law clerk and judge is not anywhere near the same nature of the discussion appellate judges have between themselves about a judicial opinion.

How decision-makers arrive at their decisions can and should influence how attorneys engage in advocacy. Attorneys should consider how the presence of more than one decision-maker may influence the degree of comprehension and retention of evidence and argument. With group decision-making, there are multiple audience members. Attorneys should think about whether there is an opportunity to appeal to one or more members in a group-decision making body, or whether there is only a single individual who will determine the outcome. At the same time, attorneys must tailor the message so as to resonate with each member of the group while at the same time not hitting a discordant tone with any of them. When advocating to a district judge, in contrast, an attorney has the ability to hone the argument to cut a path to the lone decision-maker. In short, whether the decision-maker is part of a group, or is an individual, should impact how attorneys advocate.

8. Collateral Pressures on Decision-Makers

Every decision-maker experiences influences and pressures during the decision-making process. Some of those pressures are a product of whether the decision-maker is part of a group as noted in the last discussion. But other pressures on decision-makers are collateral to the form of decision-making. Again, all decision-makers face some degree of collateral pressures while making decisions, but the nature and significance of those pressures vary dramatically among decision-makers.

Jurors experience collateral pressures primarily arising from their personal lives. The people who comprise a jury are not professional jurors. Serving as jurors is not their occupation. Their role as jurors is a temporary, unwanted, assignment that interrupts their work and lives. So jurors' family and job responsibilities remain but are on hold while they serve as jurors. Their personal responsibilities and concerns, naturally then, may influence their decision-making process by distracting their attention and concentration during trial and deliberations. Concerns about missing work, missing pay, or an angry boss may also influence jurors' ability to serve well. Family responsibilities, such as child or elder care, and other day-to-day duties of being a spouse, parent, and child—responsibilities jurors have found a way to manage in their normal lives—are upended when they lose control of their own schedules upon being sworn in as jurors. It is also entirely possible that jurors sometimes feel pressure from family, friends, or co-workers about the merits of the case on which they are serving, pressure that could even constitute juror misconduct. Last, although jurors have no deadline for reaching their verdicts, the desire to return to their normal lives creates a degree of pressure to arrive at a decision and be done with their involuntary civic duties.

Appellate judges also experience collateral pressures in their decision-making process. Time is seldom one of them. Like jurors, appellate judges have no deadlines for reaching their decisions. Rarely do cases come before appellate panels where time is of the essence in rendering an opinion. Yet, they are conscientious public servants who recognize that delays in their decisions affect the litigants' lives and, sometimes, liberty. At the same time, appellate judges are only responsible for the cases before them. When they hear oral arguments, the day is set aside and devoted to the task. When writing an opinion, appellate judges have the luxury of time to think deeply, research thoroughly, and write carefully—as we would want them to do when their opinions constitute precedent.

The collateral pressures on district judges are materially different from those facing jurors or appellate judges. All judges have significant responsibilities that come with the authority of their positions, and those responsibilities can influence how they make decisions. Many responsibilities are unique to district judges, however, that are not present with appellate judges. District judges must listen to testimony, consider evidence, and hear attorneys' arguments, but they are also responsible to enforce the evidence rules when they apply, ensure witnesses are treated with respect and not harassed, and make certain attorneys conduct themselves in a professional and ethical manner.[58] While a district judge may be trying to concentrate on the case at hand, the judge is simultaneously watching the clock, and thinking of other cases and other litigants. When presiding over jury trials, judges are always mindful of limited judicial resources and concerned about not wasting jurors' valuable time. Judges struggle to find the proper balance between permitting the parties the full benefit of having their day in court against the need to allow time for every other litigant to have their day in court as well. Judges are aware that additional briefing, more evidence, and additional argument will cost the parties more in attorneys' fees and expenses. Judges recognize they need to reach reasoned and thoughtful decisions, but also feel the pressure of the need for a speedy resolution of every case, knowing that parties need and deserve timely decisions.[59] When it comes to district judges issuing written decisions, there is a palpable tension between getting a decision out quickly, and writing a decision that is as thoroughly researched or as carefully written as what an appellate decision might be. Time is not a luxury district judges enjoy. Indeed, in federal civil cases, Rule 1 of the Federal Rules of Civil Procedure urge rapid resolution of cases by requiring judges to construe, administer, and employ them in such a manner that "secure[s] the just, speedy, and inexpensive determination of every action and proceeding."[60] In federal criminal cases, the Speedy Trial Act[61] dictates that time is of the essence for judges to move the cases to resolution. All these statutory, regulatory, and practical considerations affect the manner in which judges consider and decide cases.

Jurors, in contrast, generally don't consider any of these practical and collateral matters when they are asked to reach decisions. Nor do appellate judges face these issues when, on appeal, time constraints are largely absent. There are no equivalent statutes or rules that compel or urge appellate judges to reach speedy resolutions of appeals. The sense of urgency ever present at the district court level is largely absent when the case works its way through the appellate process.

The presence of collateral pressures can impact effective advocacy. Attorneys should be alert to whether and how collateral pressures are affecting a decision-maker's ability to concentrate on the evidence or argument. Identifying the collateral pressures and recognizing when or if they are present should influence how attorneys tailor their advocacy to counteract these influences. Knowing that judges are under pressure from these collateral sources, attorneys may need to directly address those collateral concerns when trying to persuade a judge on an issue. Attorneys may want to account for how these collateral pressures may affect the timing of when attorneys raise issued before a judge as well. For example, it may be best to raise an issue during a jury trial at a break or after the jury has been excused for the day, rather than during a sidebar when the judge will be concerned about keeping the jury waiting. Knowing these collateral pressures on judges should prompt attorneys to consider ways to modify their advocacy to be responsive to those pressures, such as by emphasizing brevity and clarity in their advocacy.

9. Time and Space Limitations

Courts place time limits on advocates in the interest of efficiency. For similar reasons, courts place page or word limits—space limits—on written submissions. The nature and extent of these limitations differ, however, depending on who decision-maker is. Those differences directly impact how attorneys advocate.

Attorneys are least restricted in their ability to advocate to judges than they are to both juries and appellate panels. With judges, the limitations take of two forms: time and space. The degree to which judges limit the time they allow attorneys to present their argument will vary greatly from court to court and judge to judge. The amount of time permitted in oral argument on motions may be the product of an individual judge's personality but will also be influenced by the judge's daily schedule and the judge's caseload. Unlike in appellate arguments, though, district judges don't impose arbitrary time limits. Judges don't put attorneys on a strict clock with a limited opportunity to talk dictated by yellow and red lightbulbs, like appellate judges do. Moreover, when advocating before a district judge, all the time allotted can be directed at the sole decision-maker. Because judges sit alone in deciding cases, they don't have to share their time and attention with other judges sitting on the panel.[62]

District judges have the authority to, and do, also place time limits on attorneys in making opening and closing arguments.[63] And sometimes, judges place limits on the length of time attorneys have to conduct direct and cross examination, or to present a case to a jury, particularly in civil cases.[64] Although it is much rarer, the law permits judges to impose similar time limits on advocates to present their cases in criminal jury trials as well.[65] With jury trials, then, it is not the decision-maker who limits the time the advocate has to persuade them, but the neutral arbiter—the judge—who does so. It follows, then, that part of effective jury trial advocacy also involves effectively persuading judges to allot more time for jury presentation.

Judges also place space limitations on attorneys' ability to advocate by imposing page limits on written submissions. But again, these space limits differ from those imposed by appellate courts. Many district judges are fairly liberal and typically more flexible than appellate courts in granting motions for filing overlength brief. Whether attorneys should file overlength briefs is another matter we will address later. The point here, however, is that although judges impose limits on attorneys' ability to advocate, those limits are seldom severe and often flexible.

With juries, attorneys' ability to advocate is limited by time. As noted, attorneys don't have the ability to advocate to jurors in writing. The only avenue of persuasion is through oral argument. Now, good attorneys know that how they present evidence and cross examination is part of the art of persuasion before juries. In that sense, the only limits placed on attorneys to advocate to jurors are those dictated by the amount of evidence there is to present and whether the judge places a time limit on the parties to present their cases. The most direct form of advocacy in jury trials, however, is through opening statements and closing arguments. In jury trials, judges almost always place time limits on these presentations. The days of hours-long or days-long closing arguments are a thing of the past.[66] In federal jury trials, opening statements are often limited to a half hour and closing arguments to an hour.

Appellate courts impose the greatest restrictions on attorneys' ability to advocate. Those limits are both in time and space. When attorneys are granted an opportunity to present oral argument—an increasingly rare event—they are strictly limited in the time allotted for them to present oral argument. The time provided each side for oral argument is often very short. Why appellate courts are so stingy on granting time to present oral argument remains a mystery. Indeed, it is somewhat ironic that appellate courts impose the strictest time limits when, as we discussed in the last section, they are subject to much less time pressures than district court judges. There was a time in our history when oral arguments before the Supreme Court lasted days.[67] Nevertheless, it is not uncommon now for appellate panels to allot attorneys a whopping ten minutes a side to present oral argument. And the time limits are enforced by pesky little lights on the lectern. Appellate panels also place space limits on attorneys. Appellate briefs come with page limits that are strictly enforced. Unlike district courts, appellate courts are much less liberal in granting motions for filing overlength briefs.

10. Decision-Maker Has Power Over Advocate

When trying to persuade another, the power differential between advocate and audience can impact how one advocates. When we, for example, try to persuade our children to perform chores, our oral advocacy occurs in the context that both our children and we know we have the power to enforce the decision through sanctions if necessary. We would attempt to persuade a king with a more deferential tone, because of the immense power a king would have over us, than we would attempt

Persuading Judges

to persuade a pauper. So, too, must we then consider the power differential that exists between an attorney and the audience the attorney seeks to persuade.

Jurors have power to make the ultimate decision about the object of the advocacy, of course, but they have no authority over the advocate. Jurors cannot discipline or sanction an attorney if they feel offended or believe the attorney has misrepresented facts or the law. Attorneys need not fear jurors, in that sense.

In contrast, judges—both trial judges and appellate judges—have a tremendous amount of power over attorneys, and both know it. Attorneys are officers of the court.[68] This means they owe a duty of fealty to the tribunal, to the justice system itself, in addition to the duty owed their clients. As we will discuss later, there isn't necessarily a conflict between the duty to zealously represent clients and the duty owed the court. As one judge explained:

> Attorneys sometimes view these roles [as zealous advocate and officer of the court] as opposed. This is a mistake. An attorney's backbone is her credibility. Good attorneys are credible attorneys because they simultaneously advocate their client's interests with zeal while presenting arguments as an officer of the court who respects rules of law and decorum.[69]

Attorneys are also bound by ethical rules to be candid with the court.[70] Indeed, attorneys are bound by many ethical rules. If a judge believes an attorney has violated any ethical rule, the judge can refer the attorney to the state ethics body for investigation and possible discipline. Moreover, judges can directly sanction attorneys, including disbarment, fines, and public or private reprimand.[71]

There exists, however, an even more subtle, but no less important, power judges have over attorneys. What judges say, and how judges render their decisions, can impact attorneys' careers for better or worse. Judges can wield a poisonous pen. By taking an attorney to task for wrongful or even poor performance, a judge soils the attorney's reputation and potentially can damage the attorney-client relationship. This is especially so when judges chose to identify the attorney by name in a written decision.[72]

This power differential between attorneys and judges is therefore quite different from that which exists between attorneys and jurors. The only power jurors have over attorneys is in the verdict they render. The power judges have over attorneys goes far, far beyond the outcome of any single case.

B. The Decision-Maker

1. Legally Trained

Jury trial advocacy correctly assumes that the jurors have no legal training. Persuasive jury advocacy, then, involves interpreting foreign legalese for lay members of the jury. Attorneys must translate legal concepts into simple terms for jurors to comprehend. Attorneys also recognize that lay people are more likely to make decisions based on an emotional basis. "[Q]uintessentially American conditions foster a culture of psychological storytelling and persuasion techniques that lead jurors to make decisions while unconsciously relying more on emotion than the disciplined application of the law to the facts."[73] Persuasive jury advocacy also requires attorneys to develop methods to appeal to jurors emotionally and rationally to convince them to find for one side or the other. Trial advocacy courses and books teach lawyers how to use common language to explain complex legal matters to jurors and to appeal to jurors' emotions and basic sense of right and wrong.

Trial advocacy also recognizes that jurors have innate biases, prejudices, preconceptions and presumptions. A significant amount of focus in jury selection involves ferreting out these inherent characteristics to inform the attorneys' motions to challenge jurors for cause and the exercise of their peremptory strikes. And, good trial attorneys will tailor the presentation of the evidence and arguments to address and counteract or exploit jurors' inherent biases, preconceptions, values and beliefs.

Some of these skills of trial advocacy may apply when attorneys are trying to persuade judges, both district court judges and appellate judges. After all, judges are human, too. Judges have emotions (perhaps some more than others) and thus can have emotional responses to evidence and arguments. Judges also have their own fair share of inherent biases and prejudices, preconceptions, and presumptions, as a result of their backgrounds, histories, and experiences.

Judges are different from jurors, however, because of their legal training. Judges have been trained, and have the mental discipline, to more successfully suppress their implicit biases, presumptions, and personal values and beliefs so that they don't influence their decisions. Judges focus on reason and logic and strive to apply the law neutrally. It follows that attorneys should adjust their advocacy in recognition of this difference.

In law school, judges learned deductive reasoning. Before they reached the bench, during their experience as practicing attorneys, judges honed their analytical skills and disciplined their minds to focus on material facts and issues. Like doctors, judges developed the ability to wall themselves off emotionally from cases and to approach cases with something akin to clinical detachment.[74] As attorneys, and even more so once obtaining a seat on the bench, judges focus on facts that have legal significance and disregard facts that don't. Unlike jurors who lack legal training, judges as factfinders are better equipped to understand which facts are important, and which are not.

Judges are also members of the same social and professional class as attorneys, sharing the same language, having similar formative experiences, and being bound by the same core rules of ethics and values.[75] When attorneys are speaking to judges, then, they are talking with one of their own. There is no need to translate legal concepts and precepts to judges. This is quite dissimilar to attorneys talking to jurors.

Because judges are legally trained and mentally disciplined to make dispassionate decisions based on reason and logic, it follows that appeals to emotion, the pathos part of classical rhetoric, not only find little purchase with judges but may be seen as insulting by suggesting that judges would make a decision based on emotion.[76] Thus, when arguing to judges, attorneys should focus on the law and the facts. Although attorneys should be emphatic on important points, they should leave drama and theatrics for juries. Judges are not persuaded by such displays; indeed, vociferous oral advocacy may have just the opposite effect than intended.[77] Judges expect attorneys to speak to them on an intellectual level, with an emphasis on reasoning and common sense and not on emotions. In short, when advocating to judges attorneys should emphasize logos over pathos.

2. Decision-Maker Knowable

The most fundamental tenet of effective public speaking is to know one's audience. The ability to persuade another person is greatly influenced by the degree to which the speaker knows the listener. It is important to have some idea of the abilities of the listener to reason and understand the message, whether the listener is likely to be receptive or resistant to the message, what experience or knowledge the listener might already have about the facts or issues at hand, and whether the listener has previously made decisions on the issue. The more advocates can know about the person or persons who they are trying to persuade, the more precisely they can craft a message tailored to resonate with the audience.

There is a tremendous difference between what attorneys can know about jurors and what attorneys can know about judges. Voir dire enables attorneys to learn limited information about prospective jurors in order for attorneys to make more informed for-cause challenges and to exercise peremptory strikes.[78] Good trial attorneys also use that information to tailor the presentation of their evidence and argument to the particular audience of jurors ultimately selected. Juror questionnaires,[79] private investigation of prospective jurors,[80] and jury consultants[81] can supplement voir dire to provide attorneys with more information about prospective jurors. In the end, however, the information trial attorneys can learn about individual jurors is limited and imperfect, restricted by access, time, and money.

Judges, on the other hand, are more of an open book. "A good lawyer tries to learn as much as possible about the judge who will decide the case."[82] As public officials, much is known about judges and attorneys can learn even more with a little effort. There is a treasure trove of information about judges in the public domain, particularly with regard to federal judges whose lengthy and detailed Senate Judicial Questionnaires are publicly filed. Many judges also provide information about their preferences and practices on court websites. Judges often speak publicly at conferences about their preferences and practices or publish articles in bar journals or law reviews on the topic. Hearings and trials take place in open court, so anyone can observe judges' practices and procedures. Finally, other attorneys are an available source of information about judges' past practices and procedures. Attorneys from outside the district can associate with local counsel who may know or may more easily come to know the judge.

Of course, the important thing is what trial attorneys do with the information that they have about decision-makers. All too often trial attorneys use the limited information they know about prospective jurors only to decide whom to challenge for cause or remove using peremptory strikes. The really good trial attorneys consider juror information in tailoring the presentation of their cases to the jurors. Good trial attorneys adjust and modify the presentation of the evidence and their arguments to better appeal to the background, abilities, and views of the jurors. Less effective trial attorneys simply present their cases as if all jurors and juries are the same. Similarly, less effective attorneys all too often present their cases to judges in hearings, bench trials, and appellate arguments as if all judges were alike. Instead, attorneys could and should adjust their presentations based on the judge's experience and familiarity with the facts and procedural history of the case.[83] To be effective advocates to judges, attorneys could find out what the judge knows about the subject matter and the legal issues. How familiar a judge is about a legal issue or factual context could greatly influence an attorney's ability to persuade the judge. The less familiar a judge is about an issue, the more space in a written brief, and more time in oral argument, may be necessary to provide sufficient background for the judge to comprehend the issues. On the other hand, when attorneys learn that the judge is quite familiar with a particular area of law or factual context in which a legal issue has arisen, the attorney can be more concise.

3. Decision-Maker's Decision's Impact on Others

Yet another difference between decision-makers in the justice system is whether they are concerned about the broader implications from their decisions, or whether their focus is primarily if not solely on the narrow consequences to the parties and on the dispute before them. If decision-makers are influenced by how their decisions will impact and influence other parties and society as a whole, to be effective advocates attorneys should address these broader implications. When, however, decision-makers are focused only on the dispute and parties before them, then attorneys' persuasive efforts must be tailored to those narrow concerns to be effective.

Generally speaking, juries, as decision-makers, have a narrow focus. Jurors have been empaneled to resolve a single dispute between the parties at trial. The scope of their decision is proscribed and limited by the verdict form and interrogatories submitted to them. Their sole task is to resolve the dispute between the two parties before them on the narrow issues presented to them, and that is all. In making their decision, jurors are seldom concerned about the broader implications of their decision. Their verdict will be binding only upon the parties before them and will have no binding precedential impact on any other court or party. Jurors generally don't, and shouldn't, be concerned about the broader political or societal implications of their decisions. Indeed, attorneys are generally prohibited in closing arguments made to juries to appeal to such broader interests.[84] When jurors base decisions on how their decisions may impact others or society as a whole, it is a form of jury nullification. It is, in that sense, a failure of the jury decision-making process in which jurors are to base their decision only on the facts of the case before them and the law that the judge provides them through jury instructions.

There are exceptions, of course, as there often are. When, in civil cases, juries are asked to consider punitive damages, jurors may take

Three. How Judges, Jurors, and Appellate Panels Differ

into account how their verdict may influence other people, whether it will be effective in deterring similar conduct not only by one of the parties before them but also similarly situated parties. Punitive damages are designed to provide both specific and general deterrence, to "send a message" to defendant and others similarly situated. Likewise, when in capital criminal cases jurors are charged with the responsibility of deciding whether the defendant should live or die, it is proper for them to consider the broader implications and impact their verdicts will have on others, not only for the defendant whose life is at stake. Jurors may also consider whether imposing the death penalty will deter others from committing similar crimes and whether mercy will send a broader message to society. These exceptions, however, prove the rule that juries generally have narrow decision-making authority unaffected by the broader implications their decisions could have on others.

District court judges are more like juries than they are like appellate panels when it comes to the impact their decisions have on others. Justice Scalia noted: "Bear in mind that trial judges are fundamentally different from appellate judges. They focus on achieving the proper result in one particular case, not on crafting a rule of law that will do justice in the generality of cases."[85] A district court judge's decision has no binding precedential authority. A district court's decision binds only the parties before the judge and no one else. No other judge is obliged to follow a district court judge's decision. Because of this, a district judge's focus is generally narrow. Their concern is resolving the dispute between the two parties before the judge. District judges don't make law, so they are less concerned with the broader implications of their decision beyond the parties in the case before them than are appellate judges whose decisions constitute binding precedent and affect more than only the parties to the instant dispute. Because district judges are far more hemmed in by prior decisions and are not allowed to shift the law, distinguishing the facts of binding precedent is much more important for attorneys advocating to district judges than it is to appellate judges.

Inferior judges—judges below the appellate level—approach decision-making from a fundamentally different perspective than appellate judges. The reality of lower-court judges is that they are problem-solvers, plain and simple, who recognize their role in the judicial system and seek to faithfully execute it.

lawyers who become judges ... seek to operate as if bound by rules not
 ise they will be punished if they do not but because they believe it is the
  ing for a judge to do. The begin to think about cases not from their

intuition about the just outcome but from the dictates of authoritative sources of law. The question that judges ask is … "What is the law, and what does it mean for this case?" Those may be difficult questions in themselves, but they significantly narrow the ambit of admissible considerations.[86]

Unlike appellate judges, lower-level judges know they are bound by precedent and limited by the facts; they seek to solve the dispute before them, nothing more.

Of course, this is not always and strictly true. Although a district court judge's decision does not constitute binding precedent, it can constitute persuasive authority. It follows, then, that judges are sometimes influenced in making their decisions by broader implications their decisions may have, particularly when the issue before them is one for which there is no binding authority. And like juries, judges' decisions are influenced by broader considerations such as the deterrence effect the decision may have on others when judges are asked to decide punitive damages and when imposing sentences in criminal cases.

Appellate panels, however, are different from both juries and judges to the extent that they have more authority to make law, to move the needle, to shift the direction the law takes. Appellate judges know that their decisions will bind all lower courts. Their decisions, then, resolve not just the dispute between appellant and appellee, but influence the outcome of cases yet to come. Appellate panels must, therefore, consider the broader implications of their decisions beyond the parties and dispute before them. Chief Justice Marshall's decision in *Marbury v. Madison*[87] is a brilliant example in which the Supreme Court's decision had a narrow impact on the plaintiff that was adverse to Marshall's own political party, but a broader implication of vesting in the Supreme Court the awesome power of deciding whether an act of Congress is constitutional, which benefited Marshall's political party.

In large part because they have binding authority on lower courts and because they can reverse lower decisions, appellate decisions command greater public attention, as they should. The press more often carry reports of appellate decisions, particularly of state and the United States Supreme Courts, because of the broader implications those decisions have beyond the parties to the lawsuit. And the attention given to appellate decisions is especially pronounced when appellate courts reverse lower court decisions and/or render decisions on controversial or politically sensitive issues. As decision-makers, appellate judges understand the power their decisions can have far beyond the narrow dispute before them. Those broader implications can influence the decisions they make and the way they make their decisions.

Three. How Judges, Jurors, and Appellate Panels Differ

It follows that effective advocates tailor their advocacy in a manner that recognizes the differences between decision-makers' concerns. Good attorneys will emphasize the impact a jury or judge's decision will have on the attorneys' individual clients in the narrow dispute before those decision-makers. With jurors, emphasis on a pathos-based argument—on the greater good or emotional appeals toward justice generally—may be less persuasive to jurors than a narrower pathos-based argument focused on the impact the decision may have on the attorney's client. Indeed, such arguments may be improper. With judges, a logos-based argument—one emphasizing the rational result demanded by application of the law to the facts—is likely to be more persuasive than any pathos-based argument focused on either the big-picture implications of the decision or its impact on the parties to the litigation.[88] Recognizing that those decision-makers are much less concerned—if concerned at all—about any broader implications their decisions may have on others, attorneys should spend little effort focused on the impact the outcome will have on anyone other than their clients. Of course, when juries or judges are concerned about broader implications, such as when deciding punitive damages or criminal punishment, good attorneys will adjust their advocacy to take into account the decision-maker's concern about these broader implications. Likewise, good appellate advocacy involves recognizing that the appellate panel, while of course concerned about resolving the narrow dispute the parties have brought on appeal, will be influenced in making its decision by the broader implications its decision will have as binding precedent on lower courts. Effective appellate advocacy involves identifying the broader implications an appellate court's decision may have and tailoring advocacy to appeal to those broader interests.

4. Decision-Maker Explains Decision

Whether decision-makers are required to explain their decision can influence how one advocates before them. Juries reflect their decisions in verdict forms and interrogatories provided by the court. In a criminal case, for example, a jury may check a box indicating the defendant is guilty or not guilty. In a civil case, jurors find for or against parties based on their claims and typically determine damages. Beyond the limited questions they answer in verdict forms and interrogatories, juries and jurors are not obliged to explain how or why they reached the decision they made. Juries don't have to explain what evidence they believed and what evidence they rejected. They don't have to explain the weight they afforded the evidence.

Persuading Judges

They don't have to explain why they decided the defendant was guilty or not guilty, or why a plaintiff proved or failed to prove a defendant was negligent. Jurors' verdicts are enigmatic in that sense. We know from jurors only what we ask of them, and nothing more. And they don't have to tell us anything more than what we ask them.

Because jurors don't have to explain their decisions, attorneys need not necessarily focus on every piece of evidence, or every element of a claim, charge, or defense. Rather, attorneys can focus on the bottom line, speaking of the evidence as a whole, emphasizing the aggregate, and brushing over the specific. Attorneys need not specifically address thorny issues, such as the credibility of specific witnesses or conflicting evidence, counting on jurors' overall sense of what the evidence proved and who should win the dispute.

Judges, however, at both district and appellate levels, generally provide written explanations in the form of opinions or orders explaining not just what they decided, but why and how they reached the decision they made. Even when judges render decisions orally, they are expected to explain the basis for their decisions if for no other reason than to make it easier for appellate courts to review the lower court's decision. When facts are in dispute, judges have to make findings of fact. They have to state what witnesses they believe and which they don't, and why. When legal tests involve multiple factors, judges generally need to address those factors in written opinion, explaining whether they found the factor proven and what weight they afforded certain facts or factors. Although judges issue many oral rulings, the rulings that matter the most on dispositive motions, are almost always reduced to writing.

Because judges typically provide an explanation for their decisions, and usually written explanations at that, this provides attorneys an opportunity through their own written advocacy to influence judges' decisions. How attorneys frame issues and organize their written and oral arguments may affect how the judges do so as well. This, in turn, may impact the scope and nature of the ultimate decision. In some instances, district court judges even give attorneys an opportunity to provide draft orders or, in bench trials, proposed findings of fact and conclusions of law. The words lawyers chose to frame issues, to persuade judges, have the capacity to influence the words the judges use to frame the same issues. When judges follow the lawyers' lead in reaching a decision on the merits of a dispute, the lawyer can directly influence the likelihood of success with the judge and on appeal.

Because district court judges must explain their factfinding in detail and address every element and every factor of applicable legal tests, attorneys cannot brush over the details and count on the overall sense of the evidence like they can with juries. To be persuasive with judges as fact-finders, then, attorneys should address the evidence in detail, specifically argue the credibility of critical testimony, and propose resolutions to conflicting evidence. Likewise, attorneys should address each element or legal factor at issue. Knowing that a judge cannot simply render a general ruling or verdict and will have to explain the basis—factual and legal—for the decisions, good judge advocates will assist the judge by providing them with the analysis the judges will have to perform. Attorneys should not leave it to chance that the reasoning the attorney believes is correct is the one the judge will adopt.

C. Conclusion

It is important to understand that the skills learned in jury trial advocacy and appellate advocacy courses are not all directly transferrable to the trial court setting. Cheerleaders for moot court programs tend to believe that skills learned there prepares students to argue in any court.[89] It is true that some skills learned in those programs help prepare students to argue on their feet generally and, to that extent, prepare students to argue before district court judges to some extent. Nevertheless, as we will explore in more detail in a later chapter, some of the jury trial advocacy and appellate advocacy skills can be ineffective with district judges, and others may actually be counterproductive. The context of advocacy to district judges is different than with juries and appellate courts. District judges also think and decide cases differently than jurors and juries and differently than appellate judges to some degree. Thus, although we believe trial and appellate advocacy courses remain very valuable, we disagree that the skills learned in trial and appellate advocacy courses adequately equip students to argue effectively before district court judges.

In summary, there are important differences in judges, jurors, juries, and appellate courts as decision-makers and in the context in which advocacy occurs before these decision-makers. Examining these difference makes it readily apparent that advocacy skills effective with one may not be effective with another. Effective advocacy requires modifying the methods of advocacy to account for the differences in context and decision-maker.

Having identified the differences in context and decision-makers and why they demand modifying methods of advocacy, we turn in the next chapter to examine the core principles of effective advocacy.

Four

The Art of Advocacy

Legal advocacy is an art. It is largely a skill set attorneys learn first through formal education, and hone through experience. There is some science behind the art, however, just as there is science behind various forms of painting, sculpture and other art forms. How decision-makers absorb, interpret, and receive information impacts advocates' ability to effectively persuade decision-makers. The art—and science—of advocacy has been the subject of study since ancient times. In this chapter we will examine the classic forms of advocacy and discuss the psychology affecting effective advocacy. In the next chapter, we'll apply these forms to persuading judges.

A. Methods of Advocacy

Advocacy, like rhetoric,[1] is the art of persuasion.[2] At its core, the art of legal persuasion contains three main elements: logos, pathos, and ethos.[3] Logos is an appeal to logic. It involves using reason to persuade the listener of the correctness of the advocate's position. It appeals to the listener's mind and analytical reasoning.[4] Pathos is an appeal to the listener's emotions, feelings, prejudices and biases.[5] This part of advocacy involves attempting to persuade the listener by triggering an emotional or visceral response. It can involve an appeal to sympathy, bias, prejudice, loyalty, patriotism and other emotional, rather than rational, bases for making decisions. Ethos relates to the credibility of the advocate. Ethos involves how an advocate makes an argument in a manner that reflects the advocate's believability, credibility and trustworthiness. Ethos also encompasses the credibility of a speaker that precedes the speaker based on reputation and previous encounters. In other words, ethos is that part of advocacy devoted to persuading the listener to trust the advocate's message.

Four. The Art of Advocacy

Effective advocates either intentionally or intuitively incorporate all three elements to some degree when striving to persuade decision-makers.[6] And there is a natural overlap of these elements of persuasion. That which makes the speaker credible (ethos) colors the decision-maker's receptiveness to the merits of the argument (logos) and to an emotional appeal (pathos). To the extent the decision-maker is moved by an emotional appeal, it likewise increases the receptivity to the logic of the argument. A logical argument makes the speaker appear more credible. And a speaker can assert a logical argument that also appeals to the justice of the outcome, the use of pathos.

The most talented attorneys, however, recognize that the focus and emphasis on the elements should vary, depending on the nature of the case. In some cases, in some settings, with some decision-makers, logic is the most compelling aspect of the argument, while in other situations an appeal to emotion is more likely to succeed. Hence the familiar saying: "If the facts are against you, argue the law. If the law is against you, argue the facts. If the law and the facts are against you, pound the table and yell like hell."[7]

To many observers, though, ethos is the key to persuasion.[8] A speaker's credibility is key to persuading a decision-maker to be receptive to persuasion. When decision-makers don't trust the speaker, they are unlikely to be persuaded no matter how logical the argument or how emotionally appealing the plea.

The credibility of a speaker is complex and depends on many things. "The primary characteristics of ethos in legal writing [are]: character, goodwill, and intelligence."[9] The same can be said, though, of ethos in legal oral argument. Character involves advocating in a way that reflects truthfulness, candor, respect and professionalism.[10] Speakers show character by being factually accurate, fully disclosing contrary authority, adverse facts, and opposing views, and by treating other parties, attorneys, and the court with respect. Goodwill means acknowledging the opposing viewpoint's legitimacy and reasonableness and refraining from ad hominem attacks and pejorative language when referring to opposing parties. Intelligence requires a speaker to demonstrate the decision-maker can trust and rely upon the speaker's sources and reasoning.

Ethos often involves more than what and how a speaker writes or orally advocates to a decision-maker. Many speakers are already known by the decision-maker. Word gets around quickly, and reputations are made and lost in short order. Speakers must recognize that their ability to persuade through ethos depends not only on what and how they say what they say in their written and oral advocacy in the particular matter at hand, but also on what the decision-maker already knows, or thinks they know, about the speaker's credibility and reliability. "For Isocrates, ethos is the speaker's prior reputation, developed during life."[11] A listener's perception of the speaker's credibility, accurate or not, impacts a speaker's ability to persuade through ethos. Thus, it's not just what a speaker says at the moment that is part of ethos, but the speaker's established reputation as well. "Every time one speaks as a lawyer, one establishes for the moment a character—an ethical identity—for oneself, for one's audience, and for those one talks about, and in addition one proposes a relation among the characters one defines."[12] Though this quote uses rather stilted language, in essence it means that a lawyer's ability to persuade through ethos depends on the reputation the lawyer builds over time.

B. Means of Advocacy

Companion to the three primary methods of advocacy, logos, ethos, and pathos, are the five cannons of rhetoric: invention, arrangement, style, memory, and delivery.[13] These can be thought of as the means to effectuate the methods of advocacy. Advocates use these cannons as a means by which to further the methods of persuasion. Invention refers to creative means of conveying a message, such as through analogy, metaphors and other forms of literary storytelling. Arrangement is how the advocate organizes a message in a rational, logical, and compelling manner. Style primarily means the type of language the advocate choses to convey the message, that is whether the language is formal or informal, technical or colloquial. Memory is a means of oral advocacy through which a speaker is able to engage visually with the audience by keeping eye contact. Delivery speaks to how one conveys the message as opposed to the content of the message: the speaker's use of movement, intonation, volume, pace, gestures, body language, and expression.

Effective legal advocacy requires attorneys to apply these various means of persuasion, these specific skills, to the methods of advocacy of legos, ethos, and pathos. Invention, for example, is a means by which attorneys can advance ethos. Analogies and metaphors allow decision-makers to identify with the attorney through mutually recognized and understood stories and comparisons. Arrangement advances logos, by increasing the clarity of the attorney's reasoning. Memory, delivery, and style are means by which attorneys can advance ethos and pathos in particular. How attorneys speak can affect the extent to which the decision-maker finds them credible and trustworthy. An attorneys' word choice, voice inflection, and other forms of written and oral communication can affect the degree to which a decision-maker's emotional cords are struck.

The means of advocacy that may be effective with one type of decision-maker may not be effective with another. Similarly, the context in which an attorney is advocating to a decision-maker may call for a greater emphasis on some means of persuasion over others. For example, the metaphors or analogies an attorney uses with judges may be more legal in nature, while those used with jurors more common. When trying to persuade judges, attorneys may want to arrange the argument to fit the order of the elements or factors the judge must address, while when trying to persuade jurors attorneys may rearrange the order to emphasize the strongest points and either ignore or bury weaker points in the middle. When advocating to judges, attorneys can speak legalese because judges speak the language; jurors do not. When delivering arguments to judges, attorneys may have less freedom to move, sometimes tied to the lectern in appellate arguments, for example. Attorneys may have less call to make dramatic use of other delivery skills as well because with judges substance counts over style, logos prevails over pathos, whereas with jurors the opposite may be more effective.

C. Conclusion

Although the best attorneys recognize the need to modify their methods and means of advocacy depending on the nature of the case and the merits of the dispute, it has been our observation that even the best attorneys fail to consider the need to modify the focus of the classic elements of advocacy based on the identity of the decision-maker. Although Aristotle was correct in discussing the elements of rhetoric that juries constitute "an audience of untrained thinkers,"[14] that is not true of judges. What may work well advocating to a group of citizens may not work well at all when advocating to a judge. As we explained in the preceding chapter, there are fundamental and important differences between judges, jurors, juries and appellate panels of judges both as decision-makers and with regard to the context in which they make decisions. These differences require advocates to modify their methods and means of advocacy if they wish to be effective. Now that we have identified the differences between juries, jurors,

Persuading Judges

appellate panels and judges in terms of context and as decision-makers and have examined the methods and means of effective legal advocacy generally, in the next chapter we will apply these principles to identify general methods and means of effectively persuading judges.

FIVE

Methods and Means of Persuading Judges

In this chapter, our aim is to share our general observations about effectively persuading judges. We begin by broadly considering the methods of logos, ethos, and pathos as they apply to persuading judges. Then we turn to consider the means of persuading judges, discussing first its two forms: written and oral. In the penultimate section, we examine how attorneys can effectively use the evidence rules when facts are in dispute, even when the evidence rules don't apply. We end this chapter with ten general practice pointers.

A. Methods of Effectively Persuading Judges

1. Ethos and Advocacy to Judges

In the preceding section, we noted that ethos is often considered the most important of the three methods of advocacy because if the listener—the decision-maker the advocate is attempting to persuade—does not trust the speaker, the use of logos and pathos won't resonate with the listener. This holds true to some extent with persuading judges. Establishing credibility with a judge is critically important if the advocate hopes to persuade the judge.

We note, though, that in some ways and to some extent, judges may disregard an advocate's lack of credibility if the strength of the reasoning compels a different result. Judges are trained to think logically and are mentally disciplined enough to more readily separate the speaker from the message than are lay people. Judges want to get it right. They are duty-bound to uphold and apply the law and not let passion and personal likes or dislikes to affect their decision. Thus it is the case, and has been with the authors, that judges will sometimes reach a legal conclusion because it is compelled by the evidence and the law, even though they don't trust the attorney, find the attorney lacks credibility, and perhaps has even made material misrepresentations. When this happens, parties prevail despite, not because of, their attorneys. Judges recognize that attorneys are agents for parties; they are not the parties themselves (or they have fools for clients). Judges recognize it would be inappropriate to rule against a party who should win on the merits of an argument simply because the messenger lacks credibility. Likewise, no matter how much a judge may trust an advocate or find the advocate credible, a judge is much less likely to allow it to overcome a weak logical argument than lay jurors may be. In that sense, when trying to persuade judges logos overrules ethos, no matter how much more important ethos may be in other advocacy settings.

That is not to say that ethos is not important or that attorneys should ignore it, trusting in judges to overlook their lack of credibility. When attorneys are credible and show the judge they can be trusted, judges are more receptive to hearing them out and being persuaded by the logic of their arguments. Legal arguments from attorneys who judges trust and in whom they have faith are providing them accurate facts and sound legal authority will resonate more readily with judges than those from attorneys who judges distrust.

Establishing credibility with judges begins before attorneys set pen to paper or open their mouths in court. Although Abraham Lincoln said an attorney's stock in trade is the attorney's time and advice,[1] credibility is also an essential part of an attorney's stock in trade.[2] An attorney's reputation for being candid, for fair dealing, and for accuracy precedes the attorney. An attorney's reputation may color the judge's perception of the attorney long before the attorney submits anything to or appears in front of the judge. Recall that one of the differences between judges, jurors, and appellate judges we identified previously is that attorneys reappear more often before the same judge than they ever do before the same jurors or even the same appellate judges. So how attorneys acted and performed in past hearings, how accurate and candid attorneys were in pleadings in prior cases, color a judge's perception of the attorney in the case then before the judge. Attorneys who seek to be effective judge advocates must strive to establish, and then maintain, a sterling reputation for credibility.

Part of the effective use of ethos in persuading judges requires a recognition that judges will also be more receptive to an advocate's message when the judge likes and respects the attorney. Attorneys who treat other attorneys, parties, witnesses, and court staff politely and with respect will

Five. Methods and Means of Persuading Judges

earn judges' respect. Attorneys who are rude, dismissive, or disrespectful of others in front of a judge will erode their ability to persuade the judge. Judges have little patience for bush league tactics and petty disputes between attorneys. Attorneys who rise above such conduct will earn judges' respect and will find judges to be much more receptive to their persuasive efforts. Attorneys who engage in sharp practices and treat others poorly will find they have created their own barriers over which they must now climb if they wish to get through to the judge.

Another part of ethos in persuading judges is treating judges appropriately. There is a significant power differential between judges and attorneys, and that difference in power exists in at least two spheres. First, the judge is the decision-maker and the attorney the supplicant. The judge has the power to make a decision which is either favorable or unfavorable to the attorney's position. As such, the advocate must tread cautiously so as not to offend the decision-maker and to earn the decision-maker's trust. This aspect of power differential exists, though, no matter who the decision-maker may be. Juries hold this same power over attorneys, as do appellate judges.

But this power differential is different with district judges because they make decisions on their own. Appellate judges reach group decisions. On a typical three-member appellate panel, attorneys can think little of one of the judges, so long as they can persuade the other two. When appearing before state supreme courts or the United States Supreme Court, attorneys need be concerned about persuading a majority of the justices. Similarly, juries make group decisions. Not so in district court. There is a single judge that holds the fate of the attorney's case in their hands.

Second, attorneys are officers of the court and judges are in charge of the court. Judges have the ability to sanction attorneys. Sanctions can range from a tongue lashing to a fine. A verbal reprimand from a judge alone can damage an attorney's reputation and, if done in front of the client, the attorney/client relationships. Judges can also make referrals to state bars for discipline, potentially jeopardizing an attorney's license and livelihood. And under court rules judges can financially penalize attorneys for violations of rules. Juries, of course, have none of these powers over attorneys.

And although attorneys are officers of appellate courts as well, it is rare for appellate judges to sanction attorneys in this sense. This is largely a product of the context of appellate advocacy. When attorneys appear before appellate courts for oral argument, there is a limited time to speak so the attorney's exposure is less. Moreover, the calm and formal setting of appellate argument, where the focus is on the law and not the facts, and the attorney has had plenty of time to prepare, is less likely to result in error. It is in the rough and tumble of district courts where the potential for friction between attorneys and judges has the greatest potential to arise and result in attorney punishments of one type or another. Attorneys spend much more time before district judges, are often more hurried, and focus more on the facts. In this less formal setting, where emotions are more likely to be on the surface and responses less thought out, the risk of incurring a judge's wrath is greater.

Recognizing these obvious and significant power differentials, attorneys must find a balanced approach to be effective judge advocates. Attorneys who appear obsequious or fawning won't earn the respect of many judges. On the other hand, talking down to judges or treating judges with disrespect will quickly damage an attorney's effectiveness. In some instances, attorneys may be older, or more experienced, or more intelligent, or more proficient in a particular area of the law, than the judge before whom they appear. Attorneys may be right, and the judge dead wrong. Be that as it may, the judge has the power to make the decision, right or wrong. An attorney who wishes to be successful in persuading the judge to make what the attorney believes to be the right decision must recognize the power imbalance. Attorneys should show respect for the office, for the position the judge holds, even if the attorney doesn't think highly of the judge as a person, a lawyer, or a jurist.

Attorneys and judges, though members of the same profession, are not equals in the courtroom when attorneys are appearing before judges as litigants. That's a simple truth that requires attorneys to tailor their advocacy in a manner that shows proper respect in addressing the judge if the attorney wants to be an effective judge advocate. It is part of the ethos of advocacy, of establishing credibility with judges. Attorneys have to find that sweet spot between obsequiousness and disdain of the judge who holds all the power over them.

2. Logos and Advocacy to Judges

In our view, logos is the key to effectively persuading judges. Judges have been trained to think, reason, and decide cases analytically and rationally by applying the law to the facts. As noted in the prior section, judges have the mental discipline to overlook an attorney's lack of credibility if the merits of the legal argument compel an answer in favor of

Five. Methods and Means of Persuading Judges

that attorney's party, or to look past an attorney's credibility if the legal argument doesn't hold water. Likewise, judges are less influenced by emotional appeals. Judges are constrained in their decision-making by binding precedent. So, unlike appellate judges, district judges are less concerned about how the decision before them may impact society as a whole or even whether the decision they make advances justice or could cause injustice in the abstract, or for others not parties to the suit. Judges focus on the cases in front of them and what outcome is dictated by the law and the facts. Logos is where it is at for judges.

With that in mind, to be effective judge advocates attorneys should emphasize logos as the primary method of persuasion. To persuade judges, attorneys need to communicate to judges in the language of the law. Knowing judges are focused on solving the problem at hand, on the legal question in dispute, attorneys should try to consider the judge's point of view. Attorneys who provide judges facts and legal reasoning in a manner that aids the judge in analyzing the complexity of the legal problem will be effective judge advocates. Knowing that judges are typically overwhelmed with work, are juggling sometimes hundreds of cases at any given time, and have many external pressures on their time and resources, effective judge advocates understand the importance of brevity and clarity.

Knowing that judges place greater emphasis on logos over pathos, there may be times when attorneys may want to directly confront a conflict between the decision reason dictates and the decision that emotion may cry for. In other words, in some cases attorneys may recognize that sympathy lies with the opposing party. The emotional appeal may favor the opponent and may even be compelling. The outcome of the decision before the court may have a direct and devastating impact on the opposing party, or the outcome of the decision may have the potential of impacting many others who are not before the court as the direct litigants. The outcome the attorney is advocating may not seem to be fair to the opposing party, even if it is legally the correct decision. When an attorney is in this situation, an effective approach to persuading a judge may be to explicitly address the elephant in the room and admit that the emotional appeal of the opposing argument is compelling but then emphasize that reason and the law dictate the opposite decision. Judges will respect an attorney's empathetic recognition of the merits of a pathos argument and will likely respond to the clarion call of logos to return to the outcome that reason dictates and the law demands, despite the impact it may have.

3. Pathos and Advocacy to Judges

Although we have repeatedly discounted the importance of pathos in effectively persuading judges, that is not to say that pathos isn't important and doesn't play some role. Judges desire to make decisions that are fair, equitable, and right in the moral sense as well as ones that are the result of sound legal reasoning. Attorneys who can use pathos hand in hand with logos to show to judges why the outcome they seek is not only dictated by the correct application of the law to the facts, but is also a fair, equitable, and just result are more likely to persuade judges to find in their favor.

Weaving pathos into a logos-focused legal argument is an art and takes a concerted effort. Direct appeals to judges' emotions will likely fall flat and perhaps even hamper the advocate's ability to persuade judges. A judge who perceives that the advocate is trying to manipulate the judge's emotions to win may be offended and insulted. The most effective way to intertwine logos and pathos is the order in which they are invoked. In other words, attorneys should consider crafting legal arguments to first show that logos—reason and the correct application of the law to the facts—compels a decision in their clients' favor and then use pathos to show that that decision will also result in a fair outcome. Attorneys who begin with pathos, who start their argument by attempting to tug on the judge's heartstrings and then shift to a logos argument of justifying what they believe to be the fair outcome by legal reasoning are going to be less effective.

Good judges are not result-oriented; they are process oriented. And even bad judges want to at least appear that they are not result-oriented. Applying the process of legal reasoning faithfully is of paramount importance for judges and the result will be what the process dictates. Attorneys who approach advocacy by emphasizing logos first, and pathos second, will find their arguments fitting within the framework of judges' analytical process.

As we noted, attorneys can know far more about judges than they can of jurors. Of course, the important thing is what trial attorneys do with the information they have about decision-makers. Some judges may value pathos-based arguments more than other judges. All too often trial attorneys present their cases to judges in hearings and bench trials as if all judges were alike, as if they were all shaped by a cookie-cutter from the same dough. Instead, attorneys should adjust their presentations based on the judge's experience and familiarity with the facts and procedural history of the case, and the degree to which they emphasize logos or pathos in their decision-making.

Five. Methods and Means of Persuading Judges

We also recognize that some judges in some situations have incredible discretion to arrive at some decisions in which pathos may have greater emphasis in effectively persuading judges. Sentencing hearings come to mind. In federal court, there is a legal process judges apply to arrive at a determination of the appropriate statutory sentencing range and an advisory sentence within the framework of the United States Sentencing Guidelines. Judges will proceed through this process with a heavy emphasis on legal reasoning, attempting to faithfully apply the law to the facts to resolve disputes to determine the parameters of the applicable statutory and Guidelines sentencing range. Up to this point, advocacy focused on logos will be most effective. Having gotten that far, federal judges then find themselves with almost unfettered discretion to impose whatever sentence they see fit within the statutory range. Federal judges are not bound to sentence offenders within the advisory Guidelines range. Instead, judges are free to vary from those ranges to impose any sentence within the statutory range. Indeed, federal judges can even have policy disagreements with Guidelines provisions and virtually ignore them. Although the sentencing statute found at Title 18, United States Code, Section 3553(a) provides a list of factors federal judges must consider in arriving at a sentence that is sufficient, but not greater than necessary, to achieve the goals of sentencing, those factors and goals are broad and vague.

In these situations, attorneys may place a greater emphasis on pathos in their efforts to persuade judges. When judges have resolved factual and legal disputes and are then left with broad discretion to arrive at a decision, there is a greater place for pathos. Even here, though, good attorneys will weave logos and pathos together. Raw appeals to a judge's emotions will be less effective than appeals that emphasize that the outcome is not only fair, but reasonable and logical. For example, a defense attorney could argue that a long sentence would be unfair for a drug-addicted defendant who grew up in a broken and dysfunctional home and has had only minor prior convictions. Or, the defense attorney could make that same argument in the context of the goals of sentencing by arguing that even a light sentence will be enough to deter the defendant who had little childhood guidance, has never served a long period in prison before, and whose judgment was impaired by their drug addiction. The attorney could argue that the length of a potential sentence won't have any deterrent effect on an offender driven to engage in criminal conduct driven by an uncontrollable addition. Placing an emotional appeal in the context of a rational framework is more likely to resonate with a judge than one that simply appeals to a judge's emotions. Trying a pathos-based argument within a logos-based framework is more likely to be effective with judges than a purely emotionally charged argument would be.

B. *Means of Effectively Persuading Judges*

Having examined the methods of effectively persuading judges generally, we will turn now to discuss some of the means by which attorneys may most effectively employ those methods in trying to persuade judges. Attorneys use two primary forms of communication when advocating to judges: written and oral. To effectively persuade judges, attorneys need to modify their approach to using these forms of communication from the approach they use in advocating to jurors and to appellate panels. A third form of communication in advocacy to judges comes through the presentation of evidence. Facts are often in dispute before judges and judges preside over evidentiary hearings. Effectively persuading judges includes modifying the means by which attorneys present evidence when judges are factfinders.

1. Written Advocacy to Judges

Regardless of context, written advocacy is directed to one or more judges, all of whom not only completed law school but also practiced law in some capacity before donning a robe. This background means that judges will apply critical thinking to any written argument. Attorneys should assume judges will detect exaggerations of the factual record or inaccurate descriptions of case holdings. When attorneys play fast and loose with the facts or the law, it detracts from their persuasiveness. Among other things, this may mean a loss of an advocate's credibility. Once lost, credibility is difficult to restore. Judges have notoriously long memories about lawyers who have given the judges reason to doubt their credibility.[3]

Apart from basic accuracy, which should be a given, effective written advocacy also requires organization, efficiency and precision. Judges have intense time demands—well beyond what most attorneys might suspect. As noted above, the decline in the number of civil jury trials has been well documented.[4] This does not mean, however, that district judges spend little time in the courtroom. As the number of jury trials has declined, the number and importance of motions has increased. As a result, Judges often preside over many hearings on a daily basis.

When judges are in chambers, instead of presiding over trials or

Five. Methods and Means of Persuading Judges

hearings in courtrooms, they are likely reading. And reading some more. Whether on a computer screen, on paper, or both, judges read a massive volume of motions, briefs, documentary exhibits, depositions, presentence reports and other case-related materials. For example, on average in our district a judge conducts more than 150 felony sentencing hearings every year. In advance of a sentencing hearing, the judge reviews a single-spaced presentence report that is typically 20 to 40 pages in length (sometimes more), sentencing memoranda filed by the parties, sentencing exhibits (including letters submitted in support of the defendant) and legal authorities the parties cite with regard to disputed sentencing issues. Thus, a hearing that may consume one hour of court time requires the judge to expend several times that much time in preparation. And judges typically have multiple hearings on any given day and week. The brief an attorney is about to submit to the judge on a pending matter is almost certainly not going to be the only document the judge will read on a particular day. Indeed, it is common for judges to read hundreds, if not thousands, of pages of materials every week.

As with any form of communication, knowing the audience and tailoring the message accordingly is critical. Here, knowing the audience means understanding a judge's workload and the voluminous reading a judge does every day. Among other things, this means that to be an effective judge advocate requires knowing (and following) the court's rules concerning the format, content, and length of briefs and other documents. These rules can be detailed and may require the inclusion of particular sections and/or attachments. At minimum, the court's rules will likely address page or word limits. Complying with these rules will go a long way toward effectively persuading judges. A concise written argument, within the court's page limits, is far more likely to be persuasive than a rambling, repetitive, lengthy written submission.

Writing a short, concise pleading requires effort, but it can be done. One easy way to do this is by eliminating unnecessary boilerplate sections, unless they are required by the court's rules. These may include "Summary Judgment Standards" or, in a sentencing brief, a section providing a general overview of federal sentencing and making the point that the United States Sentencing Guidelines are no longer mandatory.[5] At minimum, attorneys should update such sections occasionally to keep them current.

Written briefs should be well organized. The goal is to persuade a judge by using legal reasoning and walking the judge through legal analysis in a way that leads the judge to reach the conclusion advocated. That is best done when the brief is well organized and follows a structure that the legal analysis requires.[6]

Generally speaking, when trying to persuade a judge attorneys should keep pathos-based arguments to a minimum. That is not to say that attorneys shouldn't emphasize facts that point to a just result. Raw appeals to emotion, however, are ill-advised when trying to persuade judges who are trained to analyze problems using logic and reason.[7] In other words: "Just the facts (and the law), ma'am."[8] But judges are also subject to human emotions, so facts that show not only that the result is logically supported but will also lead to a just result can be persuasive. Effective advocacy to judges doesn't mean eliminating all pathos from efforts of persuasion. Rather, effectively persuading judges is a matter of finding the appropriate balance between logos, ethos, and pathos.

Attorneys should avoid making personal attacks against opposing counsel. Unless the relevant issue actually involves the alleged misconduct of counsel, such as with a motion for sanctions, a litany of complaints about another attorney is a waste of time and the lack of professionalism detracts from the attacking attorney's persuasiveness. It is equally important to avoid snide comments and the use of pejorative words to describe opposing counsel's work product. Belittling the opposing counsel's research, analysis, or writing is a personal attack on opposing counsel. Those are worse than being wasted words in a limited word-count. Judges view that type of writing as bush league behavior unbecoming a professional and an officer of the court. It harms the reputation and credibility of the attorney making the attack, not the attorney under attack.

In written work, attorneys should be as brief as possible. Longer is not better. A short, punchy argument is far better than a rambling one. Unlike many college writing projects, a court-imposed page limit is a maximum, not a minimum. Those word limits serve a function not only of encouraging better written product, it also serves to limit the drain on limited judge resources that detract from judges' ability to focus on important matters.

Attorneys should also use headings and subheadings intentionally and intelligently. Headings and subheadings can help quickly guide judges through the logic of an attorney's argument. They can aid the judge in reasoning through the issues, especially when the legal issue involves application of a legal test or consideration of various factors. Good headings and subheadings should form complete sentences.[9] For example, a subheading in a preliminary injunction motion that reads: "The hospital will prevail on the merits because the doctor violated the noncompete clause by practicing medicine in violation of the geographic limits" is much better than a generic subheading "Likelihood of success on the merits."

When attorneys file exhibits in conjunction with written pleadings, they should reference those exhibits in their pleadings. Unfortunately, it is not uncommon for attorneys to file dozens of exhibits in support of a motion or resistance, yet in the written brief reference only a few of them. Attorneys shouldn't leave it up to judges to puzzle out the significance of the attached exhibits to the arguments the attorneys are making. Every exhibit filed in support of a pleading should be referenced in a brief and its significance to the analysis explained to the judge. And attorneys should point out specifically within the referenced document exactly what it is the attorney wants the judge to focus on.

Perhaps most importantly, attorneys should put themselves in the judge's shoes. If the attorney was an objective and disinterested party charged with resolving this particular issue as a neutral arbiter, what information would the attorney want to have? How could that information be best organized and presented? When making factual assertions, what is the easiest and most effective way to direct the judge to the part of the record that supports each assertion? What information is unnecessary? The attorney's goal should be to aid the judge in reaching the correct decision in the most concise and precise manner possible. The attorney who does this well in writing will be more likely to persuade the judge.

2. Oral Advocacy to Judges

The following situation actually happens: A party's written argument includes a request for oral argument. Oral argument is granted. At oral argument, an attorney for that party states that the attorney stands on the briefing and, unless the judge has questions, has nothing to add. Wait, what? This illustrates our first point about oral advocacy—a request for oral argument is a representation that the attorney will have something important and potentially determinative to say if the judge allocates time to let the attorney do so. Attorneys set themselves up for disappointment when they fail to fulfill this representation.

Of course, oral argument may be set even without request. Whether it was the attorney's idea or not, when attorneys are summoned to present argument to the judge there are practices that can make the presentation more or less effective. Many of these overlap with the written advocacy practices discussed in the preceding section and relate to the fact that the judge's time is scarce. Thus, attorneys should know and follow the court's rules, avoid lengthy discussion of undisputed matters (such as summary judgment standards), focus on the facts and the law, avoid pathos-based appeals unless they are clearly appropriate under the circumstances, refrain from personal attacks, and keep the argument as short as reasonably possible.

When arguing to judges, it bears repeating here that attorneys should focus on the law and the facts. Although attorneys should be emphatic on important points, they should leave drama and theatrics for juries. Judges are not persuaded by such displays; indeed, vociferous oral advocacy may have just the opposite effect. Judges expect attorneys to speak to them at an intellectual level, with an emphasis on logic, reasoning and common sense and not on emotions. Attorneys who obviously attempt to play on a judge's emotions insult the judge's intelligence. In short, attorneys should emphasis logos over pathos.

To be sure, there will be cases in which the emotions involved in the legal dispute are overwhelming, and when the legally and logically correct result may not be what appears to be fair or just. These pose difficult cases for attorneys, but even more so for judges. Tragic events or consequences tug on everyone's heartstrings. These events may be the source of the legal action, such as in a tort case when a party has been injured. The emotional impact could also result from the outcome of the dispute, such as an offender being imprisoned or a litigant losing custody of a child, substantial assets, or intangible valuable property.

And so in these cases attorneys representing the suffering party may naturally try to invoke emotions if necessary to overcome a weak logical argument. When opponents emphasize emotional appeals over a rational ones, attorneys should consider directly addressing such attempts to counteract their effect. In these situations, attorneys can acknowledge the emotions, sympathize and empathize with the impacted party, but then explicitly emphasize to the judge that reason and the rule of law must prevail. That may mean emphasizing that a fair justice system doesn't always ensure a fair result in every case for everyone.

Attorneys should also be cautious not to offend judges through means other than appealing to their emotions. Attorneys sometimes make statements or arguments intended for the benefit of their clients, quasi clients (e.g., crime victims), the press, or other third parties. In an effort to curry favor with or favorable appearances before others, some attorneys will try to shift blame onto judges. For example, defense attorneys will sometimes argue that if the judge detains a defendant or imposes a particular sentence, then the judge will be responsible for tearing the defendant from his

Five. Methods and Means of Persuading Judges

family or depriving the defendant's family of a parent or financial support. Judges are understandably offended by such comments for it is the defendant and the defendant's conduct, not the judge, who jeopardized everything and caused collateral damage to others. Similarly, prosecutors may argue that failing to detain a defendant or impose a particular sentence on a defendant would constitute a miscarriage of justice for crime victims or society as a whole. Judges are equally offended by such comments because the government has the burden of proof in criminal cases. If a judge rules against the government's position, the fault lies with the prosecutor for failing to meet the burden of proof, not with the judge.

We understand that the judge is not the only member of the audience to whom an attorney's oral comments are addressed. Attorneys legitimately need to consider the effect their comments may have on their clients and others. Attorneys sometimes appropriately make statements in oral argument, for example, to placate a difficult client so as to maintain a good attorney-client relationship. Nevertheless, attorneys must understand that when they tailor their comments to curry to another member of the audience, they may adversely affect the effectiveness of their advocacy to the judge. Thus, attorneys have to recognize that tension may exist and weigh which is more important: persuading the judge or mollifying a client.

We have some final thoughts on effective oral advocacy to judges based on our own experiences presiding over the presentation of oral arguments in various types of cases.

Approach oral argument from the judge's point of view. Attorneys should recognize that the judge won't know the case like the attorneys do. As one author put it:

> The most common mistake lawyers make in oral argument, from a rhetorical point of view, is to leap into the middle of a case. You have probably lived with the case for months, deposed and interviewed witnesses, drafted pleadings, and become absorbed with the details of the case. On the other hand, if the judge ever knew anything about your case, he's probably forgotten it because in the meantime he's heard hundreds of others.[10]

Be organized. At the outset, attorneys should tell the judge what issues the attorney intends to address, and in what order. The attorney should introduce each issue as the attorney begins to discuss it so there is no confusion as to what the attorney is addressing. If multiple issues and sub-issues will be addressed, attorneys may consider using PowerPoint or similar presentation resources to help the judge follow along (and to help keep themselves on task).

Persuading Judges

Be honest. Attorneys should never exaggerate the factual record or stretch case holdings beyond their reasonable scope. They shouldn't attempt to avoid discussing unfavorable precedent. If asked to concede a point that rightly should be conceded, attorneys should do so (while, hopefully, explaining why the conceded point is not dispositive). If an attorney does not know the answer to a question, the attorney should admit it (and offer to follow up with an answer by the following day, if the judge so desires).

Be prepared. Although it is appropriate for an attorney to admit that that the attorney does not know the answer to a question, it is far better to actually know the answer. This is not always possible, as some questions are simply unforeseeable. But attorneys should know in advance which legal issues, case law authorities and factual propositions are likely to be of the most interest. An attorney who did not take the time and trouble necessary to be well-prepared for oral argument is easy to identify (it often takes only one question).

Related to the previous point, consider allowing the attorney who wrote the underlying brief to present the oral argument. A senior attorney, with substantial courtroom experience, may make a more impressive presentation but, in our experience, is also more likely to struggle when asked about the factual record or relevant legal authorities. A less-experienced attorney may not earn as many style points but might have a better grasp of the important facts and legal points. As judges tasked with sorting through the record and accurately applying the law to the facts, we prefer an attorney who can answer our questions, however awkwardly, over one who simply makes a smooth, jury-worthy presentation.

When possible, attorneys should tailor their presentations to the presiding judge. Determine in advance if the judge has addressed a similar issue in a prior, available opinion. If so, attorneys should talk about that case (even if the holding was not favorable to the attorney's position). Attorneys should ascertain if the judge has experience (from the judge's time practicing law or since taking the bench) in the particular area of the law involved in the case and determine whether to devote more or less time to educating the judge. However, there is an important distinction between tailoring and pandering. Some attorneys either research, or already know about, aspects of the judge's personal life and try to curry favor by invoking those details during their arguments. For example, if a judge is known to be a fan of Broadway musicals, an attorney may think it is helpful to include analogies to the storyline of *Les Misérables* in the course of an argument. This is going too far. Most judges prefer to keep their private and professional lives separate and may find it off-putting, if not downright creepy, when an attorney invokes the judge's hobbies or interests while attempting to persuade. By suggesting that attorneys tailor their presentations to the presiding judge, we are referring to the judge's legal experience and courtroom practices, not the judge's personal life.

Don't read your pleading. Unless told otherwise, attorneys should assume the judge has read the pleadings and is familiar with the case and the issues. Oral argument is an opportunity to engage in a conversation with a judge; it is not the time to present an oral recitation of the written pleading.[11] It is easy to waste a significant amount of time going over factual and background information with which the judge is already familiar.

Invite questions and receive them with enthusiasm. Questions from the bench can be annoying, as they interrupt the attorney's flow and may raise issues the attorney intended to address later in the presentation. If annoyed, attorneys should keep it to themselves. Questions are the judge's opportunity to zero in on the issues the judge finds to be most relevant or troubling. Attorneys shouldn't, then, treat questions as intrusions or interruptions.[12] Nor should they respond by stating that they will get to that issue later (or even that the attorney planned to address the issue later).[13] Attorneys should just answer the questions, enthusiastically and directly, and move on.

Be flexible and tune into the judge's verbal and non-verbal cues. Although every judge is different, most will make it clear when it is time to move on, or to be done. These can range from the subtle, such as looks of boredom or annoyance, to the direct ("Move on, counsel"). Attorneys should keep in mind that the judge is the audience and, ultimately, the person the attorneys are attempting to persuade. If the judge makes it clear that an attorney has made the point, the attorneys should move on.

Have a conclusion. Assuming time permits, an attorney should end with a summary of the attorney's position and a description of what, precisely, the attorney is asking the judge to do.

Suggest a solution. Judges are problem solvers. When attorneys come to the table with a suggested solution, they are more likely to have a judge adopt it than if they simply come to the judge with a problem.

3. Evidence Rules and Advocacy to Judges

Trial attorneys have been trained in the presentation of evidence with the presumption that the factfinder is a jury. They have not been trained on the need to modify that presentation when judges are factfinders.

Persuading Judges

Presenting evidence to judges is not the same as presenting evidence to jurors for several reasons. First, attorneys can and often do present some evidence to judges in advance of an evidentiary hearing. Second, judges don't sit in jury boxes during evidentiary hearings, where attorneys and witnesses are accustomed to focus evidentiary presentations. Third, when judges are factfinders, the rules of evidence either don't apply at all, or they apply in a relaxed manner. We'll discuss these nuances here.

Presenting Evidence in Advance of Hearings

In jury trials, jurors as factfinders don't see evidence until judges determine the evidence is admissible. Not so when judges are factfinders. Attorneys will often attach exhibits to their pleadings, submit them as addendum to pleadings, file them in advance of hearings or bench trials, or send them to judges in advance of the hearing or bench trial. This practice promotes efficiency because it allows judges to review exhibits in advance of the evidentiary presentation on the judge's own schedule and doesn't consume all the limited courtroom time that would otherwise be expended were the judge to see the evidence for the first time during the evidentiary presentation. It also allows the judge to study the exhibit more closely and thoroughly.

But this practice of provided judges with exhibits in advance of evidentiary presentations raises some issues pertinent to effectively persuading judges. When evidence is presented to juries, the attorneys highlight and explain the relevance and importance of the evidence through witnesses as the jury is seeing the evidence. Not so with judges who often get the evidence before the proceedings and an explanation perhaps later during the proceedings. Attorneys need to anticipate the potential problem that can arise when judges review evidence in advance of the proceeding. Without placing an exhibit in context, it is possible for judges to be confused about the purpose of exhibits, or to misunderstand their importance or meaning. To enhance judges' comprehension of exhibits and the persuasive value of exhibits, it is important then that attorneys communicate with judges in advance about the purpose and importance of exhibits in their pleadings. Attorneys should reference in their pleadings every exhibit provided to judges in advance of an evidentiary presentation and explain the purpose of the exhibit, what the attorneys want judges to see in the exhibits, and to explain why the exhibit advances the attorneys' positions.

When exhibits are lengthy, attorneys should assist judges by explaining in their pleadings what portion(s) of the lengthy exhibit is relevant as to what issue(s). It is not uncommon for attorneys to submit very long exhibits without any indication to the judge what it is the judge should be looking for in the exhibit. Attorneys may communicate this information to judges by modifying or annotating the exhibit, when possible, with highlighting or underlining or some other form of alteration to draw attention to the relevant portion of a lengthy exhibit. Alternatively, attorneys may submit only the relevant portions of an otherwise lengthy exhibit to judges or redact out irrelevant portions of a lengthy exhibit so that the judge sees only the relevant portion.

Orienting the Presentation of Evidence to a Judge

It has been our observation that attorneys don't always orient evidentiary presentations to judges as factfinders. Jury trial advocacy training devotes a lot of attention to ensuring the presentation of evidence is focused on jurors through the use of demonstrative exhibits, displaying evidence to jurors, and conditioning witnesses to make eye contact with jurors. When it comes to evidentiary presentations to judges, however, attorneys don't always adjust their presentations toward judges as factfinders.

Just as with jurors as factfinders, attorneys should orient the presentation of evidence toward judges when they are factfinders. This means, in part, using the same types of demonstrative and illustrative aids that attorneys use with jurors, orienting them toward the judge. But, attorneys should remember that judges are not jurors. They think differently, reason analytically, and come to the evidentiary hearing with experience. This isn't their first rodeo. Attorneys need not necessarily expend the time they would with jurors in educating judges about basic information if the attorney's research on the judge reveals the judge is already familiar with the subject matter in dispute.

Attorneys should also prepare and work with witnesses to ensure the evidence is presented to the judge as factfinder. By this we mean that attorneys should ensure that witnesses understand that the judge is the factfinder and the one who needs to understand and be persuaded though the witness' testimony. When witnesses are handling or explaining exhibits, for example, they should do so in a manner that the judge can see and understand them. Attorneys should also instruct witnesses to make eye contact with judges and understand the need to communicate to the judge.

Attorneys should also prepare witnesses to expect questions from judges. With rare exceptions, jurors don't ask questions of witnesses and even when they do, the questioning is not direct but is filtered through the judge and attorneys. When judges are factfinders, they may ask questions directly of witnesses. Many judges conduct their own questioning of witnesses in hearings or bench trials when they serve as factfinders, often after the attorneys have finished their own questioning. Judges do this because they are seeking clarification, not satisfied that the attorney-questioning has resolved all the issues. When witnesses are unprepared for questions from judges, it may cause the witnesses to become unnecessarily defensive or apprehensive, potentially impacting the witnesses' demeanor and credibility.

Adjusting Evidentiary Presentations When Rules Don't Apply

As we noted in a prior chapter, when attorneys are engaged in jury trial advocacy, the evidence rules always apply. When they advocate on appeal, the evidence rules are inapplicable because appellate panels are not engaged in factfinding. When attorneys engage in advocacy to judges, the evidence rules sometimes apply and sometimes don't. When attorneys advocate to judges they need to consider whether the Federal Rules of Evidence apply to the proceeding at hand, and how they need to adjust their advocacy depending on the answer to that question.

As noted, the Federal Rules of Evidence don't govern many hearings where judges are the finders of fact. Nevertheless, attorneys are trained from law school to think of admissible evidence and may unconsciously limit the scope of what they present to judges even when the rules don't apply. When the evidence rules are inapplicable, however, the proponent of evidence should recognize and take advantage of the expanded scope of information that can be presented to a judge. Opposing counsel, on the other hand, should recognize they can't object to the evidence by citing rules that don't apply. But they can and should argue why the reasons underlying the inapplicable rules should still cause the judge to give the evidence little weight.

For example, at sentencing hearings judges may consider almost anything in arriving at a sentence that is sufficient but not greater than necessary to achieve the goals of sentencing. That means a prosecutor could offer hearsay evidence on a disputed matter at the hearing. The defense attorney can't object by citing the hearsay rules but can argue the judge shouldn't give the evidence any weight, arguing that it is unreliable and wouldn't even fit within any exception to the hearsay rule. The defense attorney can argue that the evidence lacks indicia of reliability, so although the judge can consider it, the judge should not rely on it for the same reasons the evidence rules wouldn't allow a jury to even hear it.

Five. Methods and Means of Persuading Judges

To be sure, there may be other limitations on what evidence a judge may consider independent of the Federal Rules of Evidence. Local rules, the Federal Rules of Civil and Criminal Procedure, and the United States Constitution may place limitations on the evidence a judge may consider even when the Federal Rules of Evidence don't. For example, in sentencing hearings criminal defendants retain due process rights under the Fifth Amendment, which encompasses to some extent the right to confrontation under the Sixth Amendment to the United States Constitution.[14] Thus, although the Federal Rules of Evidence wouldn't bar the government from presenting hearsay testimony at a sentencing hearing, the Fifth Amendment may.

Even when evidence rules don't apply in an evidentiary hearing before a judge, it remains important for attorneys to recognize the reasoning behind the rules of evidence. That reasoning should inform what and how to present information to a judge, even when the Federal Rules of Evidence are inapplicable. Although in many proceedings a judge may consider information that wouldn't be admissible under the Federal Rules of Evidence, the judge is free to afford the information whatever weight the judge deems appropriate. It follows, then, that the closer the evidence hues to that which would be admissible under the Federal Rules of Evidence, the more likely it is that the judge will afford it greater weight. Common sense should tell attorneys that a judge is unlikely to afford much weight to uncorroborated triple hearsay, for example. Thus, when presenting information in hearings where the evidence rules don't apply, attorneys should nevertheless still attempt to present evidence that would be admissible under the rules. When they cannot do so, they should recognize why the evidence would be inadmissible under the rules, that is, identify what makes the evidence unreliable, and attempt to address that weakness through corroborating circumstances or other evidence to enhance its trustworthiness.

C. Ten Practice Pointers

In an effort to summarize the essence of our advice on effectively persuading judges, we have distilled down the core concepts of this chapter into ten practice pointers. Although it is difficult and may be oversimplified, we hope these ten practice pointers serve as an aid for attorneys to contemplate and adjust their advocacy accordingly.

1. Emphasize logic over emotion, fact over fiction

Judges, trained in legal reasoning, are more receptive to persuasion through logic than they are by emotional appeals. That doesn't mean that emotion should always be ignored or may not sometimes be important. The key is recognizing when a rational argument will carry the day and when some appeal to emotion may tip an argument over the edge by showing the rational result is also a just one.

2. Weave facts and law together (speak the language of the law)

Legal analysis involves applying the law to the facts. So to persuade judges trained in the law to engage in legal reasoning, effectively persuading judges requires attorneys to speak that language. Attorneys should use the legal tests and factors that apply to a legal issue, discuss matters in terms of elements and burdens of proof, in short approach advocacy in the way you know the judge must approach resolving the legal dispute. Effective advocacy to judges involves making the judges' task easier by showing the judges how to analyze the legal dispute in a way that resolves the dispute in your client's favor.

3. Feed the judge only essential facts

Every legal case will contain a large body of facts, but not all facts are created equal. The art of effective judge persuasion involves identifying the core facts that are material and essential to the judge's analysis and providing those facts to the judge in a clear and organized manner. Again, attorneys are more likely to succeed in persuading a judge when they make the judge's job easier. Providing judges with the key facts, and only the key facts, is like providing the judge with a list of ingredients for a recipe. All that's left is then showing the judge how to use those ingredients.

4. Be brief and specific; decrease repetition

Brevity is a key to effective advocacy.[15] This is especially so for persuading judges. "From the judges' perspective, conciseness is not aspirational, it is essential."[16] Brevity is an art. Effective advocacy to judges requires attorneys to recognize the time demands under which judges operate. The concise argument, while more difficult and time consuming

Five. Methods and Means of Persuading Judges

for the advocate to craft, is the more effective one for busy judges to comprehend.

Specificity goes hand in hand with brevity. Make it clear exactly what you want the judge to do (or not do). And for each specific request, be prepared to provide concise reasons, supported by the law and the evidence, as to why the judge should accede to that request. Within the sentencing context, for example, attorneys sometimes do little more than present a wish list of desired outcomes without explaining why the judge should accede to the requests. Although this tactic may seem to have the virtue of brevity, it is actually an unproductive use of time. Effective advocacy requires both a clear statement of the requested action and a persuasive argument as to why that action is warranted.

Finally, recognize that judges will comprehend what you say the first time you say it. Repetition won't make a weak argument stronger and can make a strong argument weaker.

5. Tailor the presentation to the essentials

As noted, one of the advantages of advocacy to judges over appellate advocacy to a panel of judges is that with district judges written page limits are more flexible, and oral arguments are not strictly limited in time. That is not to say, however, that attorneys should disregard the importance of surgical presentations. District court judges are often overwhelmed with work, so the more concise a presentation of the immediate issue the attorneys need resolved, the more persuasive it will be because the judge will more easily be able to focus on the presentation. Brevity and clarity are keys to effectively persuading judges. That said, judges recognize that attorneys sometimes need to raise multiple grounds to preserve a record on appeal. For example, a judge may be foreclosed from ruling in an attorney's favor under a particular argument because of binding precedent, but that ground may be one where there's a split in the circuits. Good advocacy to judges, in those instances, involves making it clear to the judge the primary basis upon which the attorney is relying and explicitly notes, when appropriate, that other arguments are raised to preserve a record on appeal.

6. Engage in a conversation with the judge

Effective communication involves the exchange of information. Most of the legal arena is ill-designed for effective communication. Lawyers talk

Persuading Judges

at jurors, not with them. In appellate oral arguments, attorneys rush to make their points during the limited time permitted while being interrupted and interrogated by the appellate judges. With district judges, however, attorneys and judges have an opportunity to discuss issues, to engage in a conversation about how to resolve a problem, in an effort to ensure the judge as decision-maker fully comprehends the attorneys' arguments and the attorneys fully understand the judges' concerns.

7. Understand when and how to use evidence rules

Evidence rules impose a limitation on the reception of information. Their primary function is to filter out information deemed unreliable. But when judges are decision-makers, they are also the ones deciding the admissibility of evidence, when the rules do apply. Understanding and using the reasons behind individual rules of evidence—and using that reasoning in addressing the value of evidence in arguments with judges—is the key to persuading judges about the import of evidence when the rules apply, and when they don't.

8. Learn about and advocate to the judge

Knowing your audience, and modifying your argument to appeal to your audience, is a key to effective persuasion. With judges, attorneys have an unequaled opportunity to learn about their audience and to tailor arguments precisely to strike a receptive chord (keeping in mind, of course, the admonition set forth above about not creepily invoking the judge's personal life). For attorneys to effectively take advantage of this advantage takes diligence and effort, but it will pay dividends.

9. Be candid and credible; don't exaggerate

When attorneys are advocating to judges, they are advocating to another member of the profession highly trained in legal analysis who has reason to believe they should be able to rely on attorneys as officers of the court. Nothing will more quickly damage attorneys' credibility, and damage their persuasiveness, as when attorneys exaggerate or shade the facts, or misstate or misrepresent the law. Judges are not jurors who can be bamboozled by smoke and mirrors and judges will be insulted and quickly distrust attorneys who attempt to hoodwink them. Likewise, attorneys should be realistic about the arguments they advance. Pushing the

Five. Methods and Means of Persuading Judges

envelope well beyond where a judge would ever go carries the potential of making the judge question the attorney's judgment. Of course, judges recognize that sometimes attorneys push unrealistic positions for reasons of ensuring good attorney-client relationships. Understood. But understand that attorneys engaging in this practice jeopardize good attorney-judge relationships.

10. Be professional to everyone

Treating opposing counsel, court staff, and the judge with courtesy and professionalism earn judges' respect, which will in turn make them receptive to persuasive arguments. When, though, attorneys display unprofessional treatment and disrespect of others, including opposing counsel, it carries the danger of causing judges to dislike and distrust the offending attorneys. Judges placed in that mood will be much less receptive to persuasion.

Six

Persuading Judges in Different Settings

In the preceding chapter, we provided some general observations and advice for effectively persuading judges. In this chapter, we consider the various settings and means by which attorneys will find themselves advocating to judges. Then we drill down to expand on effectively persuading judges in detail as it applies in the various settings.

When advocating before a jury, there is only the single setting and means of advocacy: a jury trial and oral persuasion. When advocating before an appellate bench, there is a single setting and two means by which attorneys can practice appellate advocacy: the written appellate brief and the oral appellate argument, when the latter is granted. When advocating before district judges, however, the settings and means can vary significantly. The different settings can influence the scope and nature of advocacy skills that an advocate can bring to bear.

Attorneys advocate to judges in a variety of proceedings based on the nature, stage, and posture of cases before the court. In some proceedings, judges serve as the factfinder and arbiter of the law. In other proceedings, judges make no findings of fact; rather, they apply the law to alleged or undisputed facts. How attorneys advocate to judges, the methods and styles attorneys uses to persuade judges in different settings, should change depending on the nature of the proceedings. Before we discuss how to advocate, then, we best first identify and discuss the nature of the proceedings in which attorneys advocate to judges.

In Part One of this chapter, we will examine the different settings in which attorneys exercise advocacy skills before judges. The first section looks at the various forms of hearings before district judges, with particular focus on whether the judge is primarily charged with fact-finding or legal conclusions. The second section examines the role of judges in jury trials. The last section examines judges' role in bench trials. In setting the

Six. Persuading Judges in Different Settings

stage in this part of the book we will focus almost entirely on federal court for two reasons. First, we are federal judges, so federal law and federal court is what we know best and where we are most comfortable. Second, the scope of state practice is too varied across fifty states for us to usefully address state court nuances in this book. The observations we make in this part will have general application, in any event, even though the context is federal court.

In Part Two of this chapter, we will drill down and examine effectively persuading judges in each of the various settings in which attorneys advocate to judges. Although the general principles and methods of persuading judges apply to some degree in each of the settings, the reader will see in Part Two of this chapter that there are nuances to effectively persuading judges depending on the setting in which attorneys have the opportunity to persuade judges.

Part One: The Settings

A. Motions and Hearings

Judges resolve motions and preside over hearings on motions in both civil and criminal cases when attorneys for opposing sides endeavor to persuade the judge to rule in the party's favor on some disputed issue. In civil cases, hearings may arise to resolve discovery disputes, dispositive motions, evidentiary issues (such as through motions in limine), and any number of other sundry matters. In criminal cases, judges hold hearings to decide bail and detention issues, determine whether to suppress evidence or dismiss indictments, resolve discovery disputes, take guilty pleas, and sentence defendants, to name a few. To effectively advocate to judges, it is important that attorneys understand that in some instances judges are factfinders and in other cases they are not.

Judges may serve as factfinders in a variety of hearings. In civil cases judges most frequently serve as factfinders in hearings on motions seeking restraining orders, motions arising from discovery disputes, and motions for summary judgment. There is potential for judges to serve as factfinders in many other civil hearings as well, of course, but these three examples will suffice for us to make our point here. The nature of fact-finding a judge performs may differ depending on the nature of the civil hearing. In some proceedings, like a hearing on a motion for a temporary restraining order, a judge may hear live testimony from witnesses and make credibility findings. In other hearings, such as in resolving discovery disputes, judges will rarely hear live testimony. Rather, judges usually find the facts regarding the underlying disputes largely, if not solely, from attorney proffers, affidavits and exhibits. In still other proceedings, such as when ruling on motions for summary judgment, judges are charged with identifying the undisputed facts and determining whether other facts are material and genuinely disputed.[1] When ruling on motions for summary judgment, judges rely on and resolve the parties' statements of undisputed facts based on the record the parties provide, which may take the form of documents, video or audio recordings, deposition transcripts, affidavits, and the like. Thus, one can see from this cursory review that the nature of a judge's fact-finding can differ significantly depending on the nature of the civil proceeding.

Opportunities for written advocacy to judges will differ significantly, depending on the nature of the proceedings. When discovery disputes arise, attorneys first attempt to resolve the disputes between themselves, sometimes cordially, often antagonistically. This often takes the form of emails exchanged between attorneys. Often, the emails are written less with the goal of sincerely attempting to find a middle ground or solution to the dispute as they are with the thought that the email chain may end up before a judge. This is a form, then, of written advocacy. A lawyer may word an email in a manner so as to couch the dispute in terms designed to show the judge the reasonableness of the author's position and the unreasonableness of the opposing counsel. It is quite common for attorneys to later attach these email strings as exhibits to motions to compel discovery or responses to such motions.

Discovery disputes will often result in written motions to compel and resistances to motions. Attorneys will often provide the court with copies of interrogatories or requests for production of documents and the opposing side's responses to such motions. Sometimes, the parties will attach responsive documents or other evidence that lies at the core of the dispute. And, as mentioned, it is common for the parties to provide the judge with copies of written emails discussing the discovery dispute.

On other occasions, discovery disputes reach the court without the opportunity for written advocacy. This may occur, for instance, during the course of a deposition when a party lodges an objection to a question and opposing counsel instructs the witness not to answer the question. When

Six. Persuading Judges in Different Settings

this happens, sometimes the lawyers pause the deposition and place a call a judge, seeking a ruling on the objection and direction as to whether the witness must answer the question. When this happens, attorneys must explain the situation to the judge orally, often over the phone. They must summarize the nature of the dispute, the circumstances that led to the objection, the question posed to the witness, and the legal and factual reasoning the lawyers believe support their position, all of which they must do quickly and orally.

On still other occasions, attorneys who find themselves in a discovery dispute may choose to seek an informal intervention by a judge by placing a call to chambers. Here, the attorneys are seeking guidance from the judge or are asking the judge to help mediate the discovery dispute in an informal manner. Here, the attorneys are seeking a practical solution to a discovery problem and hoping the judge can provide it without the lawyers having to resort to litigation over the dispute.

In addition to discovery disputes, judges handle a wide variety of motions at the district court level. Some involve factual disputes, other don't. Motions to dismiss require judges to assume the facts alleged in a complaint are true, drawing all reasonable inferences favorable to the non-moving party.[2] In those cases, advocacy to judges is limited to legal reasoning and persuasion. In other motions, judges may be presented stipulated facts when, again, the focus of the advocacy is on legal reasoning. In motions for summary judgment, however, a significant part of the written advocacy surrounds the identification and marshalling of facts material to the legal question. The same could be said of other motions, such as motions for a preliminary injunction, when advocacy to judges involves both facts and law. With any motions, oral advocacy may be available as well, depending on whether the parties ask for oral argument and whether the judge is willing to grant it.

Judges' fact-finding functions have much less variation in criminal cases than in civil cases, but judges are called upon to find facts far more often and more routinely in criminal cases. Whenever the government seeks to detain a defendant pending trial or sentencing, a judge must make a factual determination of whether the defendant poses a danger to others or the community or poses a risk of non-appearance.[3] Although a judge may rely solely upon a proffer of evidence or the undisputed portions of a probation officer's pretrial services report in ruling on a detention motion,[4] the government often presents evidence in the form of live testimony. In hearings on motions to suppress, the government will almost always present live testimony and exhibits and sometimes defendants do so as well.[5] A significant number of sentencing hearings involve contested issues, many of which require an evidentiary hearing.[6] In some contested sentencing hearings the focus is on the legal interpretation of statutory provisions or the United States Sentencing Guidelines, while in other contested sentencing hearings there are factual disputes. These later sentencing hearings can sometimes result in multiday mini-trials. Finally, federal judges preside over hearings on petitions to revoke offenders' supervised release[7] when they are alleged to have violated the terms and conditions of release. Sometimes revocation hearings involve the presentation of evidence and a judge must decide whether the offender violated the conditions of release, while in others the offender admits the violations and the judge must only decide the appropriate punishment for the violations. These hearings also sometimes turn into mini-trials that can last hours and, in rare instances, days.

For all motions and hearings on motions, civil and criminal, judges will reach legal conclusions. In some circumstances, judges are required to apply the law to the facts, regardless of whether they are judge-found facts, undisputed facts, or stipulated facts. In other instances, judges assume facts for purposes of making the legal ruling. In still other hearings, judges make purely legal rulings without any reliance on facts at all. Thus, advocacy to judges invariably involves persuading judges of the merits of legal arguments. In that sense, advocacy to judges is similar to appellate advocacy, but quite dissimilar to jury trial advocacy. But advocacy to judges differs from appellate advocacy in that, although judges will reach legal conclusions, they sometimes do so while simultaneously resolving factual disputes, whereas appellate judges reach legal conclusions on a cold factual record.

B. *Bench Trials (and Quasi Bench Trials)*

In addition to hearings, another setting where attorneys seek to persuade judges is in bench trials or other proceedings that resemble bench trials. In bench trials, judges are the factfinders. They serve in place of jurors. Sometimes judges preside over bench trials by consent of the parties. This can occur in both civil and criminal cases.[8] On other occasions, judges preside over bench trials because there is no right to a jury trial in a particular case.[9] There are times when bench trials and jury trials occur simultaneously when, for instance, the right to trial by jury attaches to some, but not all, of the claims in a civil complaint.

In federal court there are also occasionally quasi bench trial

Six. Persuading Judges in Different Settings

proceedings. For example, in Hague Convention cases[10] judges must determine if a child was wrongfully removed from a country by one parent and should be returned to that country. There is no jury involved. The factual issues may involve both whether the child was wrongfully removed from the country, and also whether there is an exception, such as a need for medical treatment, that would justify an otherwise unlawful removal. Similarly, judges sometimes preside over the equivalent of a bench trial on the issue of damages when a defendant in a civil suit is in default and the plaintiff seeks damages. When a defendant defaults by failing to defend a case, the judge will accept as true the factual allegations made in the complaint except with respect to the amount of the claimed damages.[11] A judge must hold an evidentiary hearing unless a damage claim is for a "sum certain," meaning there is no doubt as to the amount to which a plaintiff is entitled as a result of the defendant's default.[12] At such a hearing—really a bench trial over damages—the plaintiff must prove its damages by a preponderance of the evidence.[13]

C. Jury Trials

Judges preside over jury trials, where juries will make the findings of fact, but even in jury trials attorneys must still persuade judges on other matters. Before a jury trial, judges are often asked to make preliminary evidentiary rulings that may have a significant impact on the trial itself.[14] During trial, judges will rule on motions to strike prospective jurors for cause during jury selection, as well as ruling on *Batson* challenges asserting that one party has exercised peremptory strikes in a manner that violates the Constitution. Judges will rule on parties proposed jury instructions and objections to the opposing party's or the judge's own proposed jury instructions. Judges will rule on parties' evidentiary objections throughout the trial. Judges may have to rule on motions for mistrials. Judges will also rule on objections during opening statements and closing arguments. And at the close of the evidence, judges will rule on parties' motion for judgments of acquittal in criminal cases[15] and motions for directed judgment in civil cases.[16] After the verdict, judges will often rule on motions to overturn the verdicts, for new trials, or to reduce damage awards.

Advocacy to judges during in in relation to jury trials can pose particularly tricky situations for attorneys. Certainly some of that advocacy to judges in a jury trial setting will occur outside the presence of the jury. When that happens, general skills for persuading judges are largely applicable. For example, the making of for-cause challenges against prospective jurors, motions for judgment of acquittal, and motions for mistrial all usually occur outside the presence of the jury. On other occasions during jury trials, though, attorneys may have to exercise advocacy skills directed at judges in the presence of the jury. For example, when attorneys make evidentiary objections, or object during opening statements or closing arguments, and respond to such objections, the attorneys are seeking to persuade the judge to rule in their favor but are doing so cognizant that the jurors are watching and listening. Thus, when attorneys make evidentiary objections, they must do so in a way that is persuasive to the judge ruling on the objection but doesn't adversely influence the jury. Though the object is to persuade the judge at these times, the judges is not the only audience member. The words attorneys chose to use in making an evidentiary objection, and the manner and style in which they make an evidentiary objection, could appear to jurors to convey weakness or concern, or to be obstreperous or wasting the jurors' time. In other words, in these instances attorneys engage simultaneously in advocacy to judge and jury.

D. *Quasi Appellate Review Proceedings*

On occasion, judges sit in the capacity of a reviewing court. For example, parties may appeal magistrate judge decisions to district court judges. Similarly, judges sometimes sit in review of administrative law judge (ALJ) decisions, such as when ALJ's deny social security benefits to a claimant. In federal court, district judges may review appeals from state appellate court decisions. In still other settings, such as in post-conviction relief litigation, district court judges review decisions made by other judges. Here, advocacy directed at judges applies in a slightly different setting where, just like in appellate advocacy, the standard of review plays an integral role in the nature and tone of the arguments. Though in these cases judges sit as appellate panels of one, and there is no group decision-making, judges are ruling based on a cold record with varying degrees of deference sometimes given to the decision made by a lower judge or tribunal similar to how appellate panels work.

E. *Conclusion*

The various settings in which judges make decisions, both factual and legal, impacts the manner in which attorneys approach persuading

Six. Persuading Judges in Different Settings

judges. Effectively persuading judges, and sometimes effective jury trial advocacy, requires attorneys to consider the setting in which the judge is making decisions. In the previous two chapters, we identified differences between judges, jurors, juries, and appellate panels as decision-makers, and provided general guidance on effectively persuading judges. In Part One of this chapter, we just reviewed the various settings in which judges make both factual and legal decisions. Now it is time to turn to describing what we believe constitutes effectively persuading judges in these various settings.

Part Two: Effective Advocacy to Judges in Detail

Advocacy to judges occurs in two forms and several settings. The forms are written and oral advocacy. The settings include motions practice, bench trials, and jury trials. In this chapter, we will drill down into detail to examine effectively persuading judges through the two forms in each of the various settings, at each stage identifying the nuanced methods attorneys can employ to persuade judges.

A. Advocacy to Judges in Motions Practice

Motions practice involves "a contest for the mind of the judge."[17] Effectively persuading judges in motions practice can involve both written and oral advocacy. Motions practice begins with a written motion and a written response. This is the first, and sometimes only, opportunity for effectively persuading judges. Parties don't always seek, and judges don't always grant, hearings or oral arguments on motions. When there is no oral argument on a motion, the written pleadings are crucial for effectively persuading judges. Here, we will discuss first effective written advocacy in motions practice, then the question of whether and how to seek oral argument on a motion, before turning to discuss effective advocacy in connection with various types of motions.

Persuading Judges

1. Written Advocacy in Motions Practice

Effective written advocacy directed at judges begins with the need to be concise. District courts impose page limitations on motions and responses, and limitations on the filing of reply, sur-reply, and sur-sur-reply briefs for a reason. Many judges will read all of what is submitted to them out of a sense of duty and responsibility, but also because they want to understand and get it right. The more reading a judge must do, however, the more difficult it becomes for judges to issue rulings in a timely manner. With all the other cases pending requiring timely decisions, the pressures on judges to read through all the materials supplied by attorneys in connection with motions in one case makes it difficult for judges to devote concentrated effort on any single case. Because of these pressures, it is often the case that judges will read a pleading only once. These practical realities of a judge's limited time and resources lead to several conclusions about effective written advocacy. Moreover, the more words a judge must read, the more watered down the message becomes. A river of words can easily overflow a judge's capacity to absorb the message. Volume does not increase effectiveness.

First, it is important that attorneys strive to comply with page limits on motions. The page limits are not simply arbitrary lines in the sand without purpose. They exist to provide some realistic limitation on the amount of reading a judge must do to ensure that the judge can concentrate on each motion and render timely decisions. It is quite common for attorneys to request permission to file over-length briefs in support of motions. Indeed, it is a routine practice for most attorneys. Many judges will grant the motions routinely as well, concerned that to do otherwise may deprive a party of the opportunity to be fully heard. Other judges, recognizing the burden it places on them to read long briefs, routinely deny motions for permission to file overlength brief. The better practice, the more effective practice, is for attorneys to work within the page limitations and reserve asking for permission to file overlength briefs in rare cases that fully justify it. At the very least, good advocacy to judges involves attorneys learning about the judge to find out if a motion for overlength brief is routinely granted or denied. Woe betide the attorney who waits until the eleventh hour to file a motion for overlength brief only to find it denied and has an hour left before the filing deadline to somehow and somewhere cut 15 pages from the draft brief.

Truly good and effective legal writing is brief and concise. It takes a lot of effort to write concisely. There's some truth in the saying attributed

Six. Persuading Judges in Different Settings

to Mark Twain: "If I had more time, I would have written a shorter letter."[18] In practice, many briefs are unnecessarily lengthy. It is clear when reading them that the attorney put little effort into writing concisely. For a judge, reading these overlength briefs becomes an exercise in concentration. Judges will try to read these lengthy briefs searching for the nuggets of important words among the mass of pointless ones.

In contrast, short briefs, filed within the page limitations imposed by the court, capture a judge's attention immediately. Such briefs convey a message to judges that the attorneys are confident in their position. They also provide judges with the key information in a manner that judges can readily absorb and understand.

One way to achieve conciseness in motion pleadings is to dispense with boilerplate recitations about the law. Attorneys may rest assured that judges know the standards to be applied in ruling on a motion to dismiss, or a motion for summary judgment, for example. Attorneys need not include paragraphs and pages setting out such standards. A more effective and concise way of writing is to incorporate the standard in the argument on the merits of the dispute. For example, rather than waste space reciting the black letter law that a judge must accept as true the facts alleged in a complaint when ruling on a motion to dismiss a complaint, an attorney can more concisely write, "Even accepting as true the facts alleged in the complaint, it fails to state a claim because...." There's no need even to cite to the law here; the judge knows it.

Likewise, attorneys burn a lot of space in motions and responses providing the court with long string citations of authorities. District court judges are bound to follow appellate court precedent. So if there is a controlling appellate case on point, a simple citation to that one case is enough. A judge need not be persuaded that other courts followed that decision and thought it was good. To a district judge, it doesn't matter whether a controlling case is good; the judge must follow it anyway. The citation to additional authority is unnecessary.

Second, knowing that judges will read the pleadings, but often only once, it follows that attorneys often have only one chance to persuade a judge through their written advocacy. This means that they must make it count. It is important to get to the point quickly. Legal writing expert, Bryan Garner, places emphasis on the introduction to a brief so as "to win a motion in the first page and a half."[19] Make the point as simply as possible. "If you can't explain it simply, you don't understand it well enough."[20]

Attorneys should also consider that when they are writing motions for judges to read, they are communicating with a member of their own profession who is trained to think logically and analytically. Hyperbole and flowery language may be persuasive with lay jurors. It is not with judges. Generally speaking, attorneys should strip adjective and adverbs from their writing, especially when discussing facts. Likewise, attorneys use *italics*, **bold font**, and <u>underlining</u> far too often in their written advocacy; indeed, we have sometimes seen in written pleadings attorneys use <u>***all three***</u> forms of emphasis at the same time. To a judge, that is mildly insulting. Judges are capable of figuring out what is important. Using underlining, italics, or bold font suggests that the judge won't get it unless the attorney beats the judge over the head with it. All this goes to effective ethos. Part of effective persuasion is to earn the decision-maker's trust, to have the decision-make identify with the speaker and trust the speaker's assertions. Writing to a judge in a manner that reflects that the attorney understands what's important to the judge, that the judge will understand what's important to the issues in dispute, and in a manner showing proper respect for the judge's intelligence, increases the likelihood that the judge will be receptive to the logic of the attorney's argument.

Attorneys often file attachments or exhibits to accompany their briefs. All too often, these attachments are voluminous and much of it superfluous. Attorneys should consider ways of effectively conveying to the judge the key information in the attachments or exhibits. This can be accomplished by highlighting or underlining the relevant portions of the document. Indeed, attorneys should try to attach only the relevant portion of a document when possible. If the attorney feels the need to attach the entire document for purposes of appeal or to avoid having the opposing counsel suggest the attorney is attempting to hide other important portions of the document, then the attorney should identify the section of the document the attorney believes is important. Sometimes it is most effect to cut and paste that portion of the document and include it in the brief itself. The key here is to help the judge, to lead the judge to the portion of the document that the party believes is important. "Judges are not like pigs, hunting for truffles buried in briefs." *United States v. Dunkel*, 927 F.2d 955, 956 (7th Cir. 1991).

2. Seeking Oral Argument in Motions Practice

Oral arguments can be very important in persuading judges. Oral argument is more dynamic, more personal, and more flexible than written advocacy. As late Supreme Court Associate Justice Antonin Scalia put

Six. Persuading Judges in Different Settings

it succinctly, "you can put things in perspective" through oral argument in a "way a brief can't."[21] Generally speaking, judges view oral argument as very valuable, when done right, because of the opportunity for direct communication with judges.[22]

At the appellate level, oral argument is thought to have less effect in persuading appellate judges as much as it is seen as an opportunity to lose an otherwise persuasive written argument.[23] Not so much with district judges. Though district judges will have read the written pleadings and begun to formulate tentative mental conclusions from the written advocacy just like appellate judges, at the district court level attorneys have a greater opportunity to engage in a conversation with the judge, and thus a greater opportunity to persuade the judge through argument than an appellate advocate has in the more formal and time-controlled environment of an appellate argument.

Hearings, or oral arguments, are not a certainty in motions practice. Judges will often decide civil motions without hearings. This is especially true when neither party requests oral argument on the motion. Indeed, it is not uncommon for courts to adopt local rules stating that the court will rule on motions without hearings unless the parties specifically ask for oral argument.[24] Few civil motions involve the presentation of evidence, obviating the need for hearings in most instances. Because judges decide most civil motions on the pleadings, that should tell attorneys that their written advocacy is that much more important. It is only through the written advocacy that civil attorneys can persuade judges when judges rule on the pleadings. Although an attorney may request oral argument, the attorney should presume that a judge won't grant the request in a civil case when no evidence would be presented at the hearing. So good attorneys will devote more time and careful attention on the written advocacy, recognizing that it may be their only opportunity to persuade the judge.

The prevalence of oral advocacy in motions practice is greater in criminal cases than in civil cases because criminal motions practice involves more fact-finding by judges than in civil motions practice. That requires more hearings in criminal case and, naturally then, more opportunities for oral advocacy. Oral argument is not a given in criminal cases, however, when facts are not in dispute, or are established in the record.

When it is apparent that a motion won't require judge fact-finding and thus not require a hearing, part of persuading judges in motions practice involves deciding whether to seek a hearing and, if so, how to effectively request one. There are, of course, practical considerations that enter into the decision-making of whether to request oral argument. These practical considerations may involve, for example, a client's willingness or ability to pay for the time the lawyer would expend in oral argument. On other occasions, attorneys may view it as important for the client to feel they've "had their day in court." Even if the attorney doesn't personally believe oral argument would add much to the written briefing on the issue, the attorney may still request a hearing so that it makes the client feel heard. Putting aside those practical factors, though, attorneys should seek oral argument on a motion whenever they truly believe that oral argument would aid the judge in understanding the facts or legal reasoning.

All other considerations aside, as a matter of effectively persuading judges an attorney who has an opportunity to persuade a judge both in writing and in oral argument will have a greater chance of success than one that relies solely on written persuasion. When possible, then, attorneys should seek oral argument. Judges don't have to grant such requests, of course. As a practical matter, time is a scarce resource for judges, so whenever judges can decide motions on the pleadings, they tend to do so. Thus, part of effectively persuading judges involves knowing how to persuade a judge to grant oral argument on the motion.

To persuade a judge to grant oral argument, attorneys should do more than simply type "oral argument requested" below the caption of a motion or make a passing reference to a request for oral argument in the prayer for relief at the end of a written motion. Rather, effective advocacy to judges calls for an explanation by the attorney about why the judge should grant oral argument. Attorneys should explain why oral argument would help the judge. Perhaps the background of the legal dispute is particularly complex, or the law itself is complicated or uncommon. If an attorney cannot articulate why oral argument would be particularly helpful to a judge, it likely won't be.

Attorneys should request oral argument on a motion when they believe that they have something to say, something that needs further elaboration or explanation, beyond what they said in their written brief. Perhaps keeping to the written page limitation prevented an attorney from elaborating on an issue as much as the attorney thought would be helpful. Or perhaps the attorney simply doesn't know the extent to which the judge may understand the issues and believes having a conversation with the judge will help the attorney assess the need for elaboration or explanation. And sometimes, it is simply easier to explain a complex matter to a judge orally than in writing. In short, putting aside outside pressure the attorney may have from a client to request oral argument on a motion, or a client's reticence to pay the attorney's fees generated at oral argument, attorneys should carefully consider whether oral argument would add to the attorney's effort to persuade the judge.

Many judges tend to grant oral argument when requested. With this in mind, attorneys may detract from their effectiveness if they request oral argument and then fail to use the opportunity. Some attorneys request oral argument on motions as a matter of course, then appear at oral argument only to tell the judge that they have nothing to add to their brief. Judges don't look kindly on this as their schedules are busy and court time limited, so to schedule a hearing only to have an attorney state they have nothing to add to the written submission will hurt an attorney's effectiveness with judges. This, once again, goes to the ethos part of advocacy.

3. Oral Advocacy in Motions Practice

When attorneys have the opportunity to orally argue a motion to a judge, they don't want to squander the chance of persuading the judge. The first lesson is to prepare for oral argument. Attorneys should research the judge to determine if the judge is likely to have read the briefs in advance of the hearing. Some judges are known for not having done so, while others have a reputation of having thoroughly read the written submissions before every hearing. Whether the judge is familiar with the written material will significantly impact how an attorney presents oral argument. When a judge is not likely to have prepared extensively for the hearing, the attorney may have to devote more time to familiarizing the judge with the background and issues. When a judge is likely to have read the pleadings, the attorney can focus argument on some key issues or points or on explaining some particularly complex issue or area of law and dispense with the background.

Similarly, attorneys should research the judge to determine if the judge is generally familiar with the subject matter of the lawsuit, has presided over cases with similar issues, and has issued decisions on the subject matter. Again, the more familiar the judge is with the area, the more the attorney can focus in on key points. If it becomes apparent that the judge is unfamiliar with the specific are of the law or subject matter in dispute, the attorney should prepare to educate the judge about it to the extent necessary in a manner that is informative but not condescending.

Last, attorneys should research the judge to find out whether it is likely the judge will ask a lot of questions and be heavily engaged in a discussion with the attorneys. In other words, some judges are "hot benches" and ask a lot of questions, while other judges tend to be quiet and let the attorneys present their arguments, absorbing the information, but asking few questions. Knowing what type of reception the attorney is likely to encounter will affect how the attorney prepares for the oral argument.

Attorneys should consider a visual element to their oral arguments. Judges, like jurors, learn better when presented with both visual and aural information. Just as attorneys would consider preparing charts, diagrams, timelines, and other pedagogical aids in preparation for a jury trial, they should likewise consider preparing such visual aids for use in oral argument before a judge. It is important to ensure that any visual aids are easily visible to the judge; this seems obvious, but the reader might be surprised how often attorneys fail to do this. PowerPoint slides can be effective but should be limited in number and the amount of text included on each slide. PowerPoint slides should be visual aids to oral argument, not a repeat of the written brief. Text-heavy PowerPoint slides detract, rather than enhance, any oral argument, no matter who the audience is.

To be effective at oral argument before judges in motions practice, it is helpful for attorneys to consider the differences between a judge and jurors and a judge and an appellate panel. With judges, attorneys should emphasize reasoning and logic, the applicable test or factors that the judge must apply to make the decision, the burden of proof or persuasion, and so forth. Attorneys should argue the matter using the legal framework the judge will be applying in making the decision. Arguments focused on emotional appeals, drama, theatrics, will have little impact on judges.

Recall, too, that arguments before judges need not be formal affairs governed by a clock like they are before appellate panels. Attorneys should take the opportunity to gauge the judge's interest in and understanding of the issues, if appropriate to ask whether the judge has questions or concerns on a particular matter if it appears the judge does. Unlike formal appellate argument, oral argument before a district judge offers an opportunity for more of an exchange of information, a conversation. Whereas in appellate practice attorneys are there to answer the judges' questions and discouraged from ever asking questions themselves, not so with district judges. With judges, attorney have more freedom to inquire of the judge, to seek clarification, to ask about the judge's concerns and comprehension of arguments.

Although oral argument in district court is not strictly timed like it is in appellate courts, and district judges are more flexible with time constraints than appellate judges, brevity in oral argument is still important. As one trial judge observed, "[m]any lawyers snatch defeat from the jaws of victory by talking too much."[25] Judges' time is a scarce resource.

A concise, clear argument is much more persuasive than a long one. And the judge is more likely to understand and recall a short argument that quickly gets to the point, than a long rambling one. Few people remember the hour-long keynote speech at a battlefield in Pennsylvania, but almost everyone knows Lincoln's Gettysburg Address.

Having discussed generally the issues of effective writing in motions practice, whether and how to seek oral argument in motions practice, and effective oral advocacy to judges generally, we will turn next to examining effectively persuading judges in the context of several specific types of motions. The type of motion before a judge can have impact on how attorneys approach advocating to the judge; depending on the nature of the motion, attorneys may want to adjust their presentations to account for the differences between the motions, the context, the standards, and the issues. This discussion will include our advice on both written and oral advocacy, assuming the court grants the attorneys an opportunity for oral advocacy.

4. Emergency Hearings

In the category of emergency hearings we include motions for temporary restraining orders and preliminary injunctions. But the category of emergency hearings can also include any motion where a judge's speedy decision is critical, for whatever reason. These are instances when an evidentiary showing is not only likely, but in many cases necessary.[26] Here, time is often of the essence (or at least it better be, if the movant's case has any merit at all). Effective advocacy in these circumstances poses particular challenges, then, due to the time constraints and the high stakes involved.

Keep in mind that a judge is not likely to be sympathetic to self-inflicted "emergencies." For example, when an attorney knows it will be necessary to extend a deadline but waits until the last minute before filing a motion and requests expedited relief, the judge may not consider the situation to be an "emergency." Judges understand that life happens, such that a sudden illness or other unanticipated event may create the need for a last-minute request for relief. Far more often, however, the attorney simply did not get around to filing a motion to extend the deadline until the last possible minute and yet expects the judge to act on the motion immediately. This isn't a helpful or effective practice. It detracts from an attorney's reputation, part of the ethos of effective advocacy. On other occasions, a party claims there is a need for emergency action by a judge, but it turns out the party or the attorney created the emergency by failing to act promptly to address the situation until it became an emergency. Judges will not be receptive to emergency motions in these situations so when there is a possibility that the moving party was not diligent in raising the issue in a timely manner, both sides should address that issue as well as the merits of the dispute.

Written advocacy in the context of emergency motions will necessarily be rushed. The movant is motivated to get a motion filed as soon as possible, and judges may provide the opposing attorney little time to file a response. It is most critical here that attorneys strive for conciseness and brevity in their written advocacy. An emphasis should be placed on identifying the critical facts, and only the critical facts, that a judge must understand to rule on the emergency motion. The written pleadings should be shorn of any immaterial facts, and the critical facts should be summarized in as few words as possible. So, too, should the legal analysis be concise. This is not the place for boilerplate law and string citations. The legal test should be set out in tight prose, followed by application of the key facts to the test.

Because the written advocacy will be rushed and consequently should be short and perhaps not as polished as an advocate would produce with more time, effective oral advocacy will likely be particularly important. During hearings on emergency motions, attorneys should dispense with rhetorical flourishes and invectives, diatribes and discursive asides. Rather, attorneys should focus on the essential facts at issue, with only enough background for the judge to understand the setting, and with the essential legal standards and authority applicable to the issue.

It is particularly important in emergency motions that the attorneys be focused on the legal test before the court. The movant often is seeking to freeze the status quo pending resolution of the underlying dispute. Although success on the merits of the dispute is an important factor in the court's analysis of whether to grant a motion for a temporary restraining order or preliminary injunction, it is not the only factor and may not be the most important one. Indeed, whether the movant will be irreparably harmed by failing to freeze the status quo may be more important in the analysis than the chances of success on the merits.

It is important that attorneys recognize what is being asked of the judge. A district judge will be concerned about the practical implication of entering an order granting such emergency relief. The judge will be thinking about how the order will impact not just the litigants, but others as well, and will be keeping in mind the length of time it will likely be in effect while the merits of the case work their laborious way to final disposition. Effective judge advocates will address these practical concerns to help the judge resolve the equities of whether to grant emergency relief.

And in so-called emergency motions, judges will be particularly concerned about fairness to the non-moving party who has been placed in a situation of responding with little time. Movants should recognize this and to the extent possible address the fairness aspect of the crunched time frame and consider ways to ameliorate the hardship placed on the opposing party and attorney. In contrast, the opposing party may want to focus on the unfairness of the timing issue in addition to the merits of the dispute. The opposing attorney may want to address any lack of diligence by the moving party or attorney in raising the issue in a more timely manner, the adverse impact the short timeline has imposed on the attorney and client, and the manner in which the shortened timeline may prevent a full and intelligent evaluation of the merits of the dispute.

5. Discovery-Related Motions

When attorneys bring discovery disputes to a judge through motions to compel or for sanctions, they often make two primary mistakes. First, attorneys do a poor job providing judges with the essential facts, and only the essential facts, necessary for the judge to resolve the dispute. Second, attorneys bring into the courtroom the invective and antagonistic tone they have been using with each other.

Discovery disputes that get so far out of hand that they end up in front of a judge often have a lengthy and complex history. After weeks and perhaps months of conducting discovery and encountering discovery issues, exchanges of so-called good faith letters, and countless emails and phone calls, the attorneys have reached what they believe to be an impasse that requires court intervention to resolve. In discovery-related motions, attorneys then often inundate the judge with volumes of paper, including scores of interrogatories, requests for admissions, deposition pages, letters and email strings expecting the judge to read and understand it all. Or they file motions making broad assertions and references or allude to documents or depositions but then fail to give the judge the essential underlying documents. Neither of these approaches is effective with judges.

It is critical with discovery disputes that attorneys carefully cull the volumes of documents and transcripts they have, identify those that contain the essential information, and only the essential information, necessary for the judge to understand and rule on the motion, and attach only those essential documents and portions of documents to the pleadings. If a single interrogatory is at issue, the judge does not need to see all the interrogatories or the answers. If only part of a witness' testimony in a deposition is relevant, attorneys should provide the judge with the relevant portion of the deposition, not the entire deposition. Attorneys should also highlight or underline the important portions of documents drawing the judge's attention to what is important on a page, rather than expect the judge to discern the important part.

The communication between attorneys in connection to discovery disputes seems to be more full of invective and insult than in connection with any other part of litigation.[27] The tone and language attorneys use in communicating with each other over discovery disputes is, at times, extremely unprofessional. It often resembles juvenile exchanges between children on a playground. All too often, the email exchanges reveal a shocking degree of unprofessionalism, where attorneys use pejorative terms for each other and freely make accusations of misfeasance, malfeasance and incompetence. Attorneys seem to forget that their obnoxious communications could be attached as exhibits to future pleadings. Suffice it to say that these unprofessional exchanges do nothing to enhance the attorneys' credibility with judges. Hence, attorneys should use more caution and restraint before hitting "send," especially if they stop to consider the possibility that the opposing attorney may attach that email to a motion submitted to the judge. Attorneys should likewise pause before attaching such email strings to pleadings, considering whether the benefit of providing the judge with the communication outweighs the detriment of the judge having a full view of the unprofessional manner in which counsel communicated with each other.

Surprisingly, when attorneys then bring and respond to discovery dispute motions, they too often maintain the same tone in their pleadings. Judges are not interested in the personal disputes between the attorneys. Judges are not persuaded by name-calling, hyperbole, and accusations of malfeasance. Indeed, the more strenuous and strident the tone an attorney takes, the less persuasive the attorney becomes with a judge. Most judges presume attorneys are acting in good faith and behave professionally. It is very seldom the case that only one side is at fault in discovery disputes. Judges often find that there is a reasonable and practical solution to the supposed impasse between the attorneys, a solution that the attorneys could have found if only they had not let their emotions overrule their judgment. Attorneys are most effective when they are completely factually accurate, when they give the judge the facts objectively and without

Six. Persuading Judges in Different Settings

shading them, depriving the opposing side an opportunity to take issue with the recitation of the facts.

Thus, what is persuasive to a judge in relation to discovery disputes is a calm, rational, and reasonable tone in which an attorney outlines the dispute, relates the efforts made to resolve the dispute, and offers a reasonable compromise for resolving the dispute. This advances the persuasive method of ethos. Attorneys should adopt this approach not only in the written pleadings, but also in argument when a judge holds a hearing on discovery motions. Judges find attorneys who exercise professional courtesy are more persuasive and trustworthy than those who don't.

Indeed, effective advocacy should include tailoring communication about discovery disputes with opposing counsel in a way that places the advocate in the best light should that communication be appended to discovery dispute pleadings, as it most likely will. It is one thing to assert in a written pleading that the attorney has acted in a reasonable manner in connection with a discovery dispute, but if the email string reflects sharp words and bush-league practices, the protestations of reasonableness will fall on deaf ears with the judge. Attorneys should conduct communication with opposing counsel ever conscious of how a judge may later view that communication.

Attorneys often attach long email strings as exhibits to discovery-related motions, assuming the judge will read them all. Although we noted that most judges read everything submitted to them, we have found that email strings is one category of attachments that some judges simply won't read, for several reasons. First, reading an email string is laborious, requiring the reader to start at the end of the string and work backwards, too often lacking the background the attorneys had that rendered their shorthand references intelligible to the attorneys, but not to the judge. Second, judges don't want to wade into the name calling and invective all too often present in the email strings. The judge is trying to solve a discovery dispute by finding a practical solution and is uninterested in the parties' views about whether the other side has played fairly. So, rather than attach such email strings, the better practice is for attorneys to state the material facts that are reflected in the email string. If the other side disputes those facts, then they can attach the email string necessary to rebut the alleged facts.

6. Motions to Dismiss

In civil cases, parties almost invariably file dispositive motions, that is motions that ask judges to dispose of the case on the pleadings without a trial. Defendants may move to dismiss complaints under Rule 12(b) of the Federal Rules of Civil Procedure. Federal judges generally analyze motions to dismiss under the *Twombly/Iqbal* standard. Under this standard, although a complaint need not contain "detailed factual allegations," it must contain "more than an unadorned, the-defendant-unlawfully-harmed-me accusation." *Ashcroft v. Iqbal*, 556 U.S. 662, 678 (2009). "To survive a motion to dismiss, a complaint must contain sufficient factual matter, accepted as true, to state a claim to relief that is plausible on its face." *Iqbal*, 556 U.S. at 678. "[W]hen ruling on a defendant's motion to dismiss, [judges] must accept as true all of the factual allegations contained in the complaint." *Erickson v. Pardus*, 551 U.S. 89, 94 (2007). Judges must also "grant all reasonable inferences from the pleadings in favor of the nonmoving party." *United States v. Any & All Radio Station Transmission Equip.*, 207 F.3d 458, 462 (8th Cir. 2000). This is the boilerplate recitation of the standards of which judges are fully aware and need not be included in an attorney's brief.

Knowing that judges will have these standards in mind, attorneys should approach advocacy in motions to dismiss recognizing that the focus of persuasion will be on the law, not the facts. That said, when a civil complaint contains conclusions and assumptions, it is most effective for attorneys to draw the facts out from the complaint in a way that shows the judge how much of the complaint is not factual. One way to do this is to draft a fact section in the motion to dismiss that recasts the complaint to allege only the facts. This can work well when the complaint is short and the facts are few. In some cases, however, the complaint may be quite long and the alleged facts many. In those cases, recasting the facts in a fact section of the brief would consume too much of the limited space the attorney has to persuade the judge. In those instances, a method that works well is to attach as an exhibit to the motion a copy of the complaint with all assumptions and conclusions struck through, leaving only facts untouched. Then in the brief, the attorney can identify the material facts by reference to the attached and redacted complaint.

With dispositive motions, either the judge is bound by the four corners of the complaint, as in a motion to dismiss, or by the factual record provided by the parties, as with a motion for summary judgment. When, however, judges entertain oral argument on dispositive motions, attorneys should make the most of the opportunity. Attorneys shouldn't simply repeat what they wrote in the pleadings. They can assume that the judge has read the pleadings. Rather, the attorneys should key in on the reason why argument was sought in the first place. Perhaps argument is necessary because the factual context is particularly complex, and elaboration is necessary to help the judge understand the facts. If the judge sets a hearing sua sponte, then the attorneys should use the hearing as an opportunity to engage in a conversation with the judge to find out why the judge thought oral argument would be helpful. The judge most likely had a particular reason for setting the hearing. Attorneys should remember that a key difference between advocacy to a jury and advocacy to a judge is that attorneys can engage in a conversation with judges. Communication with a judge can be two-way, and attorneys should take advantage of that to ensure that they are directly responsive to issues important to the judge.

7. Motions for Summary Judgment

Both parties in a civil lawsuit may seek summary judgment, asking the judge to resolve the dispute on the merits based on an undisputed set of facts supported by the record. We take the space here to lay out the standard for judges in ruling on motions for summary judgment in federal court because it is critical in the discussion of advocacy to judges that follows.[28] Summary judgment is appropriate when "the movant shows that there is no genuine dispute as to any material fact and the movant is entitled to judgment as a matter of law."[29] When asserting that a fact is undisputed or is genuinely disputed, Rule 56 requires a party to support the assertion by "citing to particular parts of materials in the record, including depositions, documents, electronically stored information, affidavits or declarations, stipulations…, admissions, interrogatory answers, or other materials."[30] Alternatively, a party may "show that the materials cited don't establish the absence or presence of a genuine dispute, or that an adverse party cannot produce admissible evidence to support the fact."[31] In determining whether a genuine issue of material fact exists, judges must view the evidence in the light most favorable to the nonmoving party, giving that party the benefit of all reasonable inferences that can be drawn from the facts.[32] Judges cannot "weigh the evidence or attempt to determine the credibility of the witnesses."[33]

The first thing to understand about effectively persuading judges when it comes to summary judgment motions is that they pose one of the greatest burdens on judges. They are necessarily fact-intensive exercises, requiring the judge to take a deep dive into the facts in an effort to identify the material facts and then discern there's a genuine dispute about a material fact that would prevent the judge from entering summary judgment. Ruling on motions for summary judgment therefore consume more

Persuading Judges

of judges' time than any other type of motion. It follows, then, that a key to effectively persuading judges when it comes to motions for summary judgment is finding ways to make the judge's task easier.

The initial way to accomplish this is in carefully drafting the statement of uncontested material facts. Too often, attorneys exert little effort in doing this well, making the task of ruling on the motion extremely difficult and increasing the risk of error. When drafting statements of material fact, attorneys should do two things to be most effective. First, include only a single fact within a sentence. Attorneys frequently write run-on sentences including multiple facts, some of which the opposing party may dispute, and others they may not. To make it clear, the sentence should include a single fact. The opposing party can then either admit or deny that single fact. Whether it is then in dispute becomes crystal clear to the judge. Second, attorneys need to back up each alleged fact with a precise citation to the record where that fact can be found. This means not just directing the judge to a document, but to the page and paragraph and, if possible, the sentence in the document where the fact can be found. It may also aid the court if in the appendix supporting the motion or resistance, the attorney highlights or underlines the fact in the document at the relevant page so the judge can quickly find it. With other exhibits, like photographs or recordings, attorneys should find a way to isolate the precise portion of the exhibit where the judge can find the information that clearly supports the alleged fact.

Attorneys should think also about the order in which they set out their statements of fact. Organizing the facts in chronological order, or some other manner that is logical and fits within the framework of the analysis the judge will undertake, is the most helpful. Attorneys who think carefully about what judges need and then provide judges with what they need in a manner most helpful to the judges stand the greatest chance of persuading the judges to see the dispute in the light most favorable to the attorney's client. Effective advocacy involves making it as easy as possible for the judge to understand your position and conclude that it is correct.

When an opposing party resists a motion for summary judgment, there are steps an attorney can take to be more effective with the judge. First, when responding to the movant's statement of material facts, the opposing attorney should clearly state whether the fact is admitted or denied. The response to the statement of material facts is not the place to argue in opposition to the motion. Too often we see responses that don't simply admit or deny the alleged fact but, instead, assert other facts and arguments to provide "context" for the alleged fact. The arguments should be saved for the brief.

Six. Persuading Judges in Different Settings

If an alleged fact is denied, the attorney needs to cite to the record the precise location in the appendix where the judge can locate a document calling the alleged fact into question. A mere denial of a fact, without citation to the record, is not sufficient and judges won't search the record for the attorney to find the facts to support the denial.[34] Second, the opponent should follow the guidance in the prior paragraph when drafting an opposing statement of material facts. That is, each sentence should contain a single fact with citation to the precise location in the record where the judge can find support for the fact.

Complete honesty and accuracy in reciting the facts is another key to effectively persuading judges when it comes to motions for summary judgment. Attorneys can be certain that even if the opposing party does not catch an attorney playing fast and loose with the facts, the judge will. Judges will go to the record and check the facts as alleged by the parties. Nothing will more quickly hurt an advocate than for a judge to check the record and find that the attorney has twisted, shaded or been misleading about the facts. In contrast, when judges check the record and find the attorney has taken no liberties in reciting the facts and has been a hundred percent accurate, it immediately raises the judge's confidence in the reliability of that attorney, enhancing that attorney's effectiveness with the judge.

Last, in briefing and arguing a motion for summary judgment, the parties should pay close attention to the standard of review the judge must follow. That is, the judge is trying to determine if there is a genuine issue of material fact that would require resolution by a jury. It is not the case that the judge is deciding whether one side or the other wins the outcome of the case. That may be the result in ruling on the motion if the judge finds no genuine issue of material fact, but first and foremost the judge is struggling with the question of whether a jury needs to resolve the parties' dispute. Keeping this in mind will help the attorneys effectively persuade the judge.

8. Intellectual Property Cases and Other Specialized Areas of Practice

Many judges have general jurisdiction, meaning they can hear cases on any matter for which the court has jurisdiction. In federal court, for example, that means that judges may preside over a variety of highly specialized areas of law, such as intellectual property disputes, bankruptcy, and even maritime law. When attorneys appear before judges in hearings on such specialized areas of law, they will have to engage in extraordinary efforts to be truly effective judge advocates. It is important for attorneys to recognize that these are extraordinary matters for most judges. The ordinary docket of a federal judge (except in a few isolated districts that specialize in these cases) don't involve patent litigation, for example. And yet, there will be times when patent cases appear on a federal judge's docket. These will be unusual cases for most judges and very difficult for them to navigate successfully.

To be effective judge advocates when attorneys litigate legal issues before judges that are not typical for the judge's docket, it often calls upon attorneys to assume the role of guide and tutor. Before they can begin to be successful persuading the judge about the merits of the dispute, they need to help the judge understand the complex legal context in which the dispute arises. This will inevitably be a highly familiar area of the law for attorneys practicing in this area, so terms, words, and acronyms will be a second language for them. Not so for the judge. Attorneys need to recognize this and translate for the judge, not assuming a base level of knowledge.

This is when it may be especially important to conduct some research on the judge. Attorneys shouldn't assume that the judge will even know the most elementary legal principles involved in a particular specialized area of the law. No one—not even a judge—knows everything. Attorneys should determine the level of knowledge and familiarity the judge has, if any, in this area of the law. Attorneys should conduct online research to find out if the judge has ever ruled before on the particular area of the law at issue and, if so, how often. Attorneys shouldn't be afraid to even reach out to chambers to inquire from the judge's staff about the judge's familiarity with the specialized area of law.

When attorneys determine that the judge has little or no prior experience with the specialized area of law at issue, they will need to take extra efforts to educate the judge. This may start with devoting some pages in written submissions to what to the attorney may be basic background on the law and procedures inherent in the underlying litigation. For example, the typical federal district court judge has little or no bankruptcy law experience. If the parties are appealing to the district court judge a bankruptcy judge's ruling on in adversarial proceeding connected to a bankruptcy petition, it may require a short explanation to the district court judge about what an adversarial proceeding is in bankruptcy court, who the parties are in that proceeding, and what the standard is for bankruptcy judges in ruling on adversarial proceedings. Attorneys who draft a brief for a district court judge on the merits of such a dispute in same manner they draft a brief for the bankruptcy judge may find that the district court judge does not fully understand what happened below, what the dispute is about, and what the judge is supposed to do to resolve it.

In educating judges on specialized areas of law, attorneys should strip that portion of any written submission of an adversarial slant. The goal here is a neutral education of the judge. To be effective judge advocates here, the writing should convey to the judge the attorney's effort to provide the judge with a neutral tutorial. When judges discern that the attorney is intentionally attempting to aid the judge's understanding, it will be far more effective than when judges detect a subtle attempt to color or slant the explanation in a way that favors the attorney's client. Of course, attorneys should also be cautious about the tone used to provide the tutorial to the judge. In other words, attorneys should show proper respect for the judge's intelligence and don't talk down to the judge any more than attorneys should talk down to jurors. It's not the case the judge is stupid; it's a case of the judge being unfamiliar with a specialized area of law that to the attorney is second nature. Lack of knowledge doesn't mean lack of intelligence. There's a difference.

Last, requesting oral argument on motions in specialized areas of law is particularly advisable. Written advocacy lacks feedback. Attorneys may believe their written explanation of the specialized area of law and context in which the dispute has arisen is as plain as day, but it may appear as clear as mud to the judge. When attorneys are close to their specialized area of practice, what may seem clear to them may be confusing to others unfamiliar with the practice area. Oral argument can help. At a hearing on a motion, attorneys can engage with the judge in a conversation about the issues. Through that exchange, attorneys can discern the degree to which the judge has come to understand the practice area and is fully tracking the nuances of the legal dispute from reading the written pleadings. If necessary, attorneys can simply ask the judge if there is any area of the specialized practice that it would be helpful for the attorneys to explain further to aid the judge's comprehension. This can be done respectfully by explicitly acknowledging attorneys who devote their practice to the specialized area of law have a familiarity with that area that judges, responsible for a much broader scope of legal knowledge, may not have.

9. Motions in Limine

Attorneys often file motions in limine in both civil and criminal cases seeking a pretrial ruling from the judge on an evidentiary issue. At least, that is what a proper motion in limine should be. Black's Law Dictionary defines a motion in limine as "[a] pretrial request that certain inadmissible evidence not be referred to or offered at trial."[35] Or, in other words, a motion in limine is "any motion, whether made before or during trial, to exclude anticipated prejudicial evidence before the evidence is actually offered."[36] This definition, however, is too narrow. "In limine" is Latin for "at the outset."[37] In short, the word "limine" does not mean "to limit." Rather, it refers to the timing of the motion in relation to trial. Thus, attorneys may file motions in limine either to bar the admission of evidence or to seek a pretrial ruling finding that the evidence is admissible.

The Federal Rules of Evidence don't explicitly authorize in limine rulings. Nor, for that matter, do the Federal Rules of Criminal Procedure or the Federal Rules of Civil Procedure explicitly provide for motions in limine. The practice at common law of raising evidentiary issues in advance of trial by the filing of motions in limine developed under the district court's inherent authority to manage trials.[38] Some basis for the authority of a court to rule on evidentiary issues in advance of trial, however, may be found under Rule 103(d), which provides that jury proceedings should be conducted "so as to prevent inadmissible evidence from being suggested."[39] Likewise, Rule 104(a) implies the permissibility of motions in limine when it provides that "[t]he court must decide any preliminary question about whether a witness is qualified, a privilege exists, or evidence is admissible." In short, the concept of a pretrial order—an order in limine—broadly encompasses a court's ability and duty to determine preliminary issues of admissibility when most appropriate, not just a court's ability and duty to determine whether evidence should be barred in advance of trial.

A step in effectively persuading judges, when it comes to motions in limine, is learning how to use them properly. A motion in limine should be seen as a substitute for objecting to evidence at trial. Properly filed, they should be tied to the rules of evidence. Again, it is important for attorneys to recognize that in ruling on a motion in limine the judge seeks to enforce the rules of evidence in a way that provides for a fair trial before a jury, to ensure the jury bases its verdict on reliable evidence. A pretrial ruling on an evidentiary issue helps avoid prejudice and delay, and ensure an even-handed and expeditious trial, and to focus the issues the jury will consider.[40] Motions in limine further the trial court's gatekeeping responsibility to eliminate from consideration evidence that shouldn't be presented to the jury because it wouldn't be admissible for any purpose.

Some judges are openly hostile to motions in limine. In large part, this is likely a result of parties filing motions in limine for improper

Six. Persuading Judges in Different Settings

reasons. All too often, attorneys file under the guise of motions in limine motions seeking sanctions for discovery disputes, or motions for summary judgment, or the like. On other occasions, attorneys file under the caption "motion in limine" pleadings that address vague and broad categories of anticipated evidence without sufficient focus or detail such that no judge could possibly enter a pretrial order applying the Rules of Evidence because there's not enough detailed information upon which the judge can rule. For example, we have received motions in limine that broadly ask us to issue a pretrial order barring any evidence that violates the hearsay rules, without reference to any specific anticipated testimony. Similarly, some attorneys file motions in limine that list categories of obviously improper arguments (e.g., the Golden Rule, mention of insurance coverage, etc.) and ask for an order prohibiting such arguments—regardless of whether there is any basis to believe opposing counsel intends to make them. Thus, it is appropriate that we consider here when motions in limine are appropriate, and when they are not.

In light of the limited purpose of a motion in limine, "[m]otions in limine are meant to deal with discrete evidentiary issues related to trial, and are not another excuse to file dispositive motions disguised as motions in limine."[41] It follows, then, that attorneys should tailor their arguments to demonstrate why certain categories of evidence should (or shouldn't) be admitted at trial, and direct the court to specific evidence in the record that would favor or disfavor the admission of those particular categories of evidence.[42]

When filling motions in limine, attorneys should consider several things to effectively persuade the judge. First, the judge does not know the facts of the case. In contrast, attorneys are deeply enmeshed in the facts of the case to the point that they tend to assume a base level of knowledge. Too often, attorneys file motions in limine unwittingly assuming a level of knowledge about the facts the attorneys all possess, but the judge does not. To make intelligent evidentiary rulings, judges need some context. In motions in limine (and resistances to them) attorneys should provide the judge with the essential facts of the case, those facts necessary for the judge to understand the context and the basis for the evidentiary issue. That means attorneys need to consider the case from the judge's perspective, understanding what information the judge needs to make an evidentiary ruling in advance of trial.

In providing a factual context for the evidentiary issue, however, attorneys should be careful to include only the facts necessary for the judge to comprehend the context of the evidentiary issue. Keeping in mind

Persuading Judges

the demand on judges' limited time, attorneys should strip the factual description of all unnecessary and superfluous facts. There may be facts very relevant to the merits of the underlying dispute or the elements of the crime or claim, but which have nothing to do with the evidentiary dispute. And to be persuasive, the factual recitation should be a hundred percent accurate, shorn of adjectives and adverbs, and neutral. This is the place for attorneys to convey to the judge that the judge can trust and rely on them to provide the judge with accurate information upon which the judge can make difficult decisions. Attorneys should save for the jury any slant or interpretation they have on the facts.

Second, attorneys should provide the underlying evidence in dispute to the judge when possible. It is not uncommon for attorneys to file a motion in limine seeking to bar statements by a witness as hearsay or for some other reason, when the statements have been recorded or are set out in an interview report or transcript, and yet the attorneys fail to provide the judge with the underlying evidence of the statements. When attorneys provide the underlying evidence to the judge, it allows the judge to make an informed decision. Attorneys should either incorporate the evidence in the body of the motion in limine or resistance, or attach it as an exhibit. Absent having the actual evidence before it, judges are in no position to rule definitively on the matter in advance of trial. When attorneys truly seek a pretrial order indicating whether evidence will or won't be admissible at trial, it is incumbent upon them to provide the judge with the evidence in dispute in advance of trial.

Third, attorneys should recognize when an issue is not amenable to a pretrial ruling. Many evidence disputes depend completely on what happens at trial. If there is no practical way for the judge to rule in advance of trial because the evidentiary issue has not yet become ripe or lacks sufficient context in light of other evidence, attorneys shouldn't file a motion in limine on the issue. Rather, attorneys should explain that evidentiary issue in a trial brief, alerting the judge that the issue might arise so the judge can anticipate the issue and perhaps even do some research in advance of trial to be fully prepared to rule when and if the issue arises.

Attorneys shouldn't file motions in limine that do nothing more than ask the judge to enforce the rules of evidence. Broadly asking a judge to bar hearsay statements in a motion in limine, for example, is worthless. On the other hand, if there is a known statement the judge can analyze for hearsay, then the judge can make a pretrial ruling in many cases. If an attorney believes that hearsay issues might arise with a witness, but does not have sufficient information about the anticipated statements to realistically

Six. Persuading Judges in Different Settings

have the judge rule on the matter in advance of trial, it is better to bring it up in a trial memo rather than file a motion in limine when it is clear the judge cannot rule on it in advance of trial.

Last, attorneys should confer with each other before filing motions in limine to find out if the opposing side will resist. It is not uncommon for attorneys to file motions in limine seeking to bar a half dozen (frequently more) categories of evidence only to have the opposing counsel file a response not resisting the vast majority of the categories, or to have them file their own motion in limine seeking to bar the same categories of evidence. When judges receive these pleadings, it shows that the parties are failing to communicate and decreases the confidence the judge has in the attorney for the moving party. When attorneys communicate first with opposing counsel and discover there is no resistance to a motion in limine as to a particular category or piece of evidence, the attorneys can state as much in the motion, dispensing with the need to brief the merits of the evidentiary issue. Attorneys should still seek a pretrial ruling on the uncontested matter so that there is an order that the judge can enforce if necessary.

Later, we will discuss the role motions in limine should have, or should not have, in bench trials.

10. Criminal Hearings

As noted, judges preside over a lot of hearings, often evidentiary hearings, in criminal cases. Indeed, judges preside over hearings in criminal cases far more often than they do in civil cases. In criminal cases judges hold detention hearings, suppression hearings, sentencing hearings, and revocation hearings, among other sundry hearings. At some of these hearings, such as initial appearances and arraignments, the nature of the hearing is not adversarial and there is little place for advocacy by either side. In many of the hearings, however, there are contested issues, often evidentiary issues, that judges must resolve. In those hearings, there is a place for effectively persuading judges. There are several steps attorneys can take in criminal cases to be more effective advocates.

First, attorneys should recognize that, unlike juries, judges can review exhibits in advance of the hearings. In jury trials, jurors see exhibits only after the judge admits the exhibits and a party presents the exhibit at trial. When judges are factfinders, however, attorneys can, and should, provide judges with exhibits in advance of the hearing whenever possible. Providing judges the opportunity to review exhibits in advance of hearings aids judges in understanding testimony and allows time for the judge to fully review exhibits. This includes video and audio recordings as well as documents. Indeed, this is particularly true with video or audio exhibits, or lengthy written exhibits. Providing judges with copies of exhibits in advance of hearings permits a judge to review the exhibits when it best fits in the judge's schedule and at a time and place where the judge can focus on the exhibits and not feel rushed or pressed by time as the judge might if presented for the first time in the hearing.

It bears repeating that attorneys should provide the judge with only the relevant portions of the exhibit or direct the judge to the relevant portion of a larger exhibit. It is quite common for attorneys to provide us with exhibits that contain completely irrelevant material. For example, we have been provided video from an officer's body camera that contains more than an hour of recording, only a minute of two of which ended up being relevant to any issue before the Court. Other times, attorneys provide judges with exhibits, the relevance of which is not apparent on their face. For example, a prosecutor may provide the Court with multiple court documents pertaining to prior convictions in response to a defendant's objections to the scoring under the Guidelines of multiple prior convictions. Rather than rely upon the judge to try to match the exhibit to the pertinent part of the Presentence Investigation Report, the prosecutor should provide the cross-reference in the government's sentencing memorandum.

Providing judges with exhibits in advance of hearings also often cuts down on the time consumed by the hearing—scarce and valuable courtroom time. This is because the parties need not necessarily spend the time with the exhibits during the hearing that they would if it was the first time the judge saw the exhibits. Again, this is particularly true with lengthy audio and video recordings that often need not be replayed in the courtroom when the judge has already viewed them in chambers.

Attorneys should provide the judge with exhibits in advance of the hearings even if the opposing party has an evidentiary objection to them. The judge must necessarily see the exhibit to rule on its admissibility in any event. So, it is best to provide the judge with the exhibit in advance of the hearing to allow the judge time to review it in detail and thereby be more likely make a correct ruling.

Second, attorneys should tailor witness questions for presentation to a judge by omitting unnecessary background questions that attorneys may otherwise think are necessary in front of jurors to educate the jury or personalize the witness. Through education and experience, judges have a base of knowledge of criminal investigations and criminal conduct most

Six. Persuading Judges in Different Settings

jurors lack. Judges often already know common terms used in drug trafficking, for example, and don't require witnesses to explain them. Judges are also much more focused the essential facts and are less likely to be influenced by peripheral facts about witnesses such as whether they are married and have children.

That said, attorneys should nevertheless remember the need to make a good appellate record. If a particular fact is important to the case, such as firearms being tools of the drug trade, then the attorneys need to elicit those facts even if it is obvious the judge already knows that fact from other cases. Similarly, if an attorney believes that personalizing a witness by eliciting background facts might indeed influence the judge's perception of the witness (the ethos part of classical rhetoric), then the attorney should elicit the background facts.

Again, researching the judge presiding over the criminal hearing may be appropriate here. A relatively new judge whose prior legal practice was limited to civil proceedings may indeed need some education on basic criminal investigative techniques or methods and means offenders use to commit crimes. In contrast, a judge who has prior practice as a prosecutor or defense attorney, or years of experience on the bench hearing criminal cases and presiding over criminal trials, won't need superfluous testimony on basic criminal concepts.

Third, many criminal cases involve the use of cooperators, individuals who are assisting the government because they hope to receive some benefit, such as evading criminal charges or receiving a more lenient sentence. In jury trials, prosecutors necessarily worry about jurors' receptiveness to testimony from these people and defense attorneys appropriately expend a lot of time and effort making sure jurors fully understand how the motivation to evade charges or reduce a sentence could motivate these cooperating witnesses to lie or shade the truth if they believe it could benefit them in some way.

When judges are factfinders, attorneys need to recognize that judges are already fully aware of the issues inherent with cooperating government witnesses. Knowing this, attorneys should modify their approach to handling such witnesses. Prosecutors need not expend time explaining to judges how a cooperator may benefit from testifying; judges already know this. Rather, the focus should be on what the cooperator believes about how it will work. In other words, what's important here is not the mechanics of how a cooperator may actually receive a break. Rather, it's what the cooperator thinks. If a cooperator incorrectly believes that the government has promised the cooperator a reduction in sentence only if the defendant is convicted or sentenced in a particular way, it doesn't matter that the cooperation agreement says something else.

And defense attorneys should adjust their cross examination, recognizing that judges won't be influenced by labeling the cooperator as a snitch or by some other pejorative term. Such pathos-based appeals will fall flat with judges. Judges understand the process and the need for using cooperators in the criminal justice system. Judges also fully understand how the process can create a motive for cooperators to shade the truth or outright lie. To be effective judge advocates, defense counsel should concentrate on a logos-based and ethos-based attack on cross-examination, focusing more on inconsistencies in the testimony and incongruities between the cooperator's testimony and other evidence. Judges will be moved to discredit cooperating witness more by reason and doubts about such witnesses' credibility than they will by mere labeling of the cooperator as a snitch.

B. Advocacy to Judges in Bench Trials

As noted previously, cases are tried to the bench for a variety of reasons. In state court in particular, the statistics show that there are more bench trials than jury trials. In federal court, parties sometimes opt to have judges decide cases, and in other instances the federal law does not provide a right to jury trial over particular claims.

Regardless of why a jury won't be empaneled, approaching bench trials presents some unique issues that, ideally, attorneys should address during or before the final pretrial conference. Unlike in jury trials, in bench trials a lot of information can be conveyed to the judge in advance of the formal trial. This provides many opportunities for persuading the judge.

For example, unlike with juries, in bench trials there is an opportunity for the attorneys to provide the judge with detailed trial briefs in advance of trial. This is an opportunity for written advocacy that is never available to attorneys in jury trials. Through trial briefs, attorneys can concisely focus the judge on the key factual and legal disputes on which the outcome of the trial turns. An attorney can use trial briefs to persuasively provide the judge with a preview of the evidence the attorney believes will be presented at trial and explain to the judge why that evidence leads to a verdict in the client's favor.

As with hearings, in bench trials attorneys can provide the judge with

Six. Persuading Judges in Different Settings

exhibits in advance of trial. Attorneys should do so whenever possible. Most judges will review the exhibits thoroughly before trial and will spend more time with the exhibits than they might otherwise do if the only time the judge has a chance to view the exhibit is at trial. And just as with hearings, providing judges with exhibits in advance of trial often cuts down on scarce and limited courtroom time. Again, when providing exhibits to judges in advance of trial, attorneys should explain in their trial briefs the significance of the exhibits. They should also modify the exhibits through things like redactions and highlighting to direct the judge's attention to the relevant and important portions of the exhibits, especially when the exhibits are lengthy.

In bench trials, attorneys should attempt to reach stipulations on as many matters as possible. In jury trials, attorneys are sometimes understandably hesitant to stipulate to anything because of the perception or misperception lay jurors may draw from stipulations. Some attorneys worry that jurors may view stipulations as concessions of weakness, fearing jurors don't fully understand the role of stipulations. Judges, however, fully understand that a stipulation is not a concession that impacts the attorney's position on the real matters in dispute. Indeed, judges appreciate the confidence shown when attorneys stipulate to facts that are not really the rub of the dispute. Judges also deeply appreciate attorneys who narrow the issues through stipulations. This not only makes the bench trials more efficient; it is also more persuasive because it focuses the judge on the issues the attorneys believe are key.

Also, although in jury trials attorneys almost always present opening statements, in bench trials opening statements may not be needed or appropriate. This is especially true if the attorneys have already provided the court with trial briefs that inform the judge about what the parties expect the evidence will show. Attorneys need to consider the possibility that the judge may deny them an opportunity to present opening statements, even when the attorneys request the opportunity. That makes written advocacy in trial briefs that much more important. This demonstrates the need to research judges before trial briefs are due to find out whether the judge allows or favors opening statements in bench trials. Trial briefs should look very different when they are also substitutes for opening statements in bench trials.

In civil bench trials, attorneys may also have to consider how to use and present deposition testimony. In jury trials, presenting evidence through depositions is almost always a mistake and something to be done only when necessary. Jurors simply don't pay attention or absorb testimony through depositions as well as they do with live witnesses. This is true even when the party presents a videotaped deposition. It is even worse when testimony is read into evidence from a deposition.

In bench trials, however, when judges are the factfinders, attorneys should feel much more comfortable presenting testimony through depositions. Indeed, there may even be some advantages for doing so. First, judges understand what depositions are and appreciate their evidentiary value is equal to live testimony in a way jurors never will, despite court instructions to consider deposition testimony just like live testimony. Judges think analytically and are less swayed by personalities. Personal dynamism takes a far back seat to the substance of a witness's testimony when judges are factfinders. Whether live or Memorex (recorded) testimony, judges are focused on what the witness says and not as much as on how it is said. There are exceptions to every rule, of course. When a witnesses' credibility is critical, a judge can make a better assessment of credibility—just like jurors—when the testimony is presented live because it is easier to view demeanor, body language, and other intangible clues about credibility, even when the testimony might have been video-recorded.

Second, in bench trials, presenting testimony in the form of depositions may allow the judge to spend more time with the testimony and re-read the testimony as many times as needed, than the judge can with live testimony. When testimony is live, the judge—just like jurors—has one opportunity to listen and absorb the testimony. In jury trials, this is no different with the presentation of deposition testimony; it is presented to the jurors, and they have one shot at hearing it. In bench trials, however, a judge can accept deposition testimony in written form and review it at the judge's leisure. This may mean that judges can spend more time—as much time as necessary—to absorb the information contained in a deposition. And the judge can go back to that testimony as much as necessary to fully analyze the merits of the case and reach a verdict.

Sometimes parties submit deposition transcripts to the judge, with designations, for the judge to read outside the courtroom either in advance of trial or later. On the other hand, attorneys may want to consider whether it would be more persuasive, and enhance the judge's understanding of the facts, if the attorneys presented the deposition testimony in open court just as they would in a jury trial because presenting the testimony in a particular order is more comprehensible and persuasive. But, the difference with bench trials is that the attorneys can then leave the judge with written copies of the deposition after completion of the presentation of the testimony.

Six. Persuading Judges in Different Settings

As with opening statements, attorneys make closing arguments in jury trials. That may or may not happen in bench trials, depending on the need and the judge's preference. Unlike with jury trials, in bench trials there is an opportunity for attorneys to provide the court with written posttrial briefs, proposed findings of fact and conclusions of law, or some combination of these. Some judges dispense with closing arguments in favor of these posttrial written submissions.

How attorneys advocate to judges in bench trials are often matters of judicial preference. Part of effectively persuading judges in bench trials includes, therefore, knowing well in advance of trial what the presiding judge will expect, desire, and require. Researching the judge, knowing the judge's practices and preferences, becomes very important in bench trials for the attorneys to know what opportunities the attorneys may have for persuading the judge. Attorneys shouldn't appear for the first day of trial assuming the trial will proceed as a typical jury trial. Rather, they should research the judge, find out how the judge has handled other bench trials. Alternatively, attorneys may look to see if the judge has stated a preference on the court's website. Absent finding answers in any of these usual places, attorneys may contact a judge's chambers and directly ask these questions or seek a pretrial conference with the judge to obtain insight in how the judge intends to proceed at the bench trial.

The following sections will address in more detail effectively persuading judges in the various phases of a bench trial.

1. Pretrial Briefs

Pretrial briefs present an opportunity for effectively persuading judges that are never available in jury trials. Attorneys do not submit pretrial briefs to jurors, but they do to judges. Attorneys should take full advantage of this opportunity. They shouldn't consider pretrial briefs as an annoyance or afterthought or write them in a perfunctory manner.

If approached properly, pretrial briefs can serve several useful purposes. First, the process of drafting the brief should assist the attorney in trial preparation, as doing so requires thought and planning about how the attorney will present the case. Second, a well-written trial brief is akin to a written opening statement, giving an attorney the opportunity to frame the issues and provide the judge with a preview of what the evidence will show. Third, the trial brief permits an attorney to alert the judge to issues that may arise during trial, such as evidentiary concerns and scheduling problems.

Persuading Judges

As with other forms of advocacy, knowing the audience is critical. In this context, a primary consideration is the judge's preexisting knowledge of the case. If the trial judge has been assigned to the case from the start, as generally happens in federal court and in some state courts, the judge won't need a full-blown tutorial in the trial brief about the case and its procedural history. A statement that the attorney knows the judge is familiar with the case and, when possible, a reference to a prior substantive order in the case (e.g., the judge's ruling on motions for summary judgment) may suffice. By contrast, if the trial judge is relatively new to the case, an overview of the case and its procedural history may be useful.

Even when a judge may otherwise be familiar with the facts of the case through rulings on pretrial motions, attorneys should carefully consider whether the state of the record has changed due to recent discovery or disclosures, or amended pleadings or claims. Likewise, attorneys should carefully review the presentation of facts in prior pleadings to ensure that there isn't a need to alter the approach to the facts. For example, a party may have been willing to assume certain facts as true for purposes of litigating a motion for summary judgment. Now that the case is proceeding to bench trial, however, that fact may be quite material and very much in dispute. In short, in summarizing the facts in a trial brief in advance of a bench trial, attorneys should be careful to ensure that the judge is alerted to all the important facts the attorney believes will be proven by the evidence, presented in a manner that is accurate and complete, but also in a way most favorable to the attorney's client.

Being candid with the court about both favorable and unfavorable facts is particularly important in bench trials if attorneys seek to be effective judge advocates. Although in jury trials attorneys may gloss over or ignore unfavorable facts in opening statement, hoping jurors will little note nor long remember them even if the opposing party raises them in opening statement, bench trials are different. Trial briefs are in writing. Attorneys can be sure the judge will have read them in advance of trial. Because trial briefs are in writing, and judges don't have to rely only on opening statements to learn about the case, judges are more likely to catch it when attorneys omit or gloss over unfavorable facts and that may in turn affect the judge's perception of the attorney's credibility and detract from the attorney's efforts to persuade the judge.

Either way, the "opening statement" function of a pretrial brief is important. Even if the judge is intimately familiar with the facts and issues because of previous motions and proceedings, the judge does not know how the attorneys will present the case at trial. The brief should provide a preview of the attorney's case, such as who will testify, what the attorney expects them to say, and how each witness relates to the various issues in dispute. This will help the judge follow along during trial and better understand the testimony as it occurs. In addition, it can be frustrating for any finder-of-fact, judge or juror, to be subjected to testimony on an issue that appears—at least at the time—to have no relevance. A good summary of the expected evidence in a pretrial brief can aid in preventing this situation.

Trial briefs should also identify for the judge the key issues in dispute. In almost every trial, certain elements of a claim or charge are not truly in dispute between the parties. Attorneys should point out to the judge in trial briefs what the fighting issues truly are. This may also be the place to alert the judge of citations to other factually similar cases that the attorneys believe may inform the judge's analysis at the conclusion of the trial. Having these similar cases in mind while hearing the evidence during trial may greatly aid the judge in determining whether those cases are on point or distinguishable in some way from the case before the judge.

2. Motions in Limine

As we discussed, the rules of evidence generally apply in bench trials, just as they do in jury trials, though often in a more relaxed manner. Motions in limine are a means by which attorneys can seek pretrial rulings on evidentiary disputes. Motions in limine can play a pivotal role in jury trials.

As a strong general rule, though, motions in limine are ill-advised in the context of a bench trial.[43] As many courts have explained, the primary purpose of a motion in limine is to protect the jury from being exposed to inadmissible evidence.[44] Of course, a motion in limine necessarily exposes the *judge* to the evidence in controversy, as the judge must review the evidence to determine its admissibility. Thus, when the judge will act as the factfinder, the "sheltering" goal of a motion in limine simply does not apply. For the most part, such motions are not only pointless in advance of a bench trial, but downright annoying. The best practice is to highlight likely evidentiary issues in the pretrial briefs and/or the final pretrial order and then have the judge address them as they arise during trial.

Having said this, we note that there are limited instances when it might be appropriate to request resolution of an evidentiary issue before a bench trial. Judges recognize that another purpose of a motion in limine is to streamline the trial by resolving evidentiary disputes in advance.[45]

123

Although this is a worthy goal, it is usually difficult for a judge to make a final decision concerning the admissibility of evidence in the absence of the context that is usually required to determine issues such as relevancy, foundation and prejudice.[46] In our experience, motions in limine are grossly overused even with jury trials, as they are often too broad and/or unrealistically request an evidentiary ruling based on incomplete information.

Nonetheless, if a particular evidentiary issue is reasonably suitable for pretrial resolution *and* doing so would significantly impact the course or length of the trial, then a motion in limine is more likely to be favorably received. An example is when an issue exists that, if resolved in advance, could significantly shorten trial by eliminating the need for one or more witnesses. Again, however, the issue must be reasonably susceptible to resolution without developing a trial record. A motion to exclude witnesses on grounds that their testimony may be based on hearsay, or will cause unfair prejudice, or will be cumulative, likely won't meet this test.

In short, the general rule for filing motions in limine in bench trials is: Don't. Alert the judge to anticipated evidentiary issues in other filings, such as a pretrial brief, but avoid the temptation to file motions in limine. If an attorney is convinced that a particular issue falls within the limited exception of being reasonably susceptible to pretrial resolution and having the potential to significantly impact the course of trial, then the motion should (a) describe the issue narrowly and precisely, (b) explain the impact that resolving the issue will have on the trial and (c) provide the judge with all information necessary to give full consideration to the issue.

3. Opening Statements

As noted above, attorneys should ascertain in advance of trial whether the judge expects opening statements. Many judges prefer to request pretrial briefing in lieu of opening statements to allow the trial to proceed immediately to the presentation of evidence. Nevertheless, attorneys should consider their own preferences. It may be the case that if an attorney has filed a pretrial brief, the attorney sees no value in presenting an opening statement as well. On the other hand, there may be a benefit to presenting an opening statement in a bench trial. It is not uncommon as attorneys prepare for trial that their case changes because a witness becomes unavailable or says something different in trial prep. An attorney may even come to recognize the significance of certain evidence or see it in a new light than they did before. If the trial brief has presented

Six. Persuading Judges in Different Settings

a picture of the anticipated evidence that has changed since the attorney filed it, an opening statement may be important to convey to the judge nuanced changes in the anticipated evidence that have occurred since filing the trial brief. If an attorney truly believes an opening statement will help focus the judge on the key evidence the attorney believes will decide the dispute, then the attorney should ask for an opportunity to present a brief opening statement. And then the attorney should keep the promise and present a brief opening statement.

When attorneys present opening statements to judges in bench trials, there are some important differences between effective advocacy in opening statements to juries and effective advocacy to judges in presenting opening statements in a bench trial. First and foremost, attorneys should be brief in presenting opening statements to judges in bench trials. The judge almost certainly does not want, or need, an extensive introduction to the case or a preview of the evidence. This is particularly true when attorneys have filed trial briefs already. An attorney should provide an overview of the elements and issues in dispute and summarize how the attorney expects to address them, focusing in particular on the key facts that the attorney believes will be critical in the court's verdict.

Second, attorneys presenting opening statements in bench trials should skip the folksy storytelling manner adopted so often in jury trials. Stories, cultural references and historical analogies may have their place when it comes to establishing a relationship with the jury, but a judge is likely to consider them to be a waste of time. To effectively persuade judges, attorneys should stay on point.

Third, in presenting opening statement in a bench trial, attorneys should be prepared for judicial intervention, either in the form or questions or prompting to move on to another topic. Because the judge will be the factfinder, the judge may be more inclined to interrupt with questions at any stage of the trial, including during opening statements. Similarly, since the judge does not have to worry about inadvertently causing prejudice in the eyes of the jury, the judge may feel less inhibited about telling an attorney that a point has been made and it is time to move on. As with interruptions during oral arguments, attorneys should welcome these interventions as opportunities to tailor the presentation to the questions and issues the judge wants the attorney to address.

One characteristic that shouldn't change much, if at all, is the use of demonstrative aids to help the judge understand the evidence. As noted, judges comprehend information in the same manner as jurors. Visual aids enhance human comprehension and memory whether the human is a juror or judge. Although not a juror, the judge will appreciate enlargements, timelines, charts and other demonstrative items or pedagogical aids that an attorney might prepare in advance of a jury trial. These will necessarily vary from case to case and may be adjusted, to some extent, to account for the judge's preexisting knowledge of the case. Nevertheless, attorneys shouldn't assume that demonstrative aids are unnecessary simply because the case is being tried to a judge.

4. Presentation of Evidence

ORDER OF PROOF

A significant advantage of a bench trial is flexibility in the presentation of evidence. With no jury to worry about, a bench trial can, if necessary, take place in bits and pieces rather than over a period of consecutive days. If trial goes longer than planned, it can be adjourned for days (or weeks) before resuming. A witness who might otherwise be recalled during the defendant's case may be able to testify just once during a bench trial. Similarly, other witnesses can appear out of order without the concerns of confusion and prejudice that may be present in a jury trial.

Having said this, we find that it remains helpful to present the evidence in as much of a logical and orderly flow and without undue interruption as is possible under the circumstances. The ultimate goal of persuasion does not change simply because the case is being tried to a judge. Thus, if it makes logical sense for one witness to testify before another, attorneys should present them in that order if possible.

DEPOSITION TESTIMONY

Although the presentation of deposition testimony is extremely rare in federal criminal trials,[47] it is common for the parties to present such testimony during civil trials.[48] There are, of course, restrictions on a party's ability to present deposition testimony during a civil trial.[49] Assuming the conditions for presenting testimony by deposition are satisfied, attorneys must make strategic decisions about the most-effective way to present that testimony to the judge.

First, and as a threshold matter, give serious strategic thought about whether to submit deposition testimony at all. If a witness is important to the case and the witness' attendance can be procured, it is almost always best to do so, even if—by rule or stipulation—the witness's deposition testimony could be presented instead. The federal rules acknowledge "the importance of live testimony in open court."[50] This is no less true when

Six. Persuading Judges in Different Settings

trying the case to a judge rather than a jury. For the most part, if the witness has significant testimony to offer, there should be a strong preference in favor of procuring live testimony whenever possible. Of course, every trial attorney has had to rely on witnesses who, due to factors such as personality, temperament, etc., are unpredictable. If such a witness has provided useful deposition testimony, and the deposition may be presented in lieu of live testimony at trial, doing so may be the best strategic option. In most situations, however, live testimony is preferable. The flip side is that if a witness is so insignificant to the case that it is not worth the trouble to bring him or her to court, then the attorney should consider whether it is really necessary to submit deposition testimony from that witness. Attorneys should think ahead to closing argument (whether presented orally or in writing). If they are not likely to rely on the deposition testimony in support of any issue, attorneys should consider whether to submit it at all.

Second, and as addressed earlier, learn about and comply with the judge's preferences concerning deposition testimony during a bench trial. Although deposition testimony is typically presented to the jury in video form (or read aloud) in open court,[51] the judge may prefer to save courtroom time by having transcripts submitted for the judge to review outside the courtroom. If any of the depositions were videotaped, bring this to the judge's attention during the final pretrial conference. The judge may not wish to watch the entirety of a lengthy videotaped deposition but may find it useful to watch portions of the video. For example, if the witness' credibility on a particular issue is critical, the judge may wish to observe the portion of the video during which the witness testified about that issue.

Third, take the time necessary to narrow any designated deposition testimony to that which is relevant, material and non-cumulative. Most trial attorneys are savvy enough not to read an entire deposition to a jury—especially if only a small portion is relevant and material. But when submitting depositions to a judge for a bench trial, attorneys seem tempted to forego the editing process and designate large blocks of testimony (or, even worse, just submit the entire transcripts). Attorneys should avoid this temptation. Although it takes some time and thought, it is far better to show respect for the judge's time by designating only those portions of a deposition transcript that are truly necessary. It is also more persuasive because it focuses the judge's attention on the portion of the deposition the attorney wants the judge to focus on, rather than hoping the judge will read the deposition with that same focus.

Finally, if an attorney designates deposition testimony, the attorney should be sure to address that testimony in closing argument and/or the posttrial brief. A judge who has spent substantial time reading designated deposition testimony will naturally wonder why that testimony does not merit discussion as to any issue in argument. It is easy for the attorneys (and the judge) to focus on the evidence presented in open court while losing sight of the sometimes-substantial amount of evidence submitted in writing. Attorneys should be sure to tie it all together in argument.

Use of Prior Testimony

Impeachment[52] and refreshing recollection[53] are the two common, proper purposes for presenting prior testimony to a witness during trial. These are distinct purposes with separate requirements and separate strategic considerations. For the most part, these requirements and considerations are the same whether the case is being tried to a jury or a judge. However, because a judge, unlike most jurors, understands how to use prior testimony and knows the proper procedures for doing so, there is a greater risk that a judge will find the misuse of prior testimony to be unpersuasive and a waste of time. Thus, there are a few points attorneys should keep in mind when deciding whether to spend the time necessary to use prior testimony during a bench trial.

First, don't try to impeach a witness with a prior statement that is not obviously in conflict with the witness' present testimony. As one commentator has noted, confronting a witness with his or her prior statement "only works when the two statements cannot both be true."[54] Thus, "[i]f the two statements can be harmonized, explained, or rationalized, the impeachment will fail."[55] Under such circumstances, there is at least a chance that a juror may not fully grasp the witness' explanation, and thus believe that the witness has been caught in a lie. A judge, however, is likely to conclude that the attempted impeachment was nothing but a waste of time.

Second, don't waste time pursuing a minor inconsistency. Although this recommendation applies whether the case is tried to a jury or a judge, we recognize that most jurors are not in the business of viewing witness testimony on a regular basis. As such, there is a chance that some jurors may find any inconsistencies, even the minor ones that occur due to the passage of time and the imperfection of memory, to be noteworthy. A judge, by contrast, is far less likely to be impressed by the fact that a few trivial details have changed over time. If anything, pointing out a few minor inconsistencies may inadvertently drive home the point that the witness' recollection of the important facts has remained constant.

Third, and finally, don't attempt to use prior testimony unless you

Six. Persuading Judges in Different Settings

are prepared to do so promptly and efficiently. As judges attempting to adhere to tight schedules, we find few things more annoying, and less impressive, than an attorney fumbling around through stacks of papers and transcripts because the attorney believes there is something in there that might impeach the witness or refresh the witness' recollection. Doing this—especially on a repeated basis—is akin to an express announcement that the attorney is not prepared. Again, we suspect that jurors may be more forgiving of such disorganized conduct, as most have not been exposed to skilled trial advocacy on a regular basis. Judges, however, have observed (and, in some cases, engaged in) effective trial practice during their careers. They are thus more likely to question the importance of a point that the attorney was not already prepared to address.

CRIMINAL DEFENDANT TESTIMONY

In criminal cases, one of the most difficult decisions is whether the defendant should testify. Criminal defendants have the right to testify in their own defense if they want to, of course, but they have a constitutional right not to testify if they don't want to. That is a decision that the defendant alone must make but only after considering the advice of counsel. There is a legitimate concern in criminal jury trials that jurors will read guilt into a criminal defendant's decision not to testify, even though the judge has instructed them that they cannot consider a defendant's decision not to testify in any way in arriving at a verdict.

In bench trials, judges fully understand and honor a criminal defendant's decision to invoke the Fifth Amendment right to remain silent. Moreover, judges understand there may be many practical reasons why a criminal defendant would choose not to testify that has nothing to do with whether the defendant is guilty or innocent. Thus, in criminal bench trials the decision whether to have a criminal defendant testify takes on a wholly different tone. In bench trials, defense attorneys should be able to advise their clients that if they chose not to testify, the factfinder really won't use it against them or consider it in any way in reaching the verdict.

5. Objecting to Evidence

We have addressed the fact that the rules of evidence don't apply to many proceedings conducted by a judge. Trials are different. With a few minor caveats that may vary by jurisdiction, the rules of evidence are not suspended during a bench trial.[56] At the same time, since it is generally recognized that the trial judge has more flexibility in receiving questionable evidence during a bench trial,[57] attorneys need to balance the need to protect their clients' interests and preserve issues for appellate review against the risk of creating unnecessary delay and annoyance by making repeated objections during a bench trial. As we noted earlier,[58] motions in limine are disfavored in advance of a bench trial. However, this does not mean a discussion of evidentiary matters before trial is off limits. The final pretrial conference is an excellent opportunity to raise evidentiary issues and discern the judge's practices and preferences. If, for example, there is a certain category of evidence that a party finds objectionable, some judges may permit a standing objection to be made in the record to preserve the matter for appellate review. Other judges may require a separate objection each time the topic arises.

As with a jury trial, objections always involve strategic considerations.[59] Just because an attorney *can* object to evidence does not mean the attorney *should*. In our view, attorneys should be less inclined to object during a bench trial than during a jury trial. There may, of course, be instances in which the evidence at issue is critical to the case, such that its admissibility could legitimately affect the outcome. If there is a reasonable argument for exclusion of that evidence, then an objection is clearly warranted and, indeed, necessary. However, most trials don't present many situations of this nature. Attorneys should save objections for those issues that truly matter.

We acknowledge that our view about objections during bench trials is not universally held.[60] Having presided over many civil and criminal bench trials, however, we respectfully disagree with these opposing views. Preserving the record is important, of course, but only as to those material evidentiary issues that might affect the outcome of the trial (or of an appeal). Although judges may be less likely than jurors to think that an attorney is nefariously trying to hide the truth by making repeated objections, judges are *more* likely to understand and resent the real, non-evidentiary purpose of repeated objections over trivial issues (e.g., attempting to fluster the opposing attorney). Repeated objections on issues that have little or no substantive import are highly annoying, interrupt the judge's mental processing of the evidence and run the risk of impacting the judge's assessment of the attorney's credibility.

6. Judicial Questioning of Witnesses

It is generally accepted that a trial judge has the right to participate actively in the trial by, among other things, questioning witnesses.[61] Of

Six. Persuading Judges in Different Settings

course, some judges participate more actively than others. In a bench trial, when the judge is tasked with making findings of fact, it makes perfect sense that the judge might wish to ask follow-up questions of a witness to clear up any confusion or to address topics that were not covered by the attorneys. Attorneys can find this frustrating. Most trial attorneys have experienced the situation in which a favorable witness survived cross-examination unscathed, and was on the verge of being excused, only to have the judge ask a question or two that opened the door for additional examination. Since the practice is not improper, attorneys just have to grin and bear it.

Advance research about a judge's habits and practices can be helpful in determining whether that particular judge is likely to pose questions to a witness. Indeed, there is nothing wrong with making an inquiry directly to the judge during the final pretrial conference. However, when a case is set for a bench trial, few judges are likely to commit that they won't, under any circumstances, ask questions. Even judges who are known to be relatively inactive on the bench may, when assuming the role of factfinder, feel the need to ask questions of a witness.

As with questions asked of the attorneys during arguments, questions a judge poses to a witness provide clues about what the judge considers to be important. Even if the judge's questions seem to be off-point or address an issue the attorneys believe has marginal relevance, attorneys should pay close attention and attempt to discern the reasoning behind the questions. If the attorney cannot discern the reasoning, the attorney should ask. Not only will attorneys (likely) have the chance to ask the witness follow-up questions, but it may be possible to tailor closing arguments in such a way as to address the judge's apparent concern. Thus, although judicial questioning may be unwelcome at times, attorneys should expect it and attempt to use it to their advantage.

As we noted above when discussing hearings, attorneys should prepare witnesses to expect questions from judges. It shouldn't come as a surprise to a witness that the judge may have questions, too. Attorneys should prepare witnesses to respond directly to the judge's questions. Judges will likely be quicker to discern evasiveness and fudging by witnesses than many jurors, having far more experience than the average juror in hearing testimony. For their witnesses to be effective in answering judges' questions, then, attorneys should prepare the witnesses to answer the judge's questions candidly and without prevarication or evasion of any type, no matter how difficult the question may be or how damaging the answer may prove.

7. Closing Arguments

If the judge requests in-court closing arguments, the attorney should take the time to prepare and organize the argument in the same general fashion as the attorney would during a jury trial. Closing argument is an attorney's chance to persuade the factfinder that the attorney's position is correct. Again, attorneys shouldn't shy away from using presentation software, demonstrative aids and other available tools to help the judge understand the evidence. Just as when making arguments to a jury, the goal is for the factfinder to be firmly convinced that the attorney's position is correct once the attorney has concluded with the closing argument. As discussed above, attorneys shouldn't forget about deposition testimony that was submitted for the judge's review outside the courtroom. Because such testimony was not elicited "on stage," so to speak, it is especially important to remind the judge of that testimony and explain how it fits into the case.

As with opening statements, however, attorneys should make some adjustments when presenting closing arguments to a judge. For starters, the emotional appeals and persuasive tricks that may work with jurors during closing arguments are less likely to be effective when directed toward a judge.[62] Judges have been to law school and trained to analyze issues in logical terms. In addition, most judges were trial attorneys before taking the bench or, at least, have been exposed to trials and trial attorneys since doing so. The judge may have read some of the same articles[63] or attended some of the same trial practice seminars that helped hone the attorney's craft. Thus, judges will likely recognize a particular tactic and, even worse, may resent that it is being used on them. This is not to suggest that judges are entirely immune from the persuasive techniques that may work on lay jurors.[64] Persuasion remains the ultimate goal. However, knowing your audience means understanding that judges are more likely to be impressed by reason and a logical discussion of the law and the evidence than by emotional ploys and psychological tactics sometimes directed to juries.

As with other arguments to judges, attorneys should expect and welcome questions during closing arguments after a bench trial. If the judge is not going to require posttrial briefing, the closing arguments are the attorneys' last chance to explain their respective positions to the judge. By the time closing arguments are presented, the judge will be fully aware of the weaknesses in each party's case and, unlike a juror, has the opportunity to make attorneys address them. Attorneys should anticipate those questions and be ready to give judges the assurance they need to find that their clients' positions are correct.

Six. Persuading Judges in Different Settings

In a civil case involving a claim for money damages, attorneys should take the time necessary to fully address all the relevant damages issues. Defense attorneys are sometimes hesitant to devote much time to a discussion of damages during closing arguments, as the defendant's typical position is that the factfinder shouldn't reach that issue.[65] Although appearing to have conceded liability by discussing damages may be a legitimate concern in a jury trial, it shouldn't be a concern during a bench trial. Judges understand the concept of arguing in the alternative. Defense attorneys should simply tell judges that the defense does not believe the judge should reach the issue of damages but, if the judge disagrees, the defense has arguments to make about the claimed amounts. Then make those arguments. If the judge ultimately concludes that damages are appropriate, the judge will want to calculate them as accurately as possible. Being presented with only one side's arguments about damages does not further this goal.

At the conclusion of closing argument, attorneys should be very specific about what they would like the judge to do. Unlike juries, judges don't render verdicts by way of a verdict form. Simply asking the judge to "find in favor of the plaintiff" probably does not suffice if there are multiple claims, issues and requests for relief. Judges sometimes have to ask questions to the effect of: "If I find in favor of your client, what relief should I grant?" There should be no need for such questions. By the end of closing argument, the judge should know, in very specific terms, what the attorney would like the order or judgment to contain.

8. Posttrial Briefing/Proposed Findings of Fact and Conclusions of Law

Some judges will request posttrial submissions rather than (or even in addition to) in-court closing arguments. When this occurs, it is important for attorneys to understand the judge's precise expectations. Attorneys shouldn't hesitate to ask questions as necessary to clear up any confusion. Some common points of clarification are:

- Is the judge requesting written arguments on the various claims and issues or, instead, proposed findings of fact and conclusions of law?
- Does the judge expect citations to the record, which would require a delay while the court reporter prepares the transcript, or is it sufficient for the attorneys to discuss the testimony based on the attorneys' notes and recollection?

- Are there specific issues, beyond the claims and defenses that were tried to the court, that the judge would like the briefs to address? This could arise, for example, if the judge reserved ruling on an evidentiary issue during trial.
- What will be the order of briefing (simultaneous, plaintiff's brief first, etc.)?
- What procedural requirements apply (length of brief, deadlines, etc.)?

If the judge requests posttrial briefing, attorneys should take advantage of the opportunity by presenting concise, logical arguments with specific citations to the evidentiary record (particularly if a transcript is available). Effective posttrial briefs are akin, in many ways, to appellate briefs, as the factual record is complete and the goal is to convince the judge that when that record is considered in light of the applicable law, the attorney's position prevails. The same principles of advocacy to judges addressed throughout this book apply to posttrial briefing. Attorneys should avoid blatant appeals to emotion, stick to a reasoned discussion of the evidence and the law and understand that the judge is already (especially by this point) *very* familiar with the case. Attorneys should remember that a page limit, if imposed, is a maximum, not a minimum. If an attorney can present an effective written argument as to all the issues in fewer pages, the attorney should do so.

Proposed findings of fact and conclusions of law, if requested, can be challenging. Personally, we neither like them nor (with rare exceptions) request them. For understandable reasons, courts have recognized that it is a disfavored practice for a trial judge to adopt entirely one party's proposed findings and legal conclusions.[66] Because most judges wouldn't, and shouldn't, simply adopt one side's document, we question the utility of directing the parties to prepare them. Nonetheless, some judges disagree and may require the attorneys to prepare proposed findings.

If there is any benefit to requiring proposed findings, it is that the process of preparing them will, or at least should, cause the attorneys to think of the case from the judge's perspective. Although attorneys should consider the judge's perspective throughout the case, as the judge will be the ultimately decision-maker, drafting a document that is intended to read like the judge's ruling may help the attorneys focus on that perspective. Moreover, when writing in the judge's voice, rather than the voice of an advocate, attorneys may be less inclined to make *ad hominem* attacks on the opposing attorney, take obnoxious positions, or write dramatic, emotion-laden prose.

The downside is that many attorneys are good at argumentative writing but far less skilled and experienced with the neutral, analytical style of a court ruling. This can make for an awkward document—one that is far more one-sided and argumentative than what any judge would issue. It is a given that an attorney's proposed findings and conclusions will be favorable to the attorney's client (good luck collecting attorney fees if that's not the case). But unlike a brief, which is expected to be argumentative, proposed findings and conclusions should look and sound a lot like something a judge might sign. Indeed, even though the wholesale adoption of one side's proposed findings is disfavored, that does not mean it cannot happen. Attorneys should draft the proposed findings and conclusions in a reasonable, judicial manner such that if the judge decided to sign off on one side's or the other's, the judge would likely select the attorney's side.

Among other things, this means attorneys should include facts that might not be favorable to the attorney's client (but, of course, don't affect the ultimate outcome). Conceding what one must concede bolsters the attorney's credibility. As for the legal analysis, attorneys should include a fair summary of the various, competing arguments before explaining why the attorney's client's position is correct.

As noted above with regard to closing arguments, it is important to be very specific about the relief the attorney is requesting. This is true whether you are filing a posttrial brief or proposed findings and conclusions. The judge shouldn't have to guess, or comb through the record, to try to figure out what the judgment should look like if the attorney's client prevails.

C. Advocacy to Judges in Jury Trials

Even in jury trials, there is an important component of needing to persuade judges for attorneys to consider. During jury trials, the judge will make a large number of rulings on many matters including motions to strike jurors for cause, objections to jury instructions, evidentiary objections, objections during opening and closing arguments, and any number of other issues. Persuading the judge to rule in your favor at these important junctures of a jury trial can be critical. Here, we'll discuss how to effectively advocate to a judge in the context of a jury trial at various stages of the jury trial process.

Persuading Judges

1. Jury Selection

Though attorneys' primary focus during jury selection is properly on jury advocacy, there are times during the process that may call for advocating to the judge. These include arguing to strike jurors for cause and in making so-called *Batson* challenges. We'll discuss them one at a time.

But first, it's important to consider a judge's perspective of jury selection. When judges preside over jury selection, they have several considerations at the forefront of their minds. Judges are ever conscious of the imposition jury service has on citizens, and so they strive to make the jury selection process proceed as quickly, efficiently, and pleasantly as possible for jurors. This includes ensuring prospective jurors are treated with respect and their privacy is protected to the extent possible. Judges are also focused on ensuring that a fair and impartial jury is empaneled. This is a grave responsibility that sometimes requires balancing competing considerations. Judges strive to ensure that the jury is composed of a fair cross section of the community, but not at the cost of seating jurors who cannot be fair and impartial in deciding the dispute. Last, judges are always concerned about ensuring the lawyers don't violate the Constitution in exercising peremptory strikes yet recognize the importance of peremptory strikes to ensuring a fair trial.[67]

With a judge's perspective in mind, attorneys should approach making motions to strike prospective jurors for cause in a manner that reflects respect for the prospective juror and addresses the judge's concerns for balancing all the competing interests. This means that when making a motion to strike for cause, attorneys shouldn't denigrate or belittle the prospective juror. Every citizen has a right to hold opinions that may be contrary to those that would make a fair and impartial juror. Simply because a prospective juror may hold extreme views or biases does not make them a bad person. So, attorneys can and should point out how the juror's views or biases would render them too biased to be fair and impartial, but attorneys should do so with respect.

Further, in making the motion to strike for cause, attorneys should consider the gender and race of the challenged prospective juror against the rest of the panel. If the only motions to strike for cause are against one group that would make the ultimate jury less representative of a fair cross section of the community, the attorney should acknowledge it and address that concern. Though empaneling a jury that represents a fair cross section of the community is important, so too is empaneling individual jurors who are not biased for or against one side.

Six. Persuading Judges in Different Settings

Attorneys should also make for-cause challenges efficiently and concisely. The judge will be watching the clock and concerned about how much time the for-cause challenges are taking and how long the jurors will be kept waiting. To be an effective judge advocate under these circumstances, it requires the attorney to put some effort into concisely and precisely articulating why the juror should be struck for cause. Resistances to such for-cause challenges should be equally concise.

Last, once the judge has ruled on the for-cause challenge, the attorneys should accept the judge's ruling without further argument. Again, the judge will be focused on the time and will try to quickly rule on the challenge. This is not a place for prolonged debate. Attorneys have to remember the judge will be presiding over the rest of the trial. An obstreperous attorney will likely meet with less success on future issues.

As for so-called *Batson* challenges, attorneys should keep several considerations in mind if they wish to be effective judge advocates. First, dispense with personal attacks against opposing counsel. A *Batson* challenge constitutes an allegation that the opposing counsel unconstitutionally exercised a peremptory strike to remove a juror for an improper reason based on sex, race, or national origin. It can be taken as an allegation that the attorney is a bigot or racist. So, attorneys should tread carefully and professionally and not make it personal. And attorneys against whom a *Batson* challenge has been made should have a thick skin and not take the challenge personally. Judges abhor playing parent to two children spatting in the courtroom.

Judges will take *Batson* challenges very seriously because of the constitutional implications inherent in the challenge and the fundamental concern to empanel a constitutionally fair jury. Judges know and will employ the burden-shifting framework for *Batson* challenges. It follows, then, that to be effective judge advocates attorneys should frame their arguments using the burden-shifting language to place their arguments into the context of the legal analysis the judge must engage in to weigh the merits of the motion. And attorneys should be concise and precise, because the *Batson* challenge is likely the last matter the judge must resolve that's holding up the trial and keeping the jurors waiting. So, the judge will want the parties to make their arguments clearly and quickly, and the judge will likely rule quickly. Again, once the judge has ruled, the attorneys need to accept the ruling and move on. If the judge erred in denying a *Batson* challenge, the moving party can seek redress on appeal. If the judge erred in granting a *Batson* challenge, the losing attorney needs to shrug it off and not take it as a personal attack by the judge.

Persuading Judges

2. Jury Instructions

When it comes to jury instructions, attorneys often have an opportunity to engage in both written and oral advocacy. Attorneys may and are often required by local rules to submit proposed written jury instructions to the court. And judges routinely have jury instructions conferences with the attorneys to discuss proposed jury instructions. To be effective in advocating to judges about jury instructions, attorneys should consider the matter from a judge's perspective.

Judges approach jury instructions conservatively, meaning they tend to instruct juries using model or pattern jury instructions generated and approved by appellate courts. Few judges will readily accept proposed instructions that materially deviate from these pattern jury instructions because to do so risks reversal. It's not a matter of judges being risk adverse or fearing reversal because of ego. Rather, judges strive to correctly instruct jurors on the law and approved pattern instructions provide a level of confidence that if followed, the law will be correct. To be an effective judge advocate when it comes to jury instructions, it follows that attorneys should rely on such approved pattern jury instructions in the first instance. In rare cases when no pattern instruction exists for the law at issue, attorneys should provide the judge with written support for the proposed instruction, including citation to legal authorities.

The issue in most instances is not whether a pattern jury instruction is a correct statement of the law, but whether and when it is appropriate to give such an instruction. In other words, the fighting issue is often whether the judge should instruct the jury at all on an issue, such as whether the judge should instruct a jury about comparative fault or provide certain instructions on damages or the like. In those instances, good advocacy to the judge involves providing the judge with concise written legal authority supporting the party's position. To be persuasive, attorneys will need to assure the judge that the instructions, as a whole, will reflect a correct statement of the law. A focus on individual instructions alone, without considering the impact of other instructions, fails to address the judge's responsibility to ensure that the instructions taken altogether reflect a correct statement of the law.

At jury instruction conferences or hearings when the judge takes up the issue of jury instructions, attorneys are most effective when they show that they share the judge's goal of ensuring the instructions are correct. An attorney who pushes, or appears to push, for jury instructions that are debatable but favor the attorney's client may cause a judge to be cautious

Six. Persuading Judges in Different Settings

about trusting the attorney's position on any proposed instructions. In short, when it comes to jury instructions, for attorneys to be effective judge advocates they need to approach, and show they are approaching, the issue from the judge's perspective of just wanting to get the law right. This is not the place for zealous advocacy of only one side's position.

3. Depositions in Jury Trials

In civil jury trials, it is not uncommon for parties to present evidence through depositions, either by videotape or by reading in portions of depositions. Generally speaking, we believe this form of evidence presentation falls flat in persuading juries. But this isn't a book on jury trial advocacy, so we won't comment further. We recognize there are reasons why attorneys chose to, and sometimes have to, present evidence through depositions.

In jury trials, a judge's role in relation to deposition testimony is limited to ruling on objections in the depositions. During depositions, attorneys often make objections (way too many, in our view) to the testimony. The objections are made at the time to preserve the possibility of keeping that portion of the testimony out at a later date if and when a party seeks to use it for evidence. When making objections during depositions, attorneys often don't fully elaborate on the basis for the objection. Attorneys will often state, "objection as to form," whatever that means. The true basis of the objection may be to foundation, or hearsay, or some other reason under the evidence rules. Attorneys apparently believe that by stating "object as to form," they preserve their right to object to the question for any reason they can later think of when the time comes to enforce the objection.[68]

That time comes in jury trials when the parties ask the trial judge to rule on the objections made during depositions. This creates some challenges for effectively persuading the judge. First, if attorneys want judges to make informed and sound rulings on these objections, they need to provide judges with sufficient time to read the depositions, understand the objection, and rule on the objection. What happens way to often is that attorneys will provide judges with lengthy depositions containing scores of objections the day before the party wishes to present the deposition testimony. Attorneys apparently expect judges to spend their evening hours reading depositions that the attorneys could have and should have provided to the judges weeks in advance of trial.

Second, the objections made in depositions are often the vague "object

Persuading Judges

as to form"-type objections. Thus, when asking judges to rule on such vague objections, attorneys need to elaborate on the basis of the objection. To be persuasive, this may mean providing the judge with an explanation beyond simply a citation to a rule of evidence or a shorthand description such as "relevance." If depositions are properly provided to judges well in advance of trial for rulings on objections, the judges may not have a full understanding of the case or the context in which the deposition testimony arises. When evidentiary objections are made a trial, shorthand references are sufficient, and often preferred by judges, because the judge has the testimony in context of the rest of the trial. Not so when attorneys seek rulings on deposition objections in advance of trial. So, attorneys may want to take the opportunity to not only state the basis for the objection but also provide a little more of an explanation for the objection.[69]

Last, attorneys resisting the objection need to explain the basis for the resistance. Because there is no judge ruling on an objection at the time of the deposition, the transcript often contains only an objection (and often a vague one, at that) and no response from the attorney conducting the questioning. If the attorneys provide the trial judge with only a copy of the deposition transcript and ask for rulings on the objection, the judge won't have the benefit of any response by the opposing attorney. It follows, then, that in asking judges to rule on objections to deposition testimony in jury trials, the opposing party should also take the opportunity to respond to the objections in writing and explain why they believe the judge should overrule the objection. Otherwise, the opposing attorney is leaving it up to the judge to guess as to what the response to the objection might be.

4. Evidentiary Objections During Trial

Voicing objections, and responding to objections, during a jury trial is a difficult task for attorneys. When objecting or responding to an objection, an attorney is trying to persuade the judge to rule in the attorney's favor. Yet, the exercise of oral advocacy when making objections often occurs with the jury as an audience. How an attorney objects—the attorney's demeanor, tone, words—has the potential to convey an intended or unintended message to the jury. An attorney who appears to panic, jumps up wailing, and voices a loud, vehement objection may convey to jurors a message that the attorney is attempting to hide something from them that is very damaging to the attorney's client. An attorney who timely, but calmly and with moderate volume voices an objection may suggest to jurors that the attorney is simply trying to ensure the other side is playing

Six. Persuading Judges in Different Settings

fairly by the rules. Similarly, an attorney who objects often may send a message to jurors that the attorney is worried or being obstreperous, particularly if the judge repeatedly overrules the objections. Attorneys who are on the receiving end of repeated sustained objections may appear to jurors to be inept or attempting to play unfairly. In short, we understand that attorneys should consider the impact their performance in making and responding to objections may have on the jury.

Yet, the goal in making and responding to objections remains persuading the judge to rule in the attorney's favor on the objection. To understand how to be effective judge advocates in this setting, it is again important to view the matter from a judge's perspective. Judges have a lot of discretion when it comes to ruling on evidentiary objections. They are generally reluctant to keep information from jurors and so, all things being equal, judges will be more likely to overrule than sustain objections. Ruling on objections are also sometimes very difficult for judges because they are being asked to make an instantaneous ruling on an evidentiary issue that may be complex. And, let's be honest, judges may not be paying close attention to the trial at all times, and an objection may catch a judge off guard. Judges are juggling a docket with sometimes hundreds of cases pending before them and even if the judge is not working on one of those cases while sitting on the bench during a jury trial, the judge may be thinking about all those other cases. Judges are also busy watching the jurors to ensure they're paying attention, monitoring the back of the courtroom to ensure spectators are not interfering or attempting to communicate with witnesses, and the like. While sitting on the bench in a jury trial, a judge's attention is divided in many directions.

With all this in mind, here is some advice for effectively persuading judges in making and responding to objections during a jury trial. First, attorneys should voice objections loudly and clearly enough for the judge to hear. The judge may not be looking at the attorney at the time of an objection. The judge may instead be watching the witness or jurors, focusing on the testimony or monitoring jurors to ensure they are paying attention. A weak or mumbled objections may not get the judge's attention.

Second, attorneys should be familiar with the judge's preferences about objections and responses. Many judges won't allow so-called speaking objections, meaning objections in which attorneys elaborate on why they believe the evidence is inadmissible. Most judges prefer that attorneys merely recite the applicable rule of evidence or provide a shorthand description, such as "hearsay" or "relevance." Similarly, many judges don't want the proponent to respond to an objection unless requested. Judges are very familiar with the rules of evidence and will typically be able to quickly assess whether the evidence is admissible under the rules. When judges allow or request responses to objections, typically they want the responses to be equally limited to citing a rule or exception to a rule by number or description (e.g., "801(d)(2)(E)" or "co-conspirator statement").

Third, it is important for attorneys to recognize that they know more about the case and evidence than the judge. This seems obvious, but all too often attorneys operate as if the judge should fully comprehend everything without having all the knowledge. So, when evidentiary issues arise at trial, attorneys should assess whether the judge has sufficient information about the evidence to make a sound ruling. For example, in a criminal case the prosecutor may believe the evidence will show the declarant was a member of a conspiracy with the defendant and so the declarant's statements would be exempt from the hearsay rule. But, the evidence may not have yet been sufficiently developed at trial that the judge would have reason to understand the declarant's role in the conspiracy. If the defense attorney objects to a witness repeating the declarant's statement as hearsay, it may very well appear to be so to the judge. If the prosecutor has not thought this testimony out sufficiently in advance of trial to alert the judge of the facts either in a motion in limine or trial brief, the prosecutor will need to alert the judge to additional facts for the judge to be able to make a correct ruling. This is when the prosecutor may want to ask for a sidebar when the defense attorney lodges an objection.

Most judges abhor sidebar discussions as much as jurors do because they consume time and often turn out to be unnecessary. Nevertheless, most judges will trust attorneys to know when a sidebar is necessary for the orderly and fair administration of a jury trial. This is especially so when the attorney has not previously abused requests for sidebars. Attorneys should be cautious, asking for sidebars only when truly necessary. And then at sidebar, attorneys should get straight to the point and be brief.

Last, when judges rule on an objection, attorneys should accept the judge's ruling and move on. We are reminded of the scene from *A Few Good Men* in which a defense attorney character is played by Demi Moore. At one point in a proceeding, she objects to admission of some evidence. When the judge overrules the objection, she follows up with "I strenuously object!" The impact this may have on jurors aside, judges won't look kindly on their rulings being questioned in that manner. If an attorney really believes the judge has made an erroneous evidentiary ruling, and it is material, and the attorney believes that with more information or a better explanation the judge may well change the ruling, the better approach

Six. Persuading Judges in Different Settings

is for the attorney to wait for a natural break in the trial and then, during the break, respectfully ask the judge if the attorney could briefly revisit the evidentiary issue. Judges make mistakes and they know they make mistakes, so if approached appropriately and tactfully, attorneys can have a conversation with the judge about the evidentiary issue and through a calm exchange attempt to persuade the judge of the error.

5. Motions for Mistrial

It happens on occasion that an error of such magnitude occurs in a jury trial that a party believes a mistrial is in order. Attorneys should recognize that judges are inherently reluctant to declare mistrials. Judges are aware that if they declare a mistrial, all the time and resources thus far spent in trial are lost. The juror fees and expenses already expended are wasted. The jurors will have been unnecessarily inconvenienced. The trial will have to be rescheduled and will consume yet more court time. And many more citizens will have to be inconvenienced once again to seat a new jury. Effectively persuading the judge at this stage of a trial takes all this into account in how attorneys make and respond to a motion for a mistrial.

First, it should go without saying that attorneys should make motions for mistrials outside the presence of the jury, either at a sidebar or during a break. Judges will be displeased with attorneys who make dramatic, emotional motions in front of a jury in an improper effort to influence the jury's perception of the case. In contrast, judges will respect and take more seriously attorneys who recognize the magnitude of a motion for a mistrial and calmly raise the issue in a manner that won't influence the jury if the judge denies the motion.

Second, attorneys moving for mistrials should remain calm and refrain from making personal attacks against opposing counsel. Everyone makes mistakes. Absent the most blatant evidence to the contrary, attorneys should make the motion for a mistrial taking the position that, though what opposing counsel or the witness did was perhaps an honest mistake, it was so prejudicial or erroneous that the only solution is a mistrial. The attorney's tone in making the motion should be even and unemotional. Recall that judges are moved much more by logic than emotion. Attorneys moving for a mistrial, knowing judges are inherently reluctant to grant them, should focus on showing the judge logically and rationally how the mistake has jeopardized the fairness of the trial irrevocably. The moving attorney should acknowledge the inconvenience and costs associated with a mistrial and the resulting retrial but explain to the judge why in this particular case a mistrial is the appropriate and necessary remedy.

In opposing motions for mistrial, the attorneys should also remain calm and unemotional, even if the moving attorney has accused the opposing attorney of intentional misconduct. Judges will not be persuaded by attorneys who get into personal attacks or shouting matches. Judges will be much more likely to be persuaded by opposing counsel who addresses the judge, not opposing counsel, and explains why a mistrial is inappropriate. Perhaps the response will take issue with whether an error actually occurred. Here, again, logic and reason should be the focus of the opposing counsel's argument. If, however, a mistake has occurred, the opposing counsel should acknowledge the error and then look for a solution short of a mistrial. For example, if in response to a question a witness has mentioned some highly prejudicial fact that was the subject of a limine order, the attorney should acknowledge it. If the witness had been fully advised of the order and properly prepped, the attorney should say so because that may influence whether the judge believes a mistrial is an appropriate sanction for the misconduct. The opposing attorney should consider, and when appropriate suggest, other solutions short of a mistrial, such as a limiting or corrective jury instruction, or permitting the other side to offer rebutting or otherwise counterevidence of some sort. In making the argument that some other solution short of a mistrial is appropriate, the opposing counsel might want to mention the loss of time and costs associated with a mistrial, to reinforce what will already be in the back of the judge's mind when considering the appropriate ruling.

6. Motions for Judgment of Acquittal or as a Matter of Law

At the close of the government's case in a criminal trial, or the plaintiff's case in a civil trial, an attorney can move for judgment of acquittal or judgment as a matter of law, respectively, arguing that the other side has failed to prove its case and asking the judge to not submit the matter to the jury. Attorneys can renew such motions at the close of all the evidence and after the verdict has been rendered. It has been our experience that attorneys seldom make effective motions for judgment of acquittal or judgment as a matter of law. Often, attorneys put very little thought into these oral motions, making sweeping statements about credibility of witnesses and sufficiency of the evidence.

Six. Persuading Judges in Different Settings

We recognize that when attorneys are making these motions, the judge is not the only intended audience member. Sometimes attorneys make impassioned arguments not because they believe it will persuade the judge but because it will mollify a client or the client's family or others. We also recognize that attorneys sometimes make these arguments to preserve the record for appeal, even when they have no real belief that the judge will rule in the movant's favor. So, our comments here are intended for attorneys who truly believe in the motion and seek to persuade a judge to grant it.

In those cases, effectively persuading judges requires attorneys to make precise and narrow arguments tied to the evidence and the element of the crime or claim that the attorney believes is vulnerable to a directed verdict. Attorneys should recognize and acknowledge the standard by which the judge must view the evidence at this stage. Judges won't be moved by arguments about witness credibility, for example, as that is clearly a matter for jurors to assess. Rather, the moving attorney should accept the evidence in the light most favorable to the non-moving party (or verdict, if the motion is made post-verdict). Accepting the evidence in that light, the most effective motions here are ones that are focused on a particular element or perhaps two elements. Broad attacks on all the elements of every charge and every claim will seldom persuade the judge and will divert the judge's attention from what may otherwise be a persuasive argument when focused on only one or two key elements. Attorneys should identify the element(s) they feel the evidence failed to establish and then walk the judge carefully and logically through the evidence to explain why, even taken in the light most favorable to the other side, it failed to establish the contested element(s).

When opposing these motions, attorneys should recognize that judges are very reluctant to take a decision away from the jury, or to reverse a jury's decision once rendered. It follows, then, that attorneys opposing these motions should emphasize the sanctity of jury trials and the trust the system puts in jurors to reach correct decisions. And attorneys should be prepared to make detailed responses to motions for judgment of acquittal or judgment as a matter of law. It is our observation that attorneys all too often act as if they are surprised the other side made such a motion. The responses are often meandering and unfocused, fail to incorporate the standard of review, and don't connect the key evidence to the elements of the crime or claim. The most persuasive responses are those that the attorney prepared in advance, anticipating such a motion, in which the attorney is able to succinctly and quickly cite to the key evidence that supported each element of the crime or claim.

7. Objections During Opening Statements/Closing Arguments

On occasion, attorneys will object to the opposing side's opening statement or closing argument. It has been our observation that only rarely are these objections called for at all and even more rarely sustained. Even when sustained, judges will often respond to such objections by simply reminding the jury that what the attorneys say is not evidence. So, our first bit of advice here is that attorneys should be hesitant to object to an opening statement or closing argument.

When attorneys feel it necessary to make objections to opening statements or closing arguments, if they aim to persuade the judge to sustain the objection then they should voice the objection clearly, calmly, concisely and precisely. Again, we recognize that when making these objections attorneys may be trying to perform for the jury or their clients. But if they actually wish to persuade the judge to rule in their favor, attorneys need to tailor their performance in a manner that will be more likely to persuade the judge.

The objecting attorney may also consider suggesting the remedy the attorney is requesting because that may increase the likelihood of the judge sustaining the objection and granting the relief than if left for the judge to decide how to respond. For example, an objecting attorney may suggest the judge strike the opposing attorney's statement and instruct the jury to disregard it. Providing the judge with a proposed solution is more persuasive than simply alerting the judge to a problem.

Again, it is important that attorneys keep in mind what the judge knows, and more importantly, may not know, about the case, particularly at the stage of opening statements. It may not be obvious to the judge, because the judge doesn't know the case like the attorneys do, that what an attorney said in opening statement was objectionable or problematic. In these instances, it may be best for the objecting attorney to voice an objection and then ask for a sidebar so that the attorney will have an opportunity to more fully explain the issue to the judge outside the presence of the jury.

For attorneys whose opening statement or closing argument has been interrupted by an objection, often the best solution is to keep eyes on the jury and say nothing. More often than not, a judge will overrule such objections or just remind the jury that what the lawyers say is not evidence. If attorneys fear that the objection may be wrongly sustained, it is probably best at this point that the attorney ask to be heard at sidebar. There, the attorney can either try to persuade the judge that nothing objectionable

Six. Persuading Judges in Different Settings

was said or, if there was a mistake, suggest a remedy, such as asking for an opportunity for the attorney to correct his or her own misstatement.

What is ineffective advocacy for both sides is when the attorneys seem to forget that both the judge and jury are present and the attorneys engage in an argument with each other in the well of the courtroom. Being calm and collected, and addressing the judge instead of opposing counsel, is always more effect in persuading a judge to rule in an attorney's favor.

8. Ruling on Jury Questions

It is not uncommon for jurors to have questions during jury deliberation, sent to the judge through a bailiff. When this occurs, the judge will assemble the parties and attorneys to determine how to respond to the jury's question. Effective advocacy to judges at this stage involves recognizing that the judge will be motivated primarily by two considerations: (1) not creating error and (2) providing a speedy response to the waiting jury. Judges are very reluctant to answer jury questions with much more than directing the jury back to the jury instructions or telling them to reconsider all the evidence. It is when judges do more, when they attempt to come up with answers on the fly, that mistakes often occur.

When attorneys truly believe that a more direct answer to a jury question is appropriate and necessary, then they will have their work cut out for them. To be persuasive here, an attorney should first acknowledge the judge's reluctance to provide a tailored answer to a specific question. Then the attorney should propose an answer. Again, when attorneys provide judges with potential solutions, it is far more persuasive than when they simply present judges with problems. The attorney should also acknowledge any concerns opposing counsel may have and show a willingness to tweak the proposed wording in the answer in a manner that addresses those concerns. All of this will have to be done quickly to be responsive to the judge's concern that the court not keep the jurors waiting unnecessarily.

9. Ruling on Scheduling Issues

Jury trials are minor, and sometimes major, productions, requiring the coordination of many moving parts and multiple parties. Judges must find time on their busy court schedule to set aside for jury trials. The clerk of court needs lead time to summon and coordinate the arrival of sometimes scores of prospective jurors. Attorneys for both sides should orchestrate the many stages of trial preparation from identifying evidentiary issues, filing motions in limine, submitting proposed jury instructions, meeting with and preparing witnesses, identifying and marking exhibits, and the list goes on and on. Even after the jury trial begins, scheduling remains an important consideration, particularly for judges who are ever conscious and considerate of jurors' time and inconvenience.

It follows, then, that when attorneys seek continuances, or request changes in jury trial schedules, judges are often unreceptive to the attorneys' efforts. Effective advocacy to judges in addressing scheduling issues requires attorneys to recognize the judge's competing interests that influence scheduling decisions. Acknowledging and directly addressing those interests will go a long way in persuading judges to adjust jury trial schedules in a manner attorneys seek.

When it comes to scheduling a jury trial, attorneys should understand that two primary considerations drive judges' decision-making. First, judges place great importance on, and exert considerable effort to ensure, the timely and efficient resolution of cases. The federal rules are replete with commands that federal judges exercise their discretion enforcing the rules with these considerations in mind. Rule 1 of the Federal Rules of Civil Procedure provides that the Federal Rules of Civil Procedure "should be construed, administered, and employed by the court and the parties to secure the just, speedy, and inexpensive determination of every action and proceeding."[70] The Federal Rules of Criminal Procedure "are to be interpreted to provide for the just determination of every criminal proceeding, to secure simplicity in procedure and fairness in administration, and to eliminate unjustifiable expense and delay."[71] The Federal Rules of Evidence similarly command: "These rules should be construed so as to administer every proceeding fairly, eliminate unjustifiable expense and delay, and promote the development of evidence to law, to the end of ascertaining the truth and securing a just determination."[72] There is a truth to the truism that "justice delayed is justice denied." It should come as no surprise to attorneys, then, that ensuring timely resolution of disputes through jury trials is one of judges' paramount concerns when it comes to scheduling jury trials.

Second, judges' decision-making in scheduling and continuing and rescheduling jury trials is also constrained by their own court docket. Jury trials consume a lot of judicial resources. Time is a limited and finite resource available to judges. Judges and their staff members devote significant effort in scheduling jury trials, working within statutory demands for speedy trials in criminal cases, seeking to follow district guidelines

Six. Persuading Judges in Different Settings

and local rules for scheduling cases for timely resolution, and taking into account the nature and complexity of the case, the attorneys' requests, and many others considerations, including holidays and other trials already on the judge's schedule. Rescheduling a trial, then, works a significant hardship in a judge's calendar, particularly when it occurs close to the trial date, because that precious court time often cannot be filled at the last minute with another trial or other hearings, just further gumming up the works.

With all this in mind, attorneys are more effective to begin with when they devote significant effort on the front end in working with the court in scheduling the trial. Attorneys should put careful thought, particularly in civil cases that aren't constrained by the Speed Trial Act, in realistically calculating the time it will take for the parties to work through discovery and dispositive motions to be ready for trial. Then attorneys should work diligently to keep with that schedule and be ready for trial when they told the court they would be. The most effective way to persuade a judge when it comes to continuing trials is to avoid seeking to do so in the first instance whenever possible. The second most effective method is not seeking continuances often.

When, however, attorneys believe it necessary to continue a trial for some reason, effectively persuading the judge of the need for a continuance involves attorneys providing the judge with a detailed explanation of the need for the continuance, the efforts made to meet the current trial date, the opposing party's position, and a realistic proposed new trial date. Attorneys should describe efforts they have made to keep the trial on track and why, despite those best efforts, a continuance is still necessary. Too often, motions to continue trials provide judges with only vague explanations that are unpersuasive, such as "needing more time to complete discovery" or "witness availability issues." To persuade judges to continue a trial, with all the difficulty and problems it will entail, attorneys need to provide much more detail than those vague generalities. Attorneys should also make the motion to continue the trial the instant they become aware of the need. The closer the case gets to trial, the more difficult it will be to persuade judges to continue the trial. Last, attorneys may consider, in appropriate cases, to request a telephonic hearing with the judge to discuss the request. Sometimes having a conversation with the judge about the matter is a more effective means of communication than relying on a written motion alone.

Knowing the judge is a step in effectively persuading the judge when it comes to seeking continuances. Some judges routinely grant continuances, particularly as to trials or particular motions. It may not take much effort, then, to persuade these judges to grant such a motion. Other judges are known to never or rarely grant such motions. These judges will require attorneys to devote more effort to prevail on a motion to continue.

Once a jury trial is underway, part of effectively persuading judges involves efforts to make full and efficient use of jurors' time. Judges abhor keeping jurors waiting. Judges quickly become impatient when attorneys waste jurors' time by not having witnesses ready to go when called, or when attorneys fail to anticipate issues that could have been raised before or after the trial day and instead have to be taken up during trial while the jury is waiting. Judges will also have little patience for attorneys failing to have witnesses available and ready to go sufficient to fill up a trial day. And to be clear, the jurors' hate having their time wasted as well, so even if attorneys are not all that concerned about persuading judges, they should be concerned about jurors' perceptions of attorneys' competency. The more attorneys show the judge they are conscientious of jurors' valuable time, the more likely judges are to work with attorneys when they seek accommodation on other matters.

Despite attorneys' best efforts, it sometimes nevertheless becomes necessary during trials to adjust the trial schedule because of unforeseen events. Sometimes, for example, there are witness scheduling or time issues, such as when an out-of-town witness' flight is delayed. On other occasions, the day's witnesses all went through their testimony faster than anticipated, by midafternoon the attorney has run out of witnesses, and the next day's witnesses are unavailable. Attorneys can be sure that judges won't be happy about sending the jury home early and wasting valuable court time. Some judges may demand that attorneys take witnesses out of order or otherwise sanction the attorney by limiting that party's time to present the rest of the case. If, however, the attorney has shown an awareness of how important it is not to waste jurors' time, and can explain why the scheduling issue arose despite the attorney's best efforts, judges will often remain calm and work around the scheduling delay. Again, providing judges with information and solutions can help persuade judges. Advising the judge of the efforts made to avoid delay, the efforts the attorney will continue to take to avoid any further delay, and any proposal for how the lost time may be made up or filled with other necessary work that can be accomplished outside the presence of the jury (an evidence proffer, or jury instruction conference, for example), the more likely the attorney will be in persuading the judge to work with the attorney on the scheduling delay.

Seven

Teaching Integrated Legal Advocacy

In this book, we believe we have established that there is a fundamental and material difference in effective advocacy depending on who is making the decision: judge, jury, or appellate court. There are significant differences in the contexts in which advocacy occurs before these decision-makers and marked differences between decision-makers. We have also established the need for greater emphasis on training attorneys to be effective judge advocates because the litigation landscape has changed; jury trials have almost vanished and appellate oral arguments are becoming increasingly rare, while motions practice before judges have increased in number and importance. Today, the reality is that litigators will practice advocacy skills far more often before judges than they ever will before juries or appellate panels. We have also established in this book that there has been little attention paid to these differences, and virtually no education or training on skills designed to persuade judges, as opposed to jurors or a panel of appellate judges.

If our premises are correct—i.e., (1) there are significant and material differences between advocating to juries, appellate panels, and trial judges; (2) there is a greater need for knowing how to effectively persuade judges than there is for knowing how to persuade juries or appellate panels; and (3) little attention has been directed at teaching how to effectively persuade judges—then it raises the question of what should be done about it. The answer, of course, is that we need to provide more education and training on effectively persuading judges. This book is one contribution in that effort. But, the bigger question, however, is whether there isn't a better way altogether to teach advocacy to law students in a manner that recognizes the differences in advocacy and teaches the different skills in a logical manner that builds one skill on top of another.

Persuading Judges

A. *Rethinking Legal Advocacy Training*

We believe the time has come to revisit the way law schools teach legal advocacy.[1] To teach effective advocacy skills at all levels of judicial proceedings, a change is needed in the traditional backwards model of teaching second-year law students mandatory appellate advocacy skills followed by elective trial advocacy skills, while ignoring skills needed to persuade judges. That is not to say that the answer is to abandon moot court programs that have focused on trial advocacy and appellate advocacy. Traditional courses on jury trial and appellate advocacy remain valuable, despite the decrease in the number of cases that result in jury trials or appellate oral arguments. Indeed, teaching these skills in law school is, perhaps, even more critical because young attorneys will get so little practical experience in real courts. These courses teach students how to research, reason, and write; how to identify and present admissible evidence; and how to formulate and make coherent and persuasive arguments. To respond to the evolving litigation landscape then, the solution lies not in eliminating these courses but in supplementing and altering the courses.

One major flaw in the jury trial advocacy and appellate advocacy programs offered at law schools today is that they are not integrated. No thought has been given or instruction provided to students about how advocacy skills should be adapted and changed depending on the context and the decision-maker. Rather, appellate advocacy and trial advocacy programs operate independently of each other. Each focuses on its own area without effort made to compare and contrast effective advocacy practices in the very different settings.

Similarly, the appellate advocacy courses don't flow out of or extend from trial advocacy courses. Appeals in the real-world chronologically flow from trials in the lower courts. To fully understand the nature of an appeal, the scope of review, and the importance of the appellate record, attorneys need to have a founding in pretrial and trial practice first. In real life, attorneys become acutely aware on appeal of how mistakes made or decisions taken in the pretrial and trial settings directly impact the appellate record and legal issues on appeal. "[T]he work of an appellate attorney is inextricably tied to an understanding of the trial process."[2]

But in law school, the mock appellate problems are not based on the mock trial problems. The programs operate completely independent of each other, based on completely different case problems. The materials don't focus on decisions made pretrial or during trial. In trial advocacy courses, students aren't able to see the direct connection between pretrial decisions and rulings and the nature and scope of the case being tried. Rather, students are provided with materials for mock trials without having drafted the indictment or complaint, conducted discovery, or litigated dispositive motions. At most, in trial advocacy programs instructors have attorneys devote ten minutes to superficially arguing oral motions in limine to the judge immediately before the start of the mock trial. The same is true in appellate advocacy courses. Students are provided with a cold trial record, without any source materials about the pretrial litigation and without having participated in making the trial record. The connection between those pre-appeal decisions and rulings, and how they impact the nature and scope of the cold appellate record, are opaque.

In short, neither trial advocacy or appellate advocacy programs provide students with an understanding of how decisions made before trial impact the trial, and consequently, the appeal. In real life, how judges resolve motions and contested hearings, how they rule on disputes over jury instructions and admission of evidence, directly impacts how a case may be tried and the legal issues that will arise on appeal. In real life, attorneys learn the hard way that positions they took and arguments they won or lost before the district court judge often dictate the outcome of trials and appeals.

Further, trial and appellate advocacy courses fail to recognize that law students will appear far more often before judges, and engage in advocacy to judges, than they ever will before juries and appellate panels. The focus on mandatory appellate advocacy in the second year, with trial advocacy as an upper-level elective class, with no attention paid to persuading judges is about as backwards of an approach to teaching legal advocacy as could be designed, especially in today's litigation reality.

B. A Proposal for an Integrated Legal Advocacy Program

The ideal legal advocacy program would address the stages of advocacy in the order in which they occur in litigation, and have the stages integrated as they are in real life. It would place an appropriate emphasis first on learning how to persuade judges. An integrated series of course would also help students understand the differences in the forms of effective advocacy. It would further aid their comprehension of how decisions and developments at one stage of litigation directly affects later stages of litigation. If students learned first how to advocate to judges before they learned how to advocate to jurors and before they learned how to advocate on appeal, they would begin to understand the differences in advocacy skills and what is most effective at each stage. By integrating the programs, such that one flows into the other, students' ability to understanding of the litigation process will be enhanced. Students will be better able to comprehend why attorneys file motions and how the outcome of those motions dictate the nature of the evidence and the stature of the claims that proceed to trial. They will better be able to comprehend how evidence presented and decisions made at trial affect the appellate record and the nature and viability of claims on appeal.

In short, we propose that law schools adopt a new approach to teaching advocacy. Law schools should develop advocacy programs that (1) recognize that there are differences in effective advocacy to judges, juries, and appellate courts; (2) identify ways to make attorneys more effective with each decision-maker; (3) teach students how to be effective advocates in all three settings; and (4) integrate the three stages of litigation and settings in which advocacy is used.

What we propose is a series of three, one-semester, interconnected courses that would take students from pretrial litigation, through jury trial, and onto appeal using the same case problem. The first course should be on pretrial litigation and would (1) have students draft a motion and resistance to a motion and (2) argue that motion to a district judge in a mock hearing. The title of this course should be Advocacy to Judges or Persuading Judges. The Advocacy to Judges course should be a mandatory course and replace the role of the required appellate advocacy course in teaching students the basics of research, writing, and oral advocacy.[3] Indeed, an Advocacy to Judges course makes far more sense as a basic required course as far more law students will, in practice, find themselves filing motions and making arguments before district judges, administrative law judges, and other judicial officers than will ever find themselves in front of a jury or panel of appellate judges.[4]

The motion could involve either a civil motion, like a motion for summary judgment, or a criminal motion, like a motion to suppress. The ideal case problem would be one that involves the students presenting evidence. For example, it could involve a criminal case and a motion to suppress evidence, or it could involve a civil motion for summary judgment. Students would then learn the difference in advocacy in a setting where the rules of evidence don't apply.

The second course on Trial Advocacy would be an upper-level course offered to 2Ls or 3Ls in the fall semester. This course would largely be identical to the trial advocacy courses now offered in law schools, involving a mock jury trial at the end, with a few proposed alterations. First, the case problem would be the same one used in the first-year Advocacy to Judges course. Students would now be "taking to trial" the very problem in which they previously litigated pretrial motions. In doing so, students could develop a better understanding of how pretrial litigation can directly affect the posture of the case at trial. A second proposed alteration in the way traditional trial advocacy courses are taught would be a greater emphasis on the differences between a jury trial and a bench trial. Although the mock trial should still be before a jury, the course instruction should include more discussion about how advocacy would be different were the factfinder a judge and not a jury. Last, the trial advocacy course should involve comparing and contrasting the advocacy skills before a judge versus a jury. Instructors should point out to students, as we have in this book, the differences between judges and jurors and how those differences call for modifying the approach to advocacy depending on the decision-maker. There should also be a discussion of the differences between jury trial advocacy and bench trial advocacy.

The third course on Appellate Advocacy would also be an upper-level course offered to 2Ls or 3Ls in the spring semester. This course would largely be identical to the appellate advocacy courses now offered in law schools, involving brief writing and mock appellate oral arguments, but again with a few proposed alterations. First, the case problem would be the same one used in the Advocacy to Judges and Trial Advocacy courses. The benefits of the continuation of the same case problem should be obvious. Students will have a far better comprehension how pretrial rulings and the record made at trial directly impact the posture of the case on appeal. Second, the Advocacy to Judges and Trial Advocacy courses should be prerequisite courses for students taking the appellate advocacy course. Learning appellate advocacy without first having a foundation of pretrial and trial litigation presents the subject in an artificial and detached setting. When students pass through the stages of litigation in proper chronological order, they will have a significantly better comprehension of the litigation process as a whole, and how advocacy at each stage differs depending on the decision-maker. Last, as with the Trial Advocacy class, the Appellate Advocacy instructor should devote some attention to teaching students to understand the differences between appellate panels as decision-making bodies and judges and juries as decision-makers. When instructors point out the differences, as we have in this book, it will aid students in understanding and appreciating how their advocacy skills need to be modified from that they used before a judge and jury to be effective before an appellate panel.

The three-course advocacy-track program we propose would address the issues identified in this book. A first-year required course on learning how to persuade judges recognizes and would prepare students for a world of litigation where jury trials have nearly vanished and appellate oral arguments have become increasingly rare, while the need to effectively advocate to judges is increasingly important. An upper-level, two-course interconnected program of trial and appellate advocacy would, in combination with the first-year course on advocacy to judges, would provide students with an understanding of how effective advocacy is different based on the context and the decision-maker. The hope would be that students emerging from this three-semester, interconnected course, would be far better equipped with the knowledge and skills to make them effective in today's courtrooms, whomever the decision-make might be. Students would have a much deeper understanding of the course of litigation as a whole and how they relate to each other, and why it is important for them to modify their approach to advocacy depending on the setting and the decision-maker.

Conclusion

The world of litigation today looks very different than it did a couple decades ago and appears nothing like it was a century ago. Today, litigation predominantly involves efforts to persuade judges, not juries. And persuading judges is different from persuading juries. And is different from persuading panels of appellate judges.

When persuading individual judges is increasingly important, it is essential that attorneys adjust their advocacy to be more effective. As we have noted in this book, effective advocacy to a jury, or even a panel of judges, may not be effective with a single judge as decision-maker and may, in fact, be ineffective. Attorneys should carefully examine the ways in which judges are different from jurors, different from juries, and different from panels of appellate judges, and adjust their advocacy accordingly.

In this book, we have attempted to identify the differences we see in effectively persuading judges and effectively persuading juries and appellate panels. We have shared our thoughts on how attorneys can and should change their methods of advocacy to be more effective and persuasive when advocating to a judge. No doubt, some will disagree with some or all of our observations and advice. We respect that. Nevertheless, we maintain that there is a difference in the forms of advocacy depending on the decision-maker. If we have accomplished nothing else through this book, we hope we have prompted a discussion of the topic and provided some guidance to attorneys who want to become better judge advocates.

Chapter Notes

Preface

1. *See, e.g.,* STEVEN LUBERT & J.C. LORE, MODERN TRIAL ADVOCACY (5th ed. 2015); THOMAS A. MAUET, TRIAL TECHNIQUES (10th ed. 2017).

2. *See, e.g.,* John N. Sharifi, *Approaching the Bench: Trial Techniques for Defense Counsel in Criminal Bench Trials*, 28 AM. J. TRIAL ADVOC. 687, 687 (2005) (observing that "training in trial advocacy almost universally focuses only on the jury trial"); John K. Larkins, Jr., *Oral Argument on Motions*, 23 LITIGATION 16, 16 (1997) (noting how little thought or study has been given to advocacy before trial court judges).

Introduction

1. *See* John N. Sharifi, *Approaching the Bench: Trial Techniques for Defense Counsel in Criminal Bench Trials*, 28 AM. J. TRIAL ADVOC. 687, 687 (2005) (observing that "training in trial advocacy almost universally focuses only on the jury trial. Rarely, if ever, are trial advocacy techniques taught in the context of bench trials"); John K. Larkins, Jr., *Oral Argument on Motions*, 23 LITIGATION 16, 16 (1997) (noting how little thought or study has been given to advocacy before trial court judges).

2. The National Institute for Trial Advocacy text, STEVEN LUBERT & J.C. LORE, MODERN TRIAL ADVOCACY (5th ed. 2015), only references bench trials in passing in three places, and THOMAS A. MAUET, TRIAL TECHNIQUES (10th ed. 2017), addresses the topic in a final chapter of only 19 pages in a 619-page text.

3. C.J. Williams & Leonard T. Strand, *Judicial Advocacy: How to Advocate to a Judge*, 43 AM. J. TRIAL ADVOC. 281 (2020).

4. *See* Mark W. Bennett, *Essay: The Grand Poobah and Gorillas in Our Midst: Enhancing Civil Justice in the Federal Courts—Swapping Discovery Procedures in the Federal Rules of Civil and Criminal Procedures and Other Reforms Like Trial by Agreement*, 15 NEV. L.J. 1293, 1308–10 (2015) (emphasizing vanishing trials causing attorneys to no longer accurately call themselves trial attorneys); *see also* Robert P. Burns, *Advocacy in the Era of the Vanishing Trial*, 61 U. KAN. L. REV. 893, 893–94 (2013) ("It has often been remarked ruefully that 'trial lawyers' have almost all become 'litigators.'").

Chapter One

1. *See* Peter Toll Hoffman, *Law Schools and the Changing Face of Practice*, 56 N.Y.L. SCH. L. REV. 203, 205–06 (2012) (noting that young lawyers are most likely to appear before and argue motions to district court judges, rather than handle jury trials).

2. *See, e.g.,* Marc Galanter, *The Vanishing Trial: An Examination of Trials and Related Matters in Federal and State Courts*, 1 J. EMPIRICAL LEGAL STUD. 459, 460 (2004) ("In some, perhaps most, forums, the absolute number of trials has undergone a sharp decline"); John H. Langbein, *The Disappearance of Civil Trial in the United States*, 122 YALE L.J. 522 (2012) (discussing drastic decline in number of civil cases concluding at trial); Nora Freeman Engstrom, *The Diminished Trial*, 86 FORDHAM L. REV. 2131, 2135 (2018)

Notes—Chapter One

(discussing drastic decline in number of civil trials at state and federal levels); Graham K. Bryant & Kristopher R. McClellan, *The Disappearing Civil Trial: Implications for the Future of Law Practice*, 30 REGENT U. L. REV. 287, 287 (2018) (addressing "the widespread disappearance of traditional civil trials from state and federal courts across America"); Robert J. Conrad, Jr., & Katy L. Clements, *The Vanishing Criminal Jury Trial: From Trial Judges to Sentencing Judges*, 86 GEO. WASH. L. Rev. 99, 103 (2018) (noting from 2006 to 2016, jury trial criminal cases declined forty-seven percent); Ronald F. Wright, *Trial Distortion and the End of Innocence in Federal Criminal Justice*, 154 U. PA. L. REV. 79, 90–91, fig.1 (2005) (showing in 2002, federal criminal trials occurred in 4.8% of cases).

3. *See* Galanter, *supra* note 2, at 529 ("Although the number of appeals has increased, the number subject to intensive full-dress review has declined. More appeals are decided on the basis of briefs alone, without oral argument"); *see also* Nancy Winkelman, *Just a Brief Writer?*, 29 LITIG., 50, 51 (2003) (highlighting in 2002 how two-thirds of U.S. Courts of Appeals cases decided without oral argument); Nancy S. Marder, *The Conundrum of Cameras in the Courtroom*, 44 ARIZ. STATE L. J. 1489, 1544–45 (2012) (showing the trend among federal circuit courts of appeal toward holding fewer oral arguments); *See* Richard E. Finneran, *Wherefore Moot Court*, 53 Wash. U. J.L & Pol'y 121, 121 (2017) ("Appellate argument is in decline.")

4. The Declaration of Independence railed against the King "[f]or depriving us in many cases, of the benefits of Trial by Jury," among many other things. The Declaration of Independence paras. 2, 20 (1776).

5. THE REVOLUTIONARY WRITINGS OF JOHN ADAMS 55 (C. Bradley Thompson ed., 2000).

6. *See* Hon. William G. Young, *Vanishing Trials, Vanishing Juries, Vanishing Constitution*, 40 SUFFOLK L. REV. 67, 73 (2006) ("For some time now, circumstantial and anecdotal evidence has been mounting that jury trials are, with surprising rapidity, becoming a thing of the past. Institutionally, federal courts today seem unconcerned with jury trials").

7. Langbein, *supra* note 2, at 524 (2012) (citing Stephen C. Yeazell, *Re-Financing Civil Litigation*, 51 DEPAUL L. REV. 183, 185 n.9 (2001), in turn citing Stephen C. Yeazell, *The Misunderstood Consequences of Modern Civil Process*, 1994 WIS. L. REV. 631, 633 n.3 (1994), in turn citing a 1938 report by the Attorney General)); *see also* Galanter, *supra* note 2, at 464 (explaining in 1938, 18.9% of civil cases terminated by trial).

8. Langbein, *supra* note 2, at 524; *see also* Bryant, *supra* note 2, at 295 (noting in 1938, civil trials made up 19.9% of all case dispositions).

9. *See* Galanter, *supra* note 2, at 461 (examining disproportionate increase in total dispositions compared to decrease in dispositions by trial).

10. *See* Terence F. MacCarthy, *The History of the Teaching of Trial Advocacy*, 38 STETSON L. REV. 115, 123 (2008) (discussing history of trial advocacy law classes) (relating history of trial advocacy courses in law schools).

11. *See* Langbein, *supra* note 2, at 524 (denoting consistent decline in cases tried over decades).

12. *See* Galanter, *supra* note 2, at 461.

13. *See* Bryant, *supra* note 2, at 294.

14. *See Judicial Business of the United States Courts 2018*, ADMIN. OFF. U.S. CTS. (U.S. COURTS), http://www.uscourts.gov/statistics-reports/analysis-reports/judicial-business-united-states-courts (last visited Mar. 20, 2020).

15. *See* Engstrom, *supra* note 2, at 2139 (internal quotations omitted) (modification in original).

16. *See* Galanter, *supra* note 2, at 506 ("The great preponderance of trials, both civil and criminal, take place in the state courts.")

17. *See id.* at 506–07; *see also* Bryant, *supra* note 2, at 297–98 (noting civil bench and jury trials declined from 36% in 1976 to under 16% in 2002).

18. *See* Bryant, *supra* note 2, at 298 (observing that the number of civil jury trials "never approach the number of civil bench trials").

19. *See* Galanter, *supra* note 2, at 508

Notes—Chapter One

(noting "an even more pronounced 44 percent drop in the absolute number of jury trials" from 1992 to 2002).
20. *See id.* at 493
21. *See id.* at 493.
22. *See* U.S. COURTS, *supra* note 4 (showing how another .3 percent were tried in a bench trial.).
23. *See* Galanter, *supra* note 2, at 510.
24. Langbein, *supra* note 2, at 524.
25. *See generally* Engstrom, *supra* note 2, at 2133.
26. *See* Galanter, *supra* note 2, at 505; *see also* Bryant, *supra* note 2, at 314 (discussing "[t]he most obvious—and important—consequence of fewer civil trials on appellate courts is that there are fewer appeals").
27. *See* Marder, *supra* note 3, at 1545; *see also* Thomas E. Baker, *Intramural Reforms: How the U.S. Courts of Appeal Have Helped Themselves*, 22 FLA. ST. L. REV. 913, 916 (1995) (noting 1995, "between about 40% and 50% of the appeals decided on the merits by [federal] courts of appeals in recent years are being decided without oral argument").
28. *See Table B-1—U.S. Courts of Appeals Federal Judicial Caseload Statistics (March 31, 2019)*, UNITED STATES COURTS, https://www.uscourts.gov/statistics/table/b-1/federal-judicial-caseload-statstics/2019/03/31).
29. *See Table B-1—U.S. Courts of Appeals Federal Judicial Caseload Statistics (March 31, 2020)*, UNITED STATES COURTS, https://www.uscourts.gov/statistics/table/b-1/federal-judicial-caseload-statstics/2020/03/31).
30. *See Table B-1—U.S. Courts of Appeals Federal Judicial Caseload Statistics (March 31, 2021)*, UNITED STATES COURTS, https://www.uscourts.gov/statistics/table/b-1/federal-judicial-caseload-statstics/2021/03/31).
31. *See* Engstrom, *supra* note 2, at 2136 (explaining that "...over the years we have seen an uptick in pretrial motions practice (both motions to dismiss and motions for summary judgment)").
32. *See* FED. R. CIV. P. 12(b)(6); Fed R. Civ. P. 56.
33. *See* Celotex Corp. v. Catrett, 477 U.S. 317, 324–25 (1986) (ruling Rule 56 did not require party to support motion with affidavits or similar materials); Anderson v. Liberty Lobby, Inc., 477 U.S. 242, 252–56 (1986) (specifying evidentiary standards apply when ruling on motions for summary judgment); Matsushita Elec. Indus. Co., Ltd. v. Zenith Radio Corp., 475 U.S. 574, 585–88 (1986) (dictating standards courts of appeal use evaluating district courts' decision on motions for summary judgment).
34. *See* Langbein, *supra* note 2, at 567–68 (discussing impact of adoption of civil discovery rules and Rule 56 on motions practice increase); *see also* Joe S. Cecil et al., *A Quarter-Century of Summary Judgment Practice in Six Federal District Courts*, 4 J. Empirical Legal Stud. 861, 883 (2007) ("Over the 25-year period [from 1975 to 2000], the percentage of cases with one or more summary judgment motions granted in whole or in part doubled from 6 percent to 12 percent.")
35. *See* Langbein, *supra* note 2, at 568 ("Reliable empirical evidence regarding the percentage of cases resolved on summary judgment has proved difficult to obtain.")
36. *See id.* at 568–69 (noting how 2004 study concluded between 1960 and 2000 number of federal civil cases disposed of by summary judgment order increased from 1.8 percent to 7.7 percent). More recent data shows that courts granted summary judgment motions in 70% of civil rights cases and 73 percent of employment discrimination cases. *Id.*
37. Galanter, *supra* note 2, at 484.
38. *See* U.S. COURTS, *supra* note 14 (indicating criminal disposition steady between 7 to 8 percent from 1997 to 2018).
39. *See* Hoffman, *supra* note 1, at 205–06 (noting that young lawyers are most likely to appear before and argue motions to district court judges, rather than handle jury trials).
40. Larkins, *supra*, Introduction, n.2, at 16.
41. *See, e.g.*, 28 U.S.C. § 1291 (granting jurisdiction to the federal courts of appeal over "all final decisions" of the district courts). Although exceptions exist for certain interlocutory orders, *see* 28 U.S.C. § 1292, most district court decisions are unreviewable until a final decision has

been rendered that "'ends the litigation on the merits and leaves nothing for the court to do but execute the judgment.'" *Van Cauwenberghe v. Biard*, 486 U.S. 517, 521–22 (1988) (quoting *Catlin v. United States*, 324 U.S. 229, 233 (1945)).

42. *See, e.g.*, FED. R. CIV. P. 52(a)(6) ("Findings of fact, whether based on oral or other evidence, must not be set aside unless clearly erroneous, and the reviewing court must give due regard to the trial court's opportunity to judge the witnesses' credibility"); *DeMarco v. United States*, 415 U.S. 449, 450 fn. (1974) (noting that "factfinding is the basic responsibility of district courts, rather than appellate courts, and ... the Court of Appeals should not have resolved in the first instance this factual dispute which had not been considered by the District Court.")

43. *See, e.g., Anderson v. City of Bessemer City, N.C.*, 470 U.S. 564 (1985).

44. *See, e.g., United States v. Lebedev*, 932 F.3d 40, 49 (2d Cir. 2019).

45. *See, e.g., Neder v. United States*, 527 U.S. 1, 15–18 (1999) (addressing constitutional errors in the admission of evidence); *United States v. Spangler*, 810 F.3d 702, 708 (9th Cir. 2016) (addressing error in excluding an expert's testimony).

46. *See Just the Facts: U.S. Courts of Appeals*, ADMIN. OFF. U.S. CTS., https://www.uscourts.gov/news/2016/12/20/just-facts-us-courts-appeals (last visited Dec. 4, 2024).

Chapter Two

1. In 1869, 24-year-old Arabella "Bella" A. Mansfield of Mount Pleasant, Iowa (one of this book's authors' hometown), took an oath in Union Hall there, becoming the first woman in the United States to be awarded a license to practice law, a half century before women had the right to vote.

2. *See* Mark L. Jones, *Fundamental Dimensions of Law and Legal Education: An Historical Framework—A History of U.S. Legal Education Phase I: From the Founding of the Republic Until the 1860s*, 39 J. MARSHALL L. REV. 1041, 1059–60 (2006).

3. *Id.*, at 1060–62 (discussing requirements for practicing law in America before the American Civil War).

4. *Id.*, at 1066–67.

5. *Id.*, at 1067–68.

6. *Id.*, at 1067–68.

7. *See* LARRY L. TEPLY, LAW SCHOOL COMPETITIONS IN A NUTSHELL 19 (2003) (noting that moot court started at Harvard Law School and "spread quickly to other law schools); *see also* Darby Dickerson, *In re Moot Court*, 29 STETSON L. REV. 1217, 1223 (2000) (citing Harvard Law School, *First-Year Ames Moot Court*, https://orgs.law.harvard.edu/bsa/1l-ames/ (last modified Dec. 10, 1999), and JOHN RITCHIE, THE FIRST HUNDRED YEARS: A SHORT HISTORY OF THE UNIVERSITY OF VIRGINIA FOR THE PERIOD 1826–1926 34 (1978)) (recounting history of moot court programs as component of legal education).

8. *See* Hoffman, *supra* Chapter One, n.1, at 209 (highlighting history and development of case method of legal education).

9. *See* John T. Gaubatz, *Of Moots, Legal Process, and Learning to Learn the Law*, 37 U. MIAMI L. REV. 473, 481–82 (1983) (highlighting development of case method of legal education).

10. *See* Hoffman, *supra* Chapter One, n.1, at 209.

11. *See* Id. (noting that appellate advocacy programs were largely an extension of writing aspect of case method); *see also* ROBERT STEVENS, LAW SCHOOL: LEGAL EDUCATION IN AMERICA FROM THE 1850S TO THE 1980S 229 n.88 (1983) (stating that by 1948 nearly all law schools had appellate moot court programs).

12. *See* Eric E. Bergsten, *Experiential Education Through the Vis Moot*, 34 J. L. & COM. 1, 4 (2015) (explaining how "moot court" most typically refers to appellate, and not trial, advocacy).

13. *See id.* ("The typical moot court is set in an appellate court, which means that only legal issues are available for argument, not the factual issues that probably dominated the case in the trial court.")

14. *See* Barbara Kritchevsky, *Judging: The Missing Piece of the Moot Court Puzzle*, 37 U. MEM. L. REV. 45, 45–46 (2006) (emphasizing that "virtually every law school has a moot court board that

runs in-school competitions"); *see also* Gaubatz, *supra* note 9, at 87 (stating that in 1981, "most [law] schools have some moot court in their research and writing program").

15. *See* Gaubatz, *supra* note 9, at 89–90 (describing moot court program generally); *see also* Dickerson, *supra* note 7, at 1219–22 (detailing process of joining moot court team and what being on team entails).

16. *See* Finneran, *supra* Chapter One, n.3, at 125 (noting that "For most law students, moot court serves as their singular introduction to the art of appellate advocacy during their time in law school[,]" and "[f]or some, it may be their sole orientation to oral advocacy altogether"); *see also* Jennifer Kruse Hanrahan, *Truth in Action: Revitalizing Classical Rhetoric as a Tool for Teaching Oral Advocacy in American Law Schools*, 2003 B.Y.U. Educ. & L.J. 299, 305–06 (2003) (summarizing course offerings at major American law schools).

17. *See* Dickerson, *supra* note 7, at 1218 ("Moot court—or appellate advocacy—skills are typically taught as part of the first-year research and writing curriculum and are sharpened in some upperlevel [sic] electives"); *see also* Gaubatz, *supra* note 9, at 90 (explaining that moot court programs are normally "an integral part of the first-year program").

18. *See* Hoffman, *supra* Chapter One, n.1, at 210 (discussing history of development of jury trial advocacy programs in law schools); *see also* James W. McElhaney, *Toward the Effective Teaching of Trial Advocacy*, 29 U. Miami L. Rev. 198, 198 (1975) (stating that only since 1970s have law schools offered jury trial advocacy courses); Edward D. Ohlbaum, *Basic Instinct: Case Theory and Courtroom Performance*, 66 Temp. L. Rev. 1, 1 (1993) ("Until the last quarter century, law schools did not [train students in jury trial advocacy]").

19. *See* Stevens, *supra* note 11, at 214–15, 227 n.77-78 (describing training only tangentially mentioning "argumentative advocacy," and instead focusing on draftsmanship, research, and writing); *see also* Hoffman, *supra* Chapter One, n.1, at 210 (noting that mid-century skills-based training "bore scant resemblance to the trial advocacy courses of today").

20. *See* Hoffman, *supra* Chapter One, n.1, at 210 ("It was only with the founding of the National Institute for Trial Advocacy (NITA), in 1971, that things began to change and trial advocacy became an established part of the law school curriculum.")

21. *See* MacCarthy, *supra* Chapter 1, n.10, at 117 (discussing history of trial advocacy law classes).

22. *See id.* at 123 (noting the reluctance of law schools to embrace skills-based curriculum in academic setting).

23. *See* Hoffman, *supra* Chapter One, n.1, at 211 (explaining how NITA methodology regarding trial advocacy was rapidly adopted by law schools).

24. *Id.*

25. *See* Laurie A. Lewis, *Law Student Mediators Wear a Triple Crown: Skilled, Sellable, and Successful*, 50 U.S.F. L. Rev. 165, 168 n.9 (2016) ("Approximately 185 U.S. law schools offer courses in ADR, twenty-three of which self-report as having ADR class requirements."); Cynthia A. Savage, *Recommendations Regarding the Establishment of a Mediation Clinic*, 11 Cardozo J. Conflict Resol. 511, 512 (2010) (reporting number of mediation clinics in Canadian and American law schools); *see also* Joseph B. Stulberg, Donald C. Peter, Tracy L. Allen & Judith P. Myers, *Creating and Certifying the Professional Mediator-Education and Credentialing*, 28 Am. J. Trial Advoc. 75, 78 (2004) (noting that a 2003 survey showed almost half of the 184 ABA approved law schools, offer a course focused on mediation.... Eighty-seven schools offer a course in negotiation. Nine schools now are offering a specific course in dispute resolution advocacy, which presumably includes mediation advocacy. One hundred forty-one schools offer a dispute resolution survey course, which presumably covers negotiation but may or may not cover mediation"); Robert Rubinson, *Of Grids and Gatekeepers: The Socioeconomics of Mediation*, 17 Cardozo J. Conflict Resol. 873, 904 (2016) (noting "American Bar Association sponsors a 'Representation in Mediation Competition' for law students"); *see also* Douglas Pilawa, *Sifting Through the Arbitrators for the Woman, the Minority, the Newcomer*, 51 Case W.

Res. J. Int'l L. 395, 401 (2019) (describing Willem C. Vis International Commercial Arbitration Moot competition as "an international arbitration competition with thousands of law school participants").

26. *See* Nat'l Inst. for Trial Advocacy, https://www.nita.org/publications/books-dvds (last visited Feb. 27, 2025) (listing NITA's book titles and descriptions).

27. *Id.* (courses dropdown tab provides access to online courses as well as courses in twenty states).

28. https://www.johnmarshall.edu/courses/pretrial-practice-procedure/.

29. https://www.law.uchicago.edu/prospective/crimcourses#28.

30. https://www.law.berkeley.edu/php-programs/courses/fileDL.php?fID =9747.

31. https://www.law.washington.edu/coursecatalog/syllabi/2021-autumn_baileywi_b519_pre-trial_practice.pdf?44f1tko.

32. https://www.pli.edu/programs/pretrial-practice?t=live.

Chapter Three

1. *See* Kritchevsky *supra* Chapter Two, n.14, at 46–47 ("Moot court is an established part of law school life because it teaches valuable lessons that the rest of the curriculum leaves largely uncovered[,] … teaching skills that will help both in law school and in all areas of practice.") *see also* Finneran, *supra* Chapter One, n.3, at 126–28 (arguing that appellate advocacy and jury trial advocacy courses teach "the very skills that law students will need as future lawyers" and provide "exceptional preparation" for other litigation tasks, such as covering a motion hearing).

2. *See* Roger S. Haydock, David F. Herr & Jeffery W. Stempel, Fundamentals of Pretrial Litigation 637–89 (10th ed. 2016).

3. *See* Thomas A. Mauet, Pretrial 341–42, 374 (8th ed. 2012).

4. *See* Peter B. Krupp, *When Jurors Speak: A Practical Guide to Jurors Questioning Witnesses in Massachusetts*, 45 Oct. Boston Bar J. 12, 12 (2001) ("For most of this country's history, jurors have sat through trials as mute lay observers of an oftentimes technical dialogue between lawyers, judges and witnesses.")

5. *See generally* Hon. Justice Thomas D. Waterman, Hon. Judge Mark W. Bennett, & David C. Waterman, *A Fresh Look at Jurors Questioning Witnesses: A Review of Eighth Circuit and Iowa Appellate Precedents and an Empirical Analysis of Federal and State Trial Judges and Trial Lawyers*, 64 Drake L. Rev. 485, 488, 525 (2016) (noting advantages of process).

6. *See, e.g.*, Alan D. Hornstein, Appellate Advocacy in a Nutshell 242 (1998) ("Finally, and perhaps most important, questions initiated by the advocate to the court are simply inappropriate"); Antonin Scalia and Bryan A. Garner, Making Your Case: The Art of Persuading Judges, 186 (Thompson/West 2008) (addressing the context of appellate argument, "Needless to say, you should never put a substantive question to the court. You're there to answer, not to ask, and some judges may resent the role reversal").

7. *See* J. M. Balkin, *Deconstructive Practice and Legal Theory*, 96 Yale L. J. 743, 756 (1987) (noting that oral speech is "immediate, unambiguous, and sincere," while written communication can be "distant, ambiguous, and potentially misleading").

8. *See* Shirley S. Abrahamson, *Commentary on Jeffrey M. Shaman's The Impartial Judge: Detachment or Passion*, 45 DePaul L. Rev. 633, 634 (1996) (recognizing that judges "may form an early impression about a case" from briefing). *See also generally* Suzanne Ehrenberg, *Embracing the Writing-Centered Legal Process*, 89 Iowa L. Rev. 1159 (2004) (fascinating discussion of development and influence of writing-centered American legal system compared to the oral-centered English legal system).

9. *See, e.g.*, United States v. Martin, 274 F.3d 1208, 1210 (8th Cir. 2001) (approving jury instruction because it was "accurate, clear, neutral, and non-prejudicial"); Townsend v. Lumbermens Mut. Cas. Co., 294 F.3d 1232, 1246 (10th Cir. 2002) ("Rather than merely restating counsel's argument, jury instructions should be a neutral statement of the law"); Bolden v.

Notes—Chapter Three

Beaupre, Civil No. 07-4702 ADM/JSM, 2010 WL 2130858, at *4 (D. Minn. May 24, 2010) (noting that "jury instructions are to be neutral").

10. *See, e.g.*, Robert F. Forston, *Sense and Non-Sense: Jury Trial Communication*, 1975 BYU L. REV. 601, 609-10, 619-20, 631-33 (1975); Joel D. Lieberman & Bruce D. Sales, *What Social Science Teaches Us About the Jury Instruction Process*, 3 PSYCHOL. PUB. POL'Y & L. 589, 626 (1997); John P. Cronan, *Is Any of This Making Sense? Reflecting on Guilty Pleas to Aid Criminal Juror Comprehension*, 39 AM. CRIM. L. REV. 1187, 1211 (2002) (emphasizing increase in comprehension and retention when oral delivery is supplemented by written materials). Cronan opines that it is unrealistic to expect jurors, who are unfamiliar with the law, to comprehend and remember what they only hear orally. Cronan, 39 AM. CRIM. L. REV. at 1200, 1244.

11. *See, e.g.*, THOMAS A. MAUET, TRIAL TECHNIQUES 407 (5th ed. 2000) (emphasizing the need to repeat things to jurors for them to be able to remember it); H. Mitchell Caldwell, L. Timothy Perrin, Richard Gabriel, & Sharon R. Gross, *Primacy, Recency, and Pathos: Integrating Principles of Communication Into the Direct Examination*, 76 NOTRE DAME L. REV. 423, 437 (2001) (encouraging attorneys to use repetition to enhance jurors' retention of evidence); Amy Singer, *10 Common Mistakes Attorneys Make with Jurors*, 36 Trial 76, 80 (2000) ("One cardinal tenet of effective courtroom oratory is to repeat throughout the trial the case's pivotal point—the positive evidence on which the verdict will likely turn. Through repetition, the pivotal point becomes indelibly seared into the consciousness of the jurors so that it acts as their leitmotif in understanding—and thus deciding—the case"); Fred Wilkins, *Tools of Persuasion: Unfolding the Human Drama*, TRIAL, July 1994, at 80 (noting that "[j]urors are more likely to remember something heard several times"); Mark L.D. Wawro, *Effective Presentation of Experts*, 19 LITIG. 31, 35 (Spring 1993) (emphasizing the need to use repetition with experts so the juror will retain and recall the testimony).

12. *See* Theresa A. Webster, *The Creative Side of Law*, 80 MICH. BAR J. 38, 40 (2001) (urging the use of demonstrative aids as a means of enhancing juror's ability to remember the evidence).

13. *See* HORNSTEIN, *supra* note 6, at 245-46 (explaining why reading from brief is ineffective advocacy); *see also* William J. Rehnquist, *Oral Advocacy: A Disappearing Art*, 35 MERCER L. REV. 1015, 1024 (1984) ("The Supreme Court gets more advocates than it should who regard oral argument as a 'brief with gestures.'")

14. *See, e.g.*, DeMarco v. United States, 415 U.S. 449, 450 fn. (1974) (noting that "factfinding is the basic responsibility of district courts, rather than appellate courts, and … the Court of Appeals should not have resolved in the first instance this factual dispute which had not been considered by the District Court").

15. In general, appellate judges may reject the lower court's findings of fact only if those findings are clearly erroneous. *See, e.g.*, FED. R. CIV. P. 52(a)(6). ("Findings of fact, whether based on oral or other evidence, must not be set aside unless clearly erroneous, and the reviewing court must give due regard to the trial court's opportunity to judge the witnesses' credibility.") This is a "deferential standard." *See, e.g.*, Anderson v. City of Bessemer City, N.C., 470 U.S. 564 1985). Even then, though, appellate courts are not hearing evidence; they make their factual findings based on the record as it exists.

16. We discuss these classical forms of rhetorical persuasion as they apply to persuading judges in more detail in the next chapter.

17. *See generally* Hanrahan, *supra* Chapter Two, n.16, at 329 (arguing that good attorneys use classical rhetorical devices to make effective arguments).

18. *See* Mary Beth Beazley, *Writing for a Mind at Work: Appellate Advocacy and the Science of Digital Reading*, 54 DUQ. L. REV. 415, 419 (2016) ("Appellate judges, of course, must 'solve the problem' of the appeal by reviewing those attorney arguments as they appear in written briefs, and by reading the relevant case law and the 'cold record.'"); *see also* Samuel V. Schoonmaker IV & Kenneth J. Bartschi,

Notes—Chapter Three

Effective Family Law Appeals, 28 FAM. ADVOC. 6, 6 (2006) (noting that "although trial court judges have a great deal of latitude to do what they believe is fair and equitable, appellate judges review cases based on a cold record and employ formal standards of review, such as the abuse of discretion standard. Arguments that might succeed in the trial court may be doomed to failure in the appellate court").

19. *See* Kenneth D. Chestek, *The Plot Thickens: The Appellate Brief as Story*, 14 J. LEG. WRITING 127, 162 (2008) (noting "tendency of appellate brief writers to focus on the logos at the expense of the pathos").

20. *See* LAWRENCE M. FRIEDMAN, AMERICAN LAW IN THE 20TH CENTURY 266 (2002) ("It is thanks almost entirely to the jury that we have a huge, lumbering body of doctrine and practice called the law of evidence.")

21. 1 JOHN HENRY WIGMORE, A TREATISE ON THE Anglo-American SYSTEM OF EVIDENCE IN TRIALS AT COMMON LAW 125 (2d ed. 1923); *see also* LAWRENCE M. FRIEDMAN, A HISTORY OF AMERICAN LAW 135 (1st ed. 1973) (noting that American law distrusts jurors because "[t]he jury only hears part of the story; that part which the law of evidence allows").

22. FED. R. EVID. 104(c).

23. *See infra* Chapter 3(A)(5).

24. FED. R. EVID. 104(a) ("The court must decide any preliminary question about whether a witness is qualified, a privilege exists, or evidence is admissible. *In so deciding, the court is not bound by evidence rules, except those on privilege.*" (emphasis added)).

25. *See* FED. R. EVID. 1101(d) (stating Federal Rules of Evidence, "except for those on privilege" do not apply to "miscellaneous proceedings").

26. *See id.* at 1101(d)(3).

27. *See* FED. R. EVID. 1101(d)(3) (The rules (other than with respect to privileges) do not apply in the following situations: ... proceedings with respect to release on bail or otherwise").

28. *See* United States v. Matlock, 415 U.S. 164, 172–73 (1974); *see also* 3A CHARLES ALAN WRIGHT, ANDREW D. LEIPOLD, PETER J. HENNING, SARAH N. WELLING, FEDERAL PRACTICE & PROCEDURE § 689 (4th ed. 2010) (citing *Matlock*, 415 U.S. at 172–73) ("The rules of evidence do not apply in a suppression hearing and hearsay is admissible.")

29. *See* 18 U.S.C. § 3661; *see also* United States v. Watts, 519 U.S. 148, 154 (1997) (holding that lower evidentiary standard at sentencing permits sentencing court's consideration of acquitted conduct); Witte v. United States, 515 U.S. 389, 399–401 (1995) (noting that sentencing court traditionally considered range of information including criminal conduct and subsequent prosecution); Nichols v. United States, 511 U.S. 738, 747–48 (1994) (noting district courts considered defendant prior criminal conduct even when defendant was not convicted of that conduct).

30. *See* FED. R. EVID. 404(a)(1); *see also* C.J. Williams & Dasha Ternavska, *A Series of Unfortunate Events: The Admissibility of "Other Fires" Evidence in Arson Cases*, 48 CONN. L. REV. 685, 697–98 (2016) (explaining rationale behind Rule 404(a)(1)).

31. *See* FED. R. EVID. Advisory Committee Notes on Proposed Rule 406 (noting general consensus that "the uniformity of one's response to habit is far greater than the consistency with which one's conduct conforms to character or disposition").

32. *See* FED. R. EVID. Advisory Committee Notes on Proposed Rule 407 (stating that Rule 407 rests in part on "a social policy of encouraging people to take, or at least not discourage them from taking, steps in furtherance of added safety").

33. *See* Broad. Music, Inc. v. Xanthas, Inc., 855 F.2d 233, 238 (5th Cir. 1988) ("The district court erred when it admitted this evidence on the ground that hearsay is admissible in a bench trial; it is not.")

34. Fed. R. Evid. 403 ("Excluding Relevant Evidence for Prejudice, Confusion, Waste of Time, or Other Reasons").

35. *See* United States v. Musleh, 106 Fed. App'x 850, 856 (4th Cir. 2004); *see also* United States v. Hall, No. 98–6421, 2000 WL 32010, at *2 (6th Cir. 2000) (stating Rule 403 has little or no application during bench trial); Schultz v. Butcher, 24 F.3d 626, 632 (4th Cir. 1994) ("Adopting

the position taken in *Gulf States*, we hold that in the context of a bench trial, evidence should not be excluded under 403 on the ground that it is unfairly prejudicial"); Gulf States Utils. Co. v. Ecodyne Corp., 635 F.2d 517, 519 (5th Cir. 1981) (excluding relevant evidence in a bench trial on basis of unfair prejudice is useless and illogical). Courts have also acknowledged that judges have more "leeway" in receiving questionable evidence (including expert witness evidence) during a bench trial. *See, e.g.,* Attorney Gen. of Okla. v. Tyson Foods, Inc., 565 F.3d 769, 780 (10th Cir. 2009) ("[A] judge conducting a bench trial maintains greater leeway in admitting questionable evidence, weighing its persuasive value upon presentation"); Rogers v. Air Line Pilots Ass'n, Int'l, 988 F.2d 607, 612 (5th Cir. 1993) ("In a bench trial … the district court has more leeway in evaluating the admissibility of evidence since it is both the arbiter of admissibility and the finder of fact"); Thames v. Evanston Ins. Co., No. 13-CV-425-PJC, 2015 WL 3398147, at *2 (N.D. Okla. May 26, 2015) ("When set for bench trial, the Court has more leeway in its gatekeeper role, but it still must consider whether expert evidence or testimony is admissible.")

36. *See* United States v. Hassanzadeh, 271 F.3d 574, 578 (4th Cir. 2001) (holding that admission of evidence in bench trial did not violate Rule 404(b), but noting a judge can "separate the emotional impact from the probative value of this potentially prejudicial evidence").

37. *Schultz*, 24 F.3d at 632 (stating intent of Rule 403 and ability of judges to implement it).

38. In re Zurn Pex Plumbing Prods. Liab. Litig., 644 F.3d 604, 613 (8th Cir. 2011) (citing Daubert v. Merrell Dow Pharmaceuticals, Inc., 509 U.S. 579 (1993)) (outlining purpose of *Daubert* motion).

39. *See* Null v. Wainwright, 508 F.2d 340, 344 (5th Cir. 1975) ("Strict evidentiary rules of admissibility are generally relaxed in bench trials…."); *see also* United States v. Raymond, 697 F.3d 32, 39 n.6 (1st Cir. 2012) ("It is at least arguable that, in a bench trial, a district court has wider latitude in the admission of Rule 404(b) evidence" (dictum)); Celotex Corp. v. Catrett, 477 U.S. 317, 324 (1986) ("… the nonmoving party [need not] produce evidence in a form that would be admissible at trial in order to avoid summary judgment"); U.S. Dept. of Hous. & Urb. Dev. v. Cost Control Mktg. & Sales Mgmt. of Va., Inc., 64 F.3d 920, 926, 926 n.8 (4th Cir. 1995) (noting that although inadmissible evidence is "ordinarily an inadequate basis for summary judgment," the rule is "not unfailingly rigid"); Calhoun v. Bailar, 626 F.2d 145, 148 (9th Cir. 1980) ("[T]he strict rules of evidence do not apply in an administrative context.") *But see* In re Unisys Savings Plan Litig., 173 F.3d 145, 164 (3d Cir. 1999) (Becker, J., dissenting) ("The Federal Rules of Evidence apply with full force to bench trials" (citing Fed. R. Evid. 1101(b) and 9 Charles Alan Wright & Arthur R. Miller, Federal Practice & Procedure § 2411 (2d ed. 1995) ("In theory, the Federal Rules of Evidence apply equally in court trials and jury trials")). It should be noted that Rule 1101(b) does not say anything about bench trials. *See* Fed. R. Evid. 1101(b).

40. James Corp. of Opelousas v. Tangie Const. Co., Inc., No. 93-4828, 1993 WL 413912, at *3 (5th Cir. Oct. 12, 1993) (citations omitted) (identifying appropriate standard of review for challenges to evidentiary rulings); *see* BIC Corp. v. Far Eastern Source Corp., 23 Fed. App'x 36, 39 (2d Cir. 2001) ("[T]he admission of evidence in a bench trial is rarely ground for reversal, for the trial judge is presumed to be able to exclude improper inferences from his or her own decisional analysis.")

41. *See In re Unisys*, 173 F.3d at 172 (Becker, J., dissenting) ("'In nonjury cases the district court can commit reversible error by excluding evidence but it is almost impossible for it to do so by admitting evidence'" (quoting Wright & Miller, at § 2885)); *see also* Van Alen v. Dominick & Dominick, Inc., 560 F.2d 547, 552 (2d Cir. 1977) (noting that, although the trial judge ruled otherwise, "ordinarily it may be the more prudent course in a bench trial to admit into evidence doubtfully admissible records"); Dreyful Ashby, Inc. v. S/S "Rouen," No. 88 CIV. 2890 (MBM), 1989 WL 151685, at *2 (S.D.N.Y.1989) (stating

Notes—Chapter Three

that "all doubts at a bench trial should be resolved in favor of admissibility, [but] that cannot mean that standards are out the window entirely").

42. *See* RALPH ADAM FINE, THE HOW-TO-WIN TRIAL MANUAL: A NO-HOLDS-BARRED SURE-FIRE WAY TO WIN 578 (6th Ed. 2015) (opining that for a "bench trial judge to ignore the evidence that he or she has excluded from the trial requires 'a mental gymnastic which is beyond, not only [the judge's] powers, but anybody's....'" (quoting *Nash v. United States*, 54 F.2d 1006, 1007 (2d Cir. 1932)).

43. *Motion in Limine*, BLACK'S LAW DICTIONARY (11th ed. 2019) (defining a motion in limine as "[a] pretrial request that certain inadmissible evidence not be referenced to or offered at trial" and noting that attorneys typically make these motions because the evidence is so highly prejudicial that waiting to object at trial may cause a mistrial).

44. *See* Luce v. U.S., 469 U.S. 38, 41 n.4 (1984) ("Although the Federal Rules of Evidence do not explicitly authorize in limine rulings, the practice has developed pursuant to the district court's inherent authority to manage the course of trials.")

45. *See* Jonasson v. Lutheran Child and Fam. Servs., 115 F.3d 436, 440 (7th Cir. 1997).

The motion in limine is an important tool available to the trial judge to ensure the expeditious and evenhanded management of the trial proceedings. It performs a gatekeeping function and permits the trial judge to eliminate from further consideration evidentiary submissions that clearly ought not be presented to the jury because they clearly would be inadmissible for any purpose. The prudent use of the in limine motion sharpens the focus of later trial proceedings and permits the parties to focus their preparation on those matters that will be considered by the jury.
Id

46. *See* Randy Wilson, *From My Side of the Bench*, 47 THE ADVOC. (TEXAS) 92 (2009) ("[A]lthough you'd think it goes without saying, a motion in limine doesn't work with a bench trial. I wish I could say I've never seen one before in a bench trial; unfortunately, I cannot.")

47. *See* United States v. Tokash, 282 F.3d 962, 968 (7th Cir. 2002) ("Motions in limine are well-established devices that streamline trials and settle evidentiary disputes in advance, so that trials are not interrupted mid-course for the consideration of lengthy and complex evidentiary issues.")

48. *See* Larkins, *supra* Preface, n.2, at 70 ("Every appearance before a judge inevitably affects every case the lawyer or his firm has or will have before that judge"); J. Thomas Greene, *Oral Argument in the District Court*, 26 No. 3 LITIG. 3, 59 (2000) ("Remember, you may lose the particular motion, but the outcome of any case seldom turns on a single decision. Continued civility coupled with meticulous preparation inevitably will carry the day (and the judge)—if not in this case, then in the next.")

49. *See, e.g.*, Eighth Circuit Model Criminal Jury Instruction 3.16 ("Each of you must make your own conscientious decision, but only after you have considered all the evidence, discussed it fully with your fellow jurors, and listened to the views of your fellow jurors"); United States v. Williams, 547 F.3d 1187, 1203 (9th Cir. 2008) (instructing that each juror must make his or her "own conscientious decision" but "to listen to the views of your fellow jurors").

50. *See* William L. Reynolds & William M. Richman, *Justice and More Judges*, 15 J.L. & POL. 559, 563 (1999) ("[A] collegiality of judges who know one another well enough to think alike and through that group think to achieve a coherent and stable body of law.")

51. Chrisje Brants, *Wrongful Convictions and Inquisitorial Process: the Case of the Netherlands*, 80 U. CIN. L. REV. 1069, 1111–12 (2012) (discussing pitfalls of group decision making by appellate judges).

52. *Id*.

53. *See* Chris Guthrie, Jeffrey J. Rachlinski & Andrew J. Wistrich, *Blinking on the Bench: How Judges Decide Cases*, 93 CORNELL L. REV. 1, 13, 29 (2007) (explaining that judges employ intuition subconsciously to make decisions); *see also* Chris

Notes—Chapter Three

Guthrie, Jeffrey J. Rachlinski & Andrew J. Wistrich, *Can Judges Ignore Inadmissible Information? The Difficulty of Deliberately Disregarding*, 153 U. Pa. L. Rev. 1251, 1251, 1292 (2005) (concluding that judges are unable to avoid being influenced by inadmissible information); Chris Guthrie, Jeffrey J. Rachlinski & Andrew J. Wistrich, *Inside the Judicial Mind*, 86 Cornell L. Rev. 777, 778, 786 (2001) (stating that judges are just as susceptible to making errors in judgment as lay people).

54. *See* Irving L. Janis, Groupthink 7, 270–71 (2d ed. 1972) (discussing group think among jurors); *see also* Jill M. Cochran, Note, *Courting Death: 30 Years Since Furman, Is the Death Penalty Any Less Discriminatory? Looking at the Problem of Jury Discretion in Capital Sentencing*, 38 Val. U. L. Rev. 1399, 1447 (2004) (discussing negative effects of group think among jurors, particularly in death penalty cases).

55. *See* Joe S. Cecil, Valerie P. Hans, & Elizabeth C. Wiggins, *Citizen Comprehension of Difficult Issues: Lessons from Civil Jury Trials*, 40 Am. U. L. Rev. 727, 749–50 (1991) (discussing benefits of group decision-making by jurors).

56. *See id.* (describing benefits of group decision-making by jurors).

57. *See* Fed. Judicial Ctr., law Clerk Handbook: A Handbook for Law Clerks to Federal Judges 1 (Sylvan A. Sobel ed., 2d ed. 2007) ("Many judges discuss pending cases with their law clerks and confer with them about decisions"); Judge William E. Smith, *Reflections on Judicial Merit Selection, the Rhode Island Experience and Some Modest Proposals for Reform and Improvement*, 15 R. Williams U. L. Rev. 664, 697 (2010) (discussing benefits of elbow law clerk with whom judges can "bounce ideas off").

58. *See* Code of Conduct for United States Judge, Cannon 3(A)(2) (2019) (stating that judges "should maintain order and decorum in all judicial proceedings"); *see also id.*, Cannon 3(A)(3) (continuing list of judicial responsibilities).

A judge should be patient, dignified, respectful, and courteous to litigants, jurors, witnesses, lawyers, and others with whom the judge deals in an official capacity. A judge should require similar conduct by those subject to the judge's control, including lawyers to the extent consistent with their role in the adversary process.

Id.; *see* Fed. R. Evid. 611 ("The court should exercise reasonable control over the mode and order of examining witnesses and presenting evidence so as to: (1) make those procedures effective for determining the truth; (2) avoid wasting time; and (3) protect witnesses from harassment or undue embarrassment.")

59. *See* Darryl K. Brown, *Defense Counsel, Trial Judges, and Evidence Production Protocols*, 45 Tex. Tech. L. Rev. 133, 145 (2012) ("[J]udges often face significant pressure to move their dockets efficiently.") The need for efficient litigation is compelled in federal criminal cases by the Speedy Trial Act. *See* 18 U.S.C. § 3161 (2008).

60. Fed. R. Civ. P. 1; *see also* Canon 3(A)(5) ("A judge should dispose promptly of the business of the court.") The commentary to Cannon 3(A)(5) elaborates on this duty and reflects the tension between a judge's need to give parties their days in court and the limited number of days in a year.

In disposing of matters promptly, efficiently, and fairly, a judge must demonstrate due regard for the rights of the parties to be heard and to have issues resolved without unnecessary cost or delay. A judge should monitor and supervise cases to reduce or eliminate dilatory practices, avoidable delays, and unnecessary costs. Prompt disposition of the court's business requires a judge to devote adequate time to judicial duties, to be punctual in attending court and expeditious in determining matters under submission, and to take reasonable measures to ensure that court personnel, litigants, and their lawyers cooperate with the judge to that end.

Id., Cannon 3(A)(5), Comment.

61. 18 U.S.C. § 3161 et seq.

62. *See* Mark R. Kravitz, *Written and Oral Persuasion in the United States Courts: A District Judge's Perspective on Their History, Function, and Future*, 10

Notes—Chapter Three

J. App. Prac. & Process 247, 268 (2009) ("Unlike an appellate court, however, I can and do devote more than twenty or thirty minutes to each case, and I do not have to share my time with other judges.")

63. *See, e.g.*, United States v. Ransfer, 749 F.3d 914, 937 (11th Cir. 2014) (acknowledging that the period of time allotted to attorneys for closing arguments is within the sound discretion of the trial judge (quoting United States v. Carter, 760 F.2d 1568, 1581 (11th Cir. 1985))); United States v. Holt, 493 F. App'x 515, 521–22 (5th Cir. 2012) (although disagreeing with the district court's "severe limit" on closing arguments, the court held that the limitation did not constitute plain error (citing United States v. Gray, 105 F.3d 956, 963 (5th Cir. 1997))); United States v. Wright, 651 F.3d 764, 773 (7th Cir. 2011) (noting that trial judges have substantial discretion to place time limits on "peripheral issues" such as opening statements and closing arguments (quoting United States v. White, 472 F.3d 458, 462 (7th Cir. 2006))).

64. *See generally* Patrick E. Longan, *The Shot Clock Comes to Trial: Time Limits for Federal Civil Trials*, 35 Ariz. L. Rev. 663 (1993); John E. Rumel, *The Hourglass and Due Process: The Propriety of Time Limits on Civil Trials*, 26 U.S.F. L. Rev. 237 (1992).

65. *See, e.g.*, United States v. Cousar, No. 06–007, 2007 WL 4456798, at *2 (W.D. Pa. Dec. 16, 2007) ("Although it may be more common for a district court to impose time limits in a civil trial, setting time limits in a criminal trial is equally authorized.")

66. For example, in the 1907 case of State v. Haywood, a prosecutor's closing argument was eight hours long, one defense attorney's closing was ten hours long, the other defense attorney's closing was eleven hours long, and the prosecution's rebuttal was five and half hours in length. *See* Hon. J. William Hart, *Trial of the Century*, 43 Advoc. 24 (Dec. 2000). In today's world of limited attention spans, arguments of this length are unimaginable.

67. *See* Stephen M. Shapiro, *Oral Argument in the Supreme Court: The Felt Necessities of the Time*, Supreme Court Historical Society Yearbook 22, 23 (S. Ct. Historical Socy. 1985) (noting that "[t]he Supreme Court entertained these orations not only without limitation upon time but also without interruption").

68. *See* ABA Model Rules Of Prof'l Conduct Preamble (2004); *see also* Maracich v. Spears, 570 U.S. 48, 62–64 (2013) (describing an attorney as an officer of the court in the context of the attorney's "professional responsibilities" and the "proper conduct of litigation").

69. Dunn v. Wal-Mart Stores, Inc., No. 2:12–cv–01660–GMN–VCF, 2013 WL 5940099, at *3 (D. Nev. Nov. 1, 2013).

70. *See* Model Rule of Prof'l Conduct r. 3.3 ("A lawyer shall not knowingly: (1) make a false statement of material fact or law to a tribunal....")

71. *See, e.g.*, ABA Standards § 2.2–2.10 (listing the panoply of available sanctions for attorney misconduct includes disbarment, suspension, fine, public reprimand, and private reprimand); Fed. R. App. P. 46(b) & (c) (providing that a member of the bar may be subject to suspension, disbarment, or other discipline for "conduct unbecoming a member of the court's bar").

72. *See, e.g.*, Joseph P. Mastrosimone, *Benchslaps*, 2017 Utah L. Rev. 331 (2017) (discussing the practice of judges issuing so-called "benchslaps," that is publicly shaming attorneys for their conduct by identifying the attorneys by name).

73. Christopher W. Behan, *Teaching Courtroom Advocacy Principles and Skills Across Systems and Cultures*, 46 S. Ill. U. L.J. 1, 15 (2021).

74. *See* Terry A. Maroney, *Emotional and Judicial Behavior*, 99 Cal. L. Rev. 1485, 1494 (2011) (noting that "[m]any judges will, over the course of their careers, develop sound and flexible strategies for coping with emotion"). Some debate exists in academic circles about whether judges should, or even really do, separate their decision-making from their emotions. *See* Bruce A. Green & Rebecca Roiphe, *Judicial Activism in Trial Courts*, 74 N.Y.U. Ann. Surv. Am. L. 365, 379–84 (2018).

75. *See* Paul Holland, *Sharing Stories: Narrative Lawyering in Bench Trials*, 16 Clinical L. Rev. 195, 268 (2009) (noting that bench trials are different from

Notes—Chapter Three

jury trials because as "[m]embers of the same profession, judges and lawyers share a vocabulary, a code of ethics, certain formative experiences (such as law school and the bar exam) and a responsibility for justice"); Larkins, *supra* Preface, n.2, at 18 ("On one level, your unspoken attitude to the judge is, 'You and I speak the same language; we both understand the majestic principles of the law and its common sense; let us reason together.")

76. *See* Hon. David J. Newblatt, *How to Convince the Judge on Motion Day in Family Court*, 85 MICH. BAR J. 16, 17 (2006) ("Judges are trained and experienced. Judges will not be persuaded by gratuitous personal attacks. Hyperbole lost its effect long ago. We can tell baloney from substance and can tell whether you know the law and the facts. Talk to the judge at the judge's level"); Larkins, *supra* Preface, n.2, at 17 ("Although a judge, like a jury, wants to understand where justice lies in the case, a judge will rarely have a favorable reaction to an emotional or inflammatory appeal. In fact, the judge's usual reaction to such "jury argument" is to be professionally offended.")

77. *See* Brian Wice, *Oral Argument in Criminal Cases: 10 Tips for Winning the Moot Court Round*, 69 TEX. B. J. 224, 225 (2006) ("Remember that your forum is an appellate court, not a trial court, and that your audience is composed not of jurors but of appellate judges. Some of the most talented criminal trial lawyers are far from stellar when they take on the mantle of appellate warrior. Why? Because they are unable or unwilling to recognize that the same table-pounding argument and incendiary prose that may carry the day in the trial court will be laughed at by the appellate judges whom they hold hostage for 20 minutes. It is logic, not emotion, that is the foundation of a compelling oral argument.")

78. *See* Mu'Min v. Virginia, 500 U.S. 415, 431 (1991) (explaining that jury voir dire enables courts to select impartial juries and assists attorneys in exercising peremptory strikes).

79. *See generally* Rachael A. Ream, *Limited Voir Dire*, 23 CRIM. JUST. 22, 26 (2009) (discussing role of written questionnaires in jury selection).

80. *See generally* Thaddeus Hoffmeister, *Investigating Jurors in the Digital Age: One Click at a Time*, 60 U. KAN. L. REV. 611, 616 (2012) (discussing use of internet to research prospective jurors).

81. *See generally* Katherine Allen, *The Jury: Modern Day Investigation and Consultation*, 34 REV. LITIG. 529, 531 (2015) (discussing use of jury consultants in researching prospective jurors and assisting in jury selection).

82. SCALIA & GARNER, *supra* Chapter Three, n.6, at 5.

83. *See* Sara Klco & Francisco Armada, *Tips for Young Lawyers*, 37 No. 3 TRIAL ADVOC. Q. 13, 13 (2018) (urging young lawyers arguing cases before district judges to "[k]*now your audience*. Consider your judge's background and experience handling the issue you are asking him or her to address and tailor your pleadings and arguments based on that background and experience").

84. *See, e.g.,* United States v. Sanchez, 659 F.3d 1252, 1256 (9th Cir. 2011) ("Prosecutors may not urge jurors to convict a criminal defendant in order to protect community values, preserve civil order, or deter future lawbreaking. The evil lurking in such prosecutorial appeals is that the defendant will be convicted for reasons wholly irrelevant to his own guilt or innocence"); United States v. Morgan, 113 F.3d 85, 90 (7th Cir. 1997) (stating that arguments "appealing to the jurors' emotions and inviting the jury to consider the social consequences of its verdict" are improper); Pierce v. Platte-Clay Elec. Coop., Inc., 769 S.W.2d 769, 779 (Mo. 1989) (finding that the plaintiffs' counsel's arguments to the jury to "send a message" "danced dangerously close to reversible error," but was not a reversible error because "the quick objection by appellant's able counsel and the trial court's firm instruction to the jury prevented prejudice"); *but see, e.g.,* Greenleaf v. Garlock Inc., 174 F.3d 352 (3d Cir. 1999) (finding an argument that the jury should "send a message" to the defendant through its verdict permissible in a civil case, even when punitive damages are not involved).

85. SCALIA & GARNER, *supra* Chapter Three, n.6, at 7.

86. Ronald A. Cass, The Rule of Law in America 69 (2001).
87. 5 U.S. 137 (1803).
88. *See* Kathleen Dillon Narko, *Persuasion: Aristotle Still Works for Webb, Wood, and Kocoras*, 19 Chic. B. Assoc. 54, 55 (Apr. 2005) ("When arguing to a judge rather than a jury, logos takes center stage.")
89. *See* John T. Gaubatz, *Moot Court in the Modern Law School*, 31 J. Legal Educ. 87, 87 (1981) ("The [appellate advocacy] experience has the corollary benefit of preparing counsel for the task of making legal arguments before any court, and in general strengthens persuasive skills.")

Chapter Four

1. Aristotle, *Rhetorica*, in The Works of Aristotle, 1354a, 1355b (W.D. Ross Ed., Encyclopedia Britannica 1952).
2. *See* John Munkman, The Technique of Advocacy, *foreword* (Butterworth's 2001) ("Advocacy is the art of persuasion; it is also a craft"); Murphy v. Shaw, A-0906–13T1, 2014 WL 7370131, at *8 (N.J. Super. Dec. 30, 2014) ("Advocacy is the art of persuasion"); People v. Mischley, 417 N.W.2d 537, 539 (Mich. App. 1987) ("The art of advocacy is the art of persuasion.")
3. *See* Michael Frost, *Ethos, Pathos & Legal Audience*, 99 Dick. L. Rev. 85, 86 (Fall 1995) ("Roman rhetoricians and lawyers like Cicero and Quintilian, relying on Aristotle's rhetorical analyses, divided persuasive discourse, and legal arguments in particular, into three categories: logical argument (logos), emotional argument (pathos), and ethical appeal or credibility (ethos)") (footnote omitted).
4. Brett G. Scharffs, *The Character of Legal Reasoning*, 61 Wash. & Lee L. Rev. 733, 752 (2004).
5. *Id.*, at 754.
6. *See generally* Hanrahan, *supra* Chapter Two, n.16 (arguing that good lawyers use classical rhetorical devices to make effective arguments).
7. Carl Sandburg, The People, Yes 181 (1937) ("'If the law is against you, talk about the evidence,' said a battered barrister. 'If the evidence is against you, talk about the law, and, since you ask me, if the law and the evidence are both against you, then pound on the table and yell like hell.'"). Interestingly, this saying has some variations. *See* David M. Wilson, *Working Toward a Common Goal: Are You One of Us?*, 48 No. 3 DRI For Def. 14, 14 (2006) ("Lore has it that Abraham Lincoln, while lecturing a group of young lawyers, advised that 'If the facts are against you, argue the law. If the law is against you, argue the facts. If the facts and the law are against you, attack your opponent.'") (no authority cited); 2007 March 4, Fort Worth Star-Telegram, *Pounding the Table About Border Episode by Ruben Navarrette, Jr.*, Page E3, Section: Weekly Review, Fort Worth, Texas (quoting Professor Alan Dershowitz: "If the facts are on your side, Dershowitz says, pound the facts into the table. If the law is on your side, pound the law into the table. If neither the facts nor the law are on your side, pound the table"); Albert Bates, Jr., et al., *Asset Purchases, Successor Liability, and Insurance Coverage: Does the Tail Always Follow the Dog?*, 100 W. Va. L. Rev. 631, 648 n.60 (1998) ("[If] the facts are against you, argue the law. If the law is against you, argue the facts. If both the facts and the law are against you, obfuscate!").
8. *See* Anne E. Mullins, *Source-Relational Ethos in Judicial Opinions*, 54 Wake Forest L. Rev. 1089, 1091 (2019) (emphasizing that ethos "is the foundation of persuasion"). *See also* Eugene Garver, for the Sake of Argument: Practical Reasoning, Character, and the Ethics of Belief 7 (2004) ("[E]thos is the most authoritative source of belief"); Michael Smith, Advanced Legal Writing: Theories and Strategies in Persuasive Writing 125 (3d ed., 2013) ("A strong argument can be made that ethos is more important to persuasive writing than either logical argument (logos) or appeals to emotion (pathos).")
9. Mullins, *supra* note 8, at 1092.
10. *Id.*
11. William Benoit, *Isocrates and Aristotle on Rhetoric*, 20 Rhetoric Soc'y Q. 251, 257 (1990).
12. James Boyd White, *Law as Rhetoric, Rhetoric as Law: The Arts of Cultural and*

Communal Life, 52 U. CHI. L. REV. 684, 702 (1985).

13. Hanrahan, *supra* Chapter Two, n.16, at 307–08.

14. ARISTOTLE, RHETORIC, Book I, Part II, Paragraph VII (Trans. W. Rhys Roberts, Mineola, NY; Dover Publications 2004).

Chapter Five

1. OXFORD DICTIONARY OF AMERICAN LEGAL QUOTATIONS (Fred Shapiro, ed. 1993) at 257.

2. *See, e.g.*, Kent A. Jordan, *The 2018 Honorable Daniel M. Friedman Appellate Advocacy Lecture: Lessons from Lincoln on Appellate Advocacy*, 28 FED. CIR. BAR J. 1, 4 (2018) (adding credibility to an attorney's stock in trade); Michael E. Romero, *The Four "Cs" of Courtroom Presentation*, 35 COLO. LAW. 81, 81 (July 2006) (same); Martha Neil, *Leave 'Em, But Love 'Em; Keep the Door to Your Career Open by Not Slamming It on the Way Out of the Firm*, 91 A.B.A. J. 56, 56 (2005) (stating that professional reputation is a lawyer's stock in trade).

3. *See, e.g.*, Douglas E. Abrams, *Tips About Written Advocacy from the North Dakota Supreme Court*, 74 J. MO. B. 28, 31 (2018) (arguing that attorney credibility is important, noting that "judges have long memories for the advocate's past stellar performances, but also for the advocate's past shortcomings that evinced negligence or intent"); Hon. Penny J. White, *10 Things They Never Taught You in Law School*, 30 TENN. B. J. 20, 22 (1994) ("Remember also that judges, like elephants, have terribly good and long memories.")

4. *See* William V. Dorsaneo, III, *The Decline of Anglo-American Civil Jury Trial Practice*, 71 SMU L. Rev. 353, 354 (2018) ("by the twenty-first century, the use of jury trials to resolve civil disputes in America had declined, and jury trials had largely vanished.") (footnote omitted); Xavier Rodriguez, *The Decline of Civil Jury Trials: A Positive Development, Myth, or the End of Justice as We Know It?*, 45 St. MARY'S L. J. 333, 335–36 (2014) (documenting the declining percentage of federal civil cases that progress to trial by jury).

5. *See* United States v. Booker, 543 U.S. 220 (2005). Despite *Booker* being the law now for two decades, attorneys still routinely devote a page or two in sentencing briefs advising the court about the *Booker* decision and informing the court that judges are not bound by the United States Sentencing Guidelines. It must come as a surprise to these attorneys that we already know that.

6. An empirical study revealed that "the majority of judges consider legal analysis and organization—in that order—the two most important aspects of persuasive writing...." Kristen K. Robbins, *The Inside Scoop: What Federal Judges Really Think About the Way Lawyers Write*, 8 J. LEG. WRITING INST. 257, 272 (2002).

7. *See* SCALIA & GARNER, *supra* Chapter Three, n.6, at 31–32 ("Appealing to judges' emotions is misguided because it fundamentally mistakes their motivation. Good judges pride themselves on the rationality of their rulings and the suppression of their personal proclivities, including most especially their emotions. And bad judges want to be regarded as good judges. So either way, overt appeal to emotion is likely to be regarded as an insult.")

8. An edited version of the comment commonly (but perhaps incorrectly) credited to the character known as Sergeant Joe Friday in the Jack Webb television series *Dragnet. See, e.g.*, https://www.snopes.com/fact-check/just-the-facts.

9. *See* Robert Dubose, *Eight Common Writing Mistakes in Motion Practice*, 92 THE ADVOC. 16, 17 (2020) (arguing that heading should be persuasive, not neutral, and "should be a complete sentence that summarizes the argument of the section").

10. Larkins, *supra* Preface, n.2, at 17.

11. *See* Stephanie A. Vaughan, *Persuasion Is an Art But It Is Also an Invaluable Tool in Advocacy*, 61 BAYLOR L. REV. 635, 667–68 (2009) ("The most fundamental thing to remember about oral argument is that it is a conversation with the court ... not an oral recitation of a brief or [memorandum]") (quoting BRADLEY G. CLARY ET AL., ADVOCACY ON APPEAL 6, 97 (3d ed. 2008)).

12. *Cf.* James D. Dimitri, *Stepping Up*

to the Podium with Confidence: A Primer for Law Students on Preparing and Delivering an Appellate Oral Argument, 38 STETSON L. REV. 75, 95 (2008) ("Hence, you should not treat questions from the bench as an intrusion upon your argument. Rather, you should welcome questions from the bench and strive to answer them to the court's satisfaction.") (footnotes omitted).

13. *Cf.* Andrew M. Low, *Questions from the Bench*, 27-DEC. COLO. LAW. 21, 22 (1998) ("Responding to an appellate judge's question should be your number one priority in the oral argument. Never, never, never tell an appellate judge you will get to that point in a minute.")

14. *See Morrissey v. Brewer*, 408 U.S. 471, 488–89 (1972) ("[T]he minimum requirements of due process ... include ... the right to confront and cross-examine adverse witnesses (unless the hearing officer specifically finds good cause for not allowing confrontation)").

15. Marcus Tillius Cicero stated that "Brevity is the best recommendation of speech, whether in a senator or an orator."

16. Robbins, *supra* note 6, at 279 (relating the results of an empirical study of what judges thought was important in persuading them).

Chapter Six

1. *See* FED. R. CIV. P. 56. In ruling on a motion for summary judgment, a judge does "not weigh the evidence or attempt to determine the credibility of the witnesses." Kammueller v. Loomis, Fargo & Co., 383 F.3d 779, 784 (8th Cir. 2004) (citation omitted). "Rather, the court's function is to determine whether a dispute about a material fact is genuine...." Quick v. Donaldson Co., Inc., 90 F.3d 1372, 1376–77 (8th Cir. 1996).

2. *See* FED. R. CIV. P. 12(b)(6).

3. *See* Title 18, UNITED STATES CODE, Section 3142.

4. *See* UNITED STATES V. LAFONTAINE, 210 F.3d 125, 131–32 (2d Cir. 2000) (finding that the district court did not abuse its discretion by permitting the Government to proceed by way of proffer with evidence during a detention hearing); United States v. Ferranti, 66 F.3d 540, 542 (2d Cir. 1995) (finding that the district court is not bound by the rules of evidence in a detention hearing, and may rely, inter alia, upon proffer and hearsay evidence).

5. To be sure, whether an evidentiary hearing is appropriate rests in the "reasoned discretion" of the court. United States v. Walczak, 783 F.2d 852, 857 (9th Cir. 1986). *See also* United States v. D'Andrea, 648 F.3d 1, 5 (1st Cir. 2011) (holding that a defendant does not have a right to an evidentiary hearing on a motion to suppress evidence); United States v. Culotta, 413 F.2d 1343, 1345 (2d Cir. 1969) (same).

6. *See, e.g.*, United States v. Jimenez-Martinez, 83 F.3d 488, 494–95 (1st Cir. 1996) (finding error in district court's denial of defendant's motion for evidentiary hearing given questionable reliability of affidavit on which the district court relied at sentencing); United States v. Roberts, 14 F.3d 502, 521 (10th Cir. 1993) (remanding because district court did not hold evidentiary hearing to address defendants' objections to drug quantity determination or make requisite findings of fact regarding drug quantity).

7. Supervised release is a period of time after an offender has served his prison sentence during which the offender is under the supervision of the United States Probation Office and must comply with terms and conditions of release imposed by the judge at sentencing. *See* 18 U.S.C. § 3583; FED. R. CRIM. P. 32.1. Supervised release replaced the role of parole when, as part of the Sentencing Reform Act of 1984, Congress abolished indeterminate sentencing in the federal system. *See* Sentencing Reform Act of 1984, Pub L. No. 98-473, 98 Stat. 1987. *See also* Paula Kei Biderman & Jon M. Sands, *A Prescribed Failure: The Lost Potential of Supervised Release*, 6 FED. SENT. R. 204, 204 (1994). If an offender violates the terms and conditions of supervised release, a judge may continue the offender on supervision (with or without modification of the terms) or may revoke the offender's supervised release and incarcerate the offender for all or any part of the period of time the offender otherwise would have been on

Notes—Chapter Six

supervised release. *See generally* U.S. Sentencing Guidelines Manual ch. 7, pt. A; id. § 7B1.3(a).

8. *See* Fed. R. Civ. P. 38, 39; Fed. R. Crim. P. 23.

9. The Seventh Amendment to the United States Constitution preserves the right to a jury trial "(i)n Suits at common law." U.S. Const. amend. VII. Suits in equity, historically tried to the court, are not covered by the Seventh Amendment. Rule 38 of the Federal Rules simply ensures "(t)he right of trial by jury as declared by the Seventh Amendment." Fed. R. Civ. P. 38.

10. *See* Hague Convention on the Civil Aspects of International Child Abduction, Oct. 25, 1980, T.I.A.S. No. 11670, as implemented by the International Child Abduction Remedies Act, 42 U.S.C. §§ 11601–11610.

11. In re Catt, 368 F.3d 789, 793 (7th Cir. 2004).

12. KPS & Assocs., Inc. v. Designs by FMC, Inc., 318 F.3d 1, 19 (1st Cir. 2003).

13. *See, e.g.*, Oberstar v. FDIC, 987 F.2d 494, 505 n.9 (8th Cir. 1993) (describing procedures required for a party to prove damages after obtaining a default judgment).

14. *See* Fed. R. Evid. 104.

15. Fed. R. Crim. Pro. 26.

16. Fed. R. Civ. Pro. 50.

17. *See* L. Ronald Jorgensen, *Motion Practice and Persuasion*, New Jersey Lawyer, 14 (ABA Publishing 2006).

18. The quote has also been attributed to Cicero, Blaise Pascal, Abraham Lincoln, T.S. Elliot, Winston Churchill, and Will Rogers. *See, e.g.*, J. Kenneth Barbe, *The Benefits of an Open Heart*, 45 Apr. Wyo. Law 10, 10 (Apr. 2022) (attributing the quote to Mark Twain and Blaise Pascal); Martin A. Schwartz, *Do You Speak Legalese?*, 91-Apr. Fl. Bar J. 57, 58 (April 2017) (attributing the quote to Will Rogers); Margaret Oertling Cupples, *Appellate Briefing: Some Thoughts on Writing Briefs That Can Clear a Path Through the Jungle*, 30 Miss. C. L. Rev. 1, 14 (2011) (attributing the quote to Cicero, Blaise Pascal, Abraham Lincoln, Mark Twain, T.S. Eliot, and others); Raymond T. Elligett, Jr. & Amy Farrior, *The Joy of Editing: Better Appellate Briefs*, 82-June Fl. Bar J. 86, 86 (June 2008) (attributing the quote to Cicero, Blaise Pascal, T.S. Elliot, Winston Churchill). We're hopeful it will soon be attributed to us.

19. Bryan Garner, The Redbook, at 320 (West Group 2002).

20. Justice Michael B. Hyman, *A Few Notions on Motions*, 110 Ill. B. J. 46, 47 (Nov. 2022) (quoting an unknown source).

21. Justice Antonin Scalia, 13 Scribes J. Legal Writing 51, 68 (2010).

22. Vaughan, *supra* Chapter Five, n.11, at 134 ("Judges consider oral argument to be 'terribly, terribly important,'" because the ability to have direct communication with the judges is invaluable.") (quoting Mark R. Kravitz, *Written and Oral Persuasion in the United States Courts: A District Judge's Perspective on Their History, Function, and Future*, 10 App. Prac. & Process 247, 271 (2009)).

23. The Honorable Ruth Bader Ginsburg, *Remarks on Appellate Advocacy*, 50 S.C. L. Rev. 567, 570 (1999) (noting that Justice Ginsburg considered oral arguments "a hold-the-line operation" where she saw "few victories snatched at oral argument" but witnessed "several potential winners become losers in whole or in part because of clarification elicited at argument").

24. *See, e.g.*, Rule 7(c), Local Rules of the United States District Courts for the Northern and Southern Districts of Iowa.

25. Michael Greene, *How to Persuade a Trial Judge; It's Not Rocket Science*, 72 Or. St. B. Bull. 34, 34 (Oct. 2011).

26. Federal Rule of Civil Procedure 65(b) provides, for instance, that if a court grants a temporary restraining order without notice, "the motion for a preliminary injunction shall be set down for hearing at the earliest possible time and takes precedence of all matters except older matters of the same character...." Fed. R. Civ. P. 65(b).

27. *See* Dahl v. City of Huntington Beach, 84 F.3d 363, 366 (9th Cir. 1996) ("'[I]f there is a hell to which disputatious, uncivil, vituperative lawyers go, let it be one in which the damned are eternally locked in discovery disputes with other

Notes—Chapter Six

lawyers of equally repugnant attributes.'" (*quoting* Krueger v. Pelican Prod. Corp., No-CIV-87-2385-A (W.D. Okla. Feb. 24, 1989)).

28. The standard is similar, if not identical, in most state courts as well.

29. Fed. R. Civ. P. 56(a).

30. Fed. R. Civ. P. 56(c)(1)(A).

31. Fed. R. Civ. P. 56(c)(1)(B).

32. *See Tolan v. Cotton*, 572 U.S. 650, 651 (2014).

33. *Id.*, at 656.

34. *See* United States v. Dunkel, 927 F.2d 955, 956 (7th Cir. 1991) ("Judges are not like pigs, hunting for truffles buried in briefs.")

35. Motion in Limine, Black's Law Dictionary.

36. *Luce v. United States*, 469 U.S. 38, 40 n.2 (1984).

37. In Limine, Black's Law Dictionary.

38. *See Luce*, 469 U.S. at 41 n.4.

39. Fed. R. Evid. 103(d). *See also Figgins v. Advance Am. Cash Advance Ctrs. of Mich., Inc.*, 482 F. Supp.2d 861 (E.D. Mich. 2007) (explaining that Rule 103(d) is a source of authority for a court to rule on motions in limine).

40. *See, e.g.*, United States v. Brawner, 173 F.3d 966, 970 (6th Cir. 1999) (holding federal rules of evidence, civil procedure and criminal procedure and interpretive rulings of the Supreme Court all encourage parties to use pretrial procedures, such as motions in limine, to narrow the issues and minimize disruptions at trial); Jonasson v. Lutheran Child and Family Servs., 115 F.3d 436, 440 (7th Cir. 1997); Bradley v. Pittsburgh Bd. of Educ., 913 F.2d 1064, 1069 (3d Cir. 1990) ("motion in limine is designed to narrow the evidentiary issues for trial and to eliminate unnecessary trial interruptions").

41. *Dunn ex rel. Albery v. State Farm Mut. Auto. Ins. Co.*, 264 F.R.D. 266, 274 (E.D. Mich. 2009) (citation and internal quotation marks omitted).

42. *See, e.g.*, Williams v. Johnson, 747 F. Supp.2d 10, 14 (D. D.C. 2010); United States ex rel. El-Amin v. George Washington Univ., 533 F. Supp.2d 12, 19 (D. D.C. 2008).

43. *See, e.g.*, Wilson, *supra* Chapter Three, n.46, at 92 ("although you'd think it goes without saying, a motion in limine doesn't work with a bench trial. I wish I could say I've never seen one before in a bench trial; unfortunately, I cannot").

44. *See, e.g.*, Malibu Media, LLC v. Tashiro, 1:13–cv–00205–WTL–MJD, 2015 WL 1717170, at *2 (S.D. Ind. Apr. 14, 2015) ("As noted above, the purpose of a motion in limine is to protect the jury from confusion or inadmissible evidence"); Team Play, Inc. v. Boyer, No. 03 C 7240, 2005 WL 3320746, at *1 (N.D. Ill. Dec. 5, 2005) ("The purpose of a motion in limine is to exclude inadmissible evidence that may confuse or prejudice a jury, but evidence should not be so excluded unless it would clearly be inadmissible on all potential grounds.")

45. *See, e.g.*, United States v. Tokash, 282 F.3d 962, 968 (7th Cir. 2002) ("Motions in limine are well-established devices that streamline trials and settle evidentiary disputes in advance, so that trials are not interrupted mid-course for the consideration of lengthy and complex evidentiary issues.")

46. *See, e.g.*, Middleby Corp. v. Hussmann Corp., No. 90 C 2744, 1993 WL 151290, at *1 (N.D. Ill. May 7, 1993) ("Evidentiary rulings should be deferred until trial so that questions of foundation, competency, relevancy and potential prejudice may be resolved in proper context.")

47. *See* Fed. R. Crim. P. 15(a) (permitting a prospective witness to be deposed to preserve testimony for trial only under "exceptional circumstances and in the interest of justice"); *see also* United States v. Drogoul, 1 F.3d 1546, 1552 (11th Cir. 1993) ("The primary reasons for the law's normal antipathy toward depositions in criminal cases are the factfinder's usual inability to observe the demeanor of deposition witnesses, and the threat that poses to the defendant's Sixth Amendment confrontation rights.") (footnote omitted).

48. *See generally* Fed. R. Civ. P. 32 (describing circumstances under which deposition testimony may be used during a civil proceeding); *see also* Sach Oliver, *Depositions Are Trial*, 55-JUN Trial 16 (2019) ("The modern civil trial typically has multiple witnesses presented by video

Notes—Chapter Six

deposition testimony. Your next deposition may be the trial testimony.")

49. *See* FED. R. CIV. P. 32(a) (describing situations during which a party may use deposition testimony).

50. FED. R. CIV. P. 32(a)(4)(E).

51. *See* FED. R. CIV. P. 32(c) ("On any party's request, deposition testimony offered in a jury trial for any purpose other than impeachment must be presented in nontranscript form, if available, unless the court for good cause orders otherwise"); *see also* Jeffrey J. Kroll, *Effective Use of Depositions at Trial*, 30 No. 1 LITIGATION 47, 48 (2003) (noting the pitfalls of making jurors "listen to a talking head for hours at a time" and stating that "[t]he use of videotape in trial is almost expected these days").

52. *See* FED. R. EVID. 801(d)(1)(A)(excluding from the definition of hearsay a witness' prior sworn statement that is inconsistent with the witness' testimony); FED. R. EVID. 613(a) (acknowledging that a witness may be examined about a prior statement); *see also* Steven Lubet, *Understanding Impeachment*, 15 AM J. TRIAL ADVOC. 483, 497–522 (Spring 1992) (describing the procedures and strategies for impeaching a witness with a prior inconsistent statement).

53. *See* FED. R. EVID. 612 (acknowledging the permissive use of a writing to refresh recollection and providing options for the adverse party); FED. R. EVID. 803(5) (creating exception to the hearsay rule for prior recorded recollections for the purpose of refreshing recollection under certain circumstances). Although these rules extend to other writings and records, in addition to prior sworn testimony, we are focusing here on the use of prior testimony during a bench trial.

54. Lubet, *supra* note 52, at 492.

55. *Id.*

56. *See, supra* Chapter 3(A)(5).

57. *See* Attorney Gen. of Okla. v. Tyson Foods, Inc., 565 F.3d 769, 780 (10th Cir. 2009) ("[A] judge conducting a bench trial maintains greater leeway in admitting questionable evidence, weighing its persuasive value upon presentation.")

58. *See supra* Chapter 6, Part Two (B)(2).

59. *See, e.g.,* Edward D. Ohlbaum, *Objections and Offers: Tell It Again, Sam*, 25 No. 3 LITIGATION 8, 14, 73 (Spring 1999) (discussing strategic factors to consider when deciding whether to object to evidence during a jury trial).

60. *See, e.g.,* Sharifi, *supra* Preface, n.1, at 695–97 (advocating for the increased use of objections during criminal bench trials for various reasons, including preserving the record, rattling the prosecutor and impressing the trial judge with the attorney's mastery of the rules of evidence); FINE, *supra* note 124, at 577–78 (asserting "there is no down-side to objecting" and asserting that "in the bench trial you should object to the admission of evidence that you believe runs afoul of the rules of evidence.") (emphasis in original).

61. *See, e.g.,* Loue v. Dore, 103 F.3d 1040, 1045 (1st Cir. 1997) ("It is, moreover, beyond cavil that a trial judge in the federal system retains the common law power to question witnesses and to analyze, dissect, explain, summarize, and comment on the evidence.") (citing Quercia v. United States, 289 U.S. 466, 469 (1933)).

62. *See* Larkins, *supra* note 1, at 17 ("Although a judge, like a jury, wants to understand where justice lies in the case, a judge will rarely have a favorable reaction to an emotional or inflammatory appeal. In fact, the judge's usual reaction to such a 'jury argument' is to be professionally offended.")

63. Many articles have been written about the art and psychology of jury persuasion. *See, e.g.,* Jonathan M. Lytle, *Persuasion in the Courtroom: Six Social Psychological Principles for Winning*, 53-APR ORANGE COUNTY (CA) LAW. 24 (2011); Richard C. Waites, *Courtroom Psychology and Trial Advocacy*, 66 TEXAS B.J. 587 (2003); James H. Roberts, Jr., *The SEC of Closing Arguments*, 23 AM. J. TRIAL ADVOC. 203 (1999) (describing the "Story," "Emotion" and "Communication" approach).

64. *See generally* Guthrie et al., *supra* Chapter Three, n.53 (describing results of cognitive study that measured the effects of certain cognitive illusions (framing, anchoring, etc.) on a group of United States Magistrate Judges and concluding that judges, like other humans, are vulnerable to those illusions).

65. *See, e.g.*, Kevin W. Murphy, *Closing Argument: Addressing Damages in Aviation Wrongful Death Cases*, 73 J. Air L. & Com. 463, 484 (2008) ("Some defense attorneys fear that any discussion of damages implicitly carries with it an admission of liability"); Kerry E. Notestine, *Closing Arguments*, 29-Fall Brief 72, 75 (1999) ("However, debate circulates among defense attorneys about whether or not to address damages during closing argument.")

66. *See, e.g.,* In re Jess, 169 F.3d 1204, 1209 (9th Cir. 1999) ("we have frequently criticized a trial court's wholesale adoption of a party's proposed findings"); Marchant v. City of Little Rock, 741 F.2d 201, 203 (8th Cir. 1984) ("for a district court to adopt a party's proposed findings and conclusions verbatim is a strongly disfavored practice").

67. *See* Lewis v. United States, 146 U.S. 370, 378–79 (1892) (recognizing the right of peremptory challenge is essential to ensuring the impartiality of the jury).

68. There is some support for this belief in some courts before some judges, but other courts and other judges find such vague objections fail to preserve anything. *Compare* Mayor & City Counsel of Baltimore v. Theiss, 354 Md. 234, 729 A.2d 965 976 (1999) (finding an "objection as to form," with no further explanation, is an improper objection), *with* In re St. Jude Med., Inc., No. 1396, 2002 WL 1050311, at *5 (D. Minn. May 24, 2002) ("Objecting counsel shall say simply the word 'objection,' and no more, to preserve all objections as to form.")

69. On the topic of deposition objections and improper deposition conduct, we highly recommend the published decision by our former colleague, Judge Mark W. Bennett, in *Security Nat'l Bank of Sioux City, Iowa v. Abbott Labs.*, 299 F.R.D. 595, 601 (N.D. Iowa 2014), *vacated on other grounds*, 800 F.3d 936 (8th Cir. 2015). Although the well-earned sanction Judge Bennett imposed was vacated on appeal, his decision provides a thorough and thoughtful analysis of attorney conduct during depositions. Among other things, *Security National Bank* illustrates the fact that even though a judge is not present during a deposition, an attorney's conduct and statements during the deposition may very well come to the attention of the trial judge before or during trial.

70. Fed. R. Civ. P. 1.

71. Fed. R. Crim. P. 2.

72. Fed. R. Evid. 102.

Chapter Seven

1. This portion of the book is based on an earlier article on the topic published by one of the authors. *See* C.J. Williams, *Advocating Altering Advocacy Academics: A Proposal to Change the Pedagogical Approach to Legal Advocacy*, 25 Suffolk J. Trial & App. Advoc. 203 (2020).

2. Karen A. Williams, *Trial Advocacy: The Use of Trial Skills in Non-Trial Experiences*, 29 Stetson L. Rev. 1229, 1237 (2000).

3. *See* Hanrahan, *supra* Chapter Two, n.16, at 300 (observing that "[i]ncreasingly, judges have complained of the lack of talented and skilled orators that argue in their courtrooms[,]" and noting that "[u]nfortunately, most law students have only one experience with oral argument (the first-year moot court competition), and even less receive actual training in oral argument during law school").

4. *See* Hoffman, *supra* Chapter One, n.1, at 207 (arguing that law schools offer far too little instruction on handing pretrial motions, noting they are "precisely the tasks newly admitted lawyers [are] likely to confront during their first years of practice"); Finneran, *supra* Chapter One, n.3, at 127–28 (noting that new attorneys rarely even get to question a witness during jury trials and are much more likely to cover a motion hearing); Greene, *supra* Chapter Three, n.48, at 4 (stating a firm belief "that oral argument is of equal if not greater importance in the district courts than it is in the courts of appeals").

Bibliography

Books

Ronald A. Cass, The Rule of Law in America (2001)
Fed. Judicial Ctr., law Clerk Handbook: A Handbook for Law Clerks to Federal Judges (Sylvan A. Sobel ed., 2d ed. 2007)
Ralph Adam Fine, The How-to-Win Trial Manual: A No-Holds-Barred Sure-Fire Way to Win (6th ed. 2015)
Lawrence M. Friedman, American Law in the 20th Century (2002)
Lawrence M. Friedman, A History of American Law (1st ed. 1973)
Bryan Garner, The Redbook (West Group 2002)
Eugene Garver, For the Sake of Argument: Practical Reasoning, Character, and the Ethics of Belief (2004)
Roger S. Haydock, David F. Herr & Jeffery W. Stempel, Fundamentals of Pretrial Litigation (10th ed. 2016)
Alan D. Hornstein, Appellate Advocacy in a Nutshell (1998)
Irving L. Janis, Groupthink (2d ed. 1972)
Steven Lubert & J.C. Lore, Modern Trial Advocacy (5th ed. 2015)
Thomas A. Mauet, Pretrial (8th ed. 2012)
Thomas A. Mauet, Trial Techniques (10th ed. 2017)
The Revolutionary Writings of John Adams (C. Bradley Thompson ed., 2000)
John Ritchie, The First Hundred Years: A Short History of the University of Virginia for the Period 1826–1926 (1978)
Carl Sandburg, The People, Yes (1937)
Antonin Scalia & Bryan A. Garner, Making Your Case: The Art of Persuading Judges (Thompson/West 2008)
Michael Smith, Advanced Legal Writing: Theories and Strategies in Persuasive Writing (3d ed. 2013)
Robert Stevens, Law School: Legal Education in America from the 1850s to the 1980s (1983)
Larry L. Teply, Law School Competitions in a Nutshell (2003)
John Henry Wigmore, A Treatise on the Anglo-American System of Evidence in Trials at Common Law (2d ed. 1923)
Charles Alan Wright, Andrew D. Leipold, Peter J. Henning & Sarah N. Welling, Federal Practice & Procedure (4th ed. 2010)
Charles Alan Wright & Arthur R. Miller, Federal Practice & Procedure (2d ed. 1995)

Law Review Articles

Shirley S. Abrahamson, *Commentary on Jeffrey M. Shaman's The Impartial Judge: Detachment or Passion*, 45 DePaul L. Rev. 633 (1996)

Bibliography

Douglas E. Abrams, *Tips About Written Advocacy from the North Dakota Supreme Court*, 74 J. Mo. B. 28 (2018)

Katherine Allen, *The Jury: Modern Day Investigation and Consultation*, 34 Rev. Litig. 529 (2015)

Thomas E. Baker, *Intramural Reforms: How the U.S. Courts of Appeal Have Helped Themselves*, 22 Fla. St. L. Rev. 913 (1995)

J.M. Balkin, *Deconstructive Practice and Legal Theory*, 96 Yale L. J. 743 (1987)

Albert Bates, Jr., et al., *Asset Purchases, Successor Liability, and Insurance Coverage: Does the Tail Always Follow the Dog?*, 100 W. Va. L. Rev. 631 (1998)

Mary Beth Beazley, *Writing for a Mind at Work: Appellate Advocacy and the Science of Digital Reading*, 54 Duq. L. Rev. 415 (2016)

Christopher W. Behan, *Teaching Courtroom Advocacy Principles and Skills Across Systems and Cultures*, 46 S. Ill. U. L.J. 1 (2021)

Mark W. Bennett, *Essay: The Grand Poobah and Gorillas in Our Midst: Enhancing Civil Justice in the Federal Courts—Swapping Discovery Procedures in the Federal Rules of Civil and Criminal Procedures and Other Reforms Like Trial by Agreement*, 15 Nev. L.J. 1293 (2015)

William Benoit, *Isocrates and Aristotle on Rhetoric*, 20 Rhetoric Soc'y Q. 251 (1990)

Eric E. Bergsten, *Experiential Education Through the Vis Moot*, 34 J. L. & Com. 1 (2015)

Paula Kei Biderman & Jon M. Sands, *A Prescribed Failure: The Lost Potential of Supervised Release*, 6 Fed. Sent. R. 204 (1994)

Chrisje Brants, *Wrongful Convictions and Inquisitorial Process: the Case of the Netherlands*, 80 U. Cin. L. Rev. 1069 (2012)

Darryl K. Brown, *Defense Counsel, Trial Judges, and Evidence Production Protocols*, 45 Tex. Tech. L. Rev. 133 (2012)

Graham K. Bryant & Kristopher R. McClellan, *The Disappearing Civil Trial: Implications for the Future of Law Practice*, 30 Regent U. L. Rev. 287 (2018)

Robert P. Burns, *Advocacy in the Era of the Vanishing Trial*, 61 U. Kan. L. Rev. 893 (2013)

H. Mitchell Caldwell, L. Timothy Perrin, Richard Gabriel & Sharon R. Gross, *Primacy, Recency, and Pathos: Integrating Principles of Communication Into the Direct Examination*, 76 Notre Dame L. Rev. 423 (2001)

Joe S. Cecil et al., *A Quarter-Century of Summary Judgment Practice in Six Federal District Courts*, 4 J. Empirical Legal Stud. 861 (2007)

Joe S. Cecil, Valerie P. Hans & Elizabeth C. Wiggins, *Citizen Comprehension of Difficult Issues: Lessons from Civil Jury Trials*, 40 Am. U. L. Rev. 727 (1991)

Kenneth D. Chestek, *The Plot Thickens: The Appellate Brief as Story*, 14 J. Leg. Writing 127 (2008)

Jill M. Cochran, Note, *Courting Death: 30 Years Since Furman, Is the Death Penalty any less Discriminatory? Looking at the Problem of Jury Discretion in Capital Sentencing*, 38 Val. U. L. Rev. 1399 (2004)

Robert J. Conrad, Jr., & Katy L. Clements, *The Vanishing Criminal Jury Trial: From Trial Judges to Sentencing Judges*, 86 Geo. Wash. L. Rev. 99 (2018)

John P. Cronan, *Is Any of This Making Sense? Reflecting on Guilty Pleas to Aid Criminal Juror Comprehension*, 39 Am. Crim. L. Rev. 1187 (2002)

Darby Dickerson, *In re Moot Court*, 29 Stetson L. Rev. 1217 (2000)

James D. Dimitri, *Stepping Up to the Podium with Confidence: A Primer for Law Students on Preparing and Delivering an Appellate Oral Argument*, 38 Stetson L. Rev. 75 (2008)

William V. Dorsaneo, III, *The Decline of Anglo-American Civil Jury Trial Practice*, 71 SMU L. Rev. 353 (2018)

Robert Dubose, *Eight Common Writing Mistakes in Motion Practice*, 92 The Advoc. 16 (2020)

Suzanne Ehrenberg, *Embracing the Writing-Centered Legal Process*, 89 Iowa L. Rev. 1159 (2004)

Nora Freeman Engstrom, *The Diminished Trial*, 86 Fordham L. Rev. 2131 (2018)

Bibliography

Richard E. Finneran, *Wherefore Moot Court*, 53 Wash. U. J.L & Pol'y 121 (2017)
Robert F. Forston, *Sense and Non-Sense: Jury Trial Communication*, 1975 BYU L. Rev. 601 (1975)
Michael Frost, *Ethos, Pathos & Legal Audience*, 99 Dick. L. Rev. 85 (Fall 1995)
Marc Galanter, *The Vanishing Trial: An Examination of Trials and Related Matters in Federal and State Courts*, 1 J. Empirical Legal Stud. 459 (2004)
John T. Gaubatz, *Moot Court in the Modern Law School*, 31 J. Legal Educ. 87 (1981)
John T. Gaubatz, *Of Moots, Legal Process, and Learning to Learn the Law*, 37 U. Miami L. Rev. 473 (1983)
Ruth Bader Ginsburg, *Remarks on Appellate Advocacy*, 50 S.C. L. Rev. 567 (1999)
Bruce A. Green & Rebecca Roiphe, *Judicial Activism in Trial Courts*, 74 N.Y.U. Ann. Surv. Am. L. 365 (2018)
J. Thomas Greene, *Oral Argument in the District Court*, 26 No. 3 Litig. 3 (2000)
Michael Greene, *How to Persuade a Trial Judge; It's Not Rocket Science*, 72 Or. St. B. Bull. 34 (Oct. 2011)
Chris Guthrie, Jeffrey J. Rachlinski & Andrew J. Wistrich, *Blinking on the Bench: How Judges Decide Cases*, 93 Cornell L. Rev. 1 (2007)
Chris Guthrie, Jeffrey J. Rachlinski & Andrew J. Wistrich, *Can Judges Ignore Inadmissible Information? The Difficulty of Deliberately Disregarding*, 153 U. Pa. L. Rev. 1251 (2005)
Chris Guthrie, Jeffrey J. Rachlinski & Andrew J. Wistrich, *Inside the Judicial Mind*, 86 Cornell L. Rev. 777 (2001)
Jennifer Kruse Hanrahan, *Truth in Action: Revitalizing Classical Rhetoric as a Tool for Teaching Oral Advocacy in American Law Schools*, 2003 B.Y.U. Educ. & L.J. 299 (2003)
Hon. J. William Hart, *Trial of the Century*, 43 Advoc. 24 (Dec. 2000)
Peter Toll Hoffman, *Law Schools and the Changing Face of Practice*, 56 N.Y.L. Sch. L. Rev. 203 (2012)
Thaddeus Hoffmeister, *Investigating Jurors in the Digital Age: One Click at a Time*, 60 U. Kan. L. Rev. 611 (2012)
Paul Holland, *Sharing Stories: Narrative Lawyering in Bench Trials*, 16 Clinical L. Rev. 195 (2009)
Justice Michael B. Hyman, *A Few Notions on Motions*, 110 Ill. B. J. 46 (Nov. 2022)
Mark L. Jones, *Fundamental Dimensions of Law and Legal Education: An Historical Framework—A History of U.S. Legal Education Phase I: From the Founding of the Republic Until the 1860s*, 39 J. Marshall L. Rev. 1041 (2006)
Kent A. Jordan, *The 2018 Honorable Daniel M. Friedman Appellate Advocacy Lecture: Lessons from Lincoln on Appellate Advocacy*, 28 Fed. Cir. Bar J. 1 (2018)
L. Ronald Jorgensen, *Motion Practice and Persuasion*, New Jersey Lawyer, 14 (ABA Publishing 2006)
Sara Klco & Francisco Armada, *Tips for Young Lawyers*, 37 No. 3 Trial Advoc. Q. 13 (2018)
Mark R. Kravitz, *Written and Oral Persuasion in the United States Courts: A District Judge's Perspective on Their History, Function, and Future*, 10 J. App. Prac. & Process 247 (2009)
Barbara Kritchevsky, *Judging: The Missing Piece of the Moot Court Puzzle*, 37 U. Mem. L. Rev. 45 (2006)
Jeffrey J. Kroll, *Effective Use of Depositions at Trial*, 30 No. 1 Litigation 47 (2003)
Peter B. Krupp, *When Jurors Speak: A Practical Guide to Jurors Questioning Witnesses in Massachusetts*, 45 Oct. Boston Bar J. 12 (2001)
John H. Langbein, *The Disappearance of Civil Trial in the United States*, 122 Yale L. J. 522 (2012)
John K. Larkins, Jr., *Oral Argument on Motions*, 23 Litigation 16 (1997)
Laurie A. Lewis, *Law Student Mediators Wear a Triple Crown: Skilled, Sellable, and Successful*, 50 U.S.F. L. Rev. 165 (2016)
Joel D. Lieberman & Bruce D. Sales, *What Social Science Teaches Us About the Jury Instruction Process*, 3 Psychol. Pub. Pol'y & L. 589 (1997)

Bibliography

Patrick E. Longan, *The Shot Clock Comes to Trial: Time Limits for Federal Civil Trials*, 35 ARIZ. L. REV. 663 (1993)

Andrew M. Low, *Questions From The Bench*, 27-DEC. COLO. LAW. 21 (1998)

Steven Lubet, *Understanding Impeachment*, 15 AM J. TRIAL ADVOC. 483 (Spring 1992)

Jonathan M. Lytle, *Persuasion in the Courtroom: Six Social Psychological Principles for Winning*, 53-APR ORANGE COUNTY (CA) LAW. 24 (2011)

Terence F. MacCarthy, *The History of the Teaching of Trial Advocacy*, 38 STETSON L. REV. 115 (2008)

Nancy S. Marder, *The Conundrum of Cameras in the Courtroom*, 44 ARIZ. STATE L. J. 1489 (2012)

Terry A. Maroney, *Emotional and Judicial Behavior*, 99 CAL. L. REV. 1485 (2011)

Joseph P. Mastrosimone, *Benchslaps*, 2017 UTAH L. REV. 331 (2017)

James W. McElhaney, *Toward the Effective Teaching of Trial Advocacy*, 29 U. MIAMI L. REV. 198 (1975)

Anne E. Mullins, *Source-Relational Ethos in Judicial Opinions*, 54 WAKE FOREST L. REV. 1089 (2019)

Kevin W. Murphy, *Closing Argument: Addressing Damages in Aviation Wrongful Death Cases*, 73 J. AIR L. & COM. 463 (2008)

Kathleen Dillon Narko, *Persuasion: Aristotle Still Works for Webb, Wood, and Kocoras*, 19 CHIC. B. ASSOC. 54 (Apr. 2005)

Martha Neil, *Leave 'Em, But Love 'Em; Keep the Door to Your Career Open by Not Slamming it on the Way Out of the Firm*, 91 A.B.A. J. 56 (2005)

Hon. David J. Newblatt, *How to Convince the Judge on Motion Day in Family Court*, 85 MICH. BAR J. 16 (2006)

Kerry E. Notestine, *Closing Arguments*, 29-FALL BRIEF 72 (1999)

Edward D. Ohlbaum, *Basic Instinct: Case Theory and Courtroom Performance*, 66 TEMP. L. REV. 1 (1993)

Edward D. Ohlbaum, *Objections and Offers: Tell it Again, Sam*, 25 No. 3 LITIGATION 8 (1999)

Sach Oliver, *Depositions Are Trial*, 55-JUN TRIAL 16 (2019)

Douglas Pilawa, *Sifting Through the Arbitrators for the Woman, the Minority, the Newcomer*, 51 CASE W. RES. J. INT'L L. 395 (2019)

Rachael A. Ream, *Limited Voir Dire*, 23 CRIM. JUST. 22 (2009)

William J. Rehnquist, *Oral Advocacy: A Disappearing Art*, 35 MERCER L. REV. 1015 (1984)

William L. Reynolds & William M. Richman, *Justice and More Judges*, 15 J.L. & POL. 559 (1999)

Kristen K. Robbins, *The Inside Scoop: What Federal Judges Really Think About the Way Lawyers Write*, 8 J. LEG. WRITING INST. 257 (2002).

James H. Roberts, Jr., *The SEC of Closing Arguments*, 23 AM. J. TRIAL ADVOC. 203 (1999)

Xavier Rodriguez, *The Decline of Civil Jury Trials: A Positive Development, Myth, or the End of Justice as We Know It?*, 45 ST. MARY'S L. J. 333 (2014)

Michael E. Romero, *The Four "Cs" of Courtroom Presentation*, 35 COLO. LAW. 81 (July 2006)

Robert Rubinson, *Of Grids and Gatekeepers: The Socioeconomics of Mediation*, 17 CARDOZO J. CONFLICT RESOL. 873 (2016)

John E. Rumel, *The Hourglass and Due Process: The Propriety of Time Limits on Civil Trials*, 26 U.S.F. L. REV. 237 (1992)

Cynthia A. Savage, *Recommendations Regarding the Establishment of a Mediation Clinic*, 11 CARDOZO J. CONFLICT RESOL. 511 (2010)

Justice Antonin Scalia, 13 SCRIBES J. LEGAL WRITING 51 (2010)

Brett G. Scharffs, *The Character of Legal Reasoning*, 61 WASH. & LEE L. REV. 733 (2004)

Samuel V. Schoonmaker IV & Kenneth J. Bartschi, *Effective Family Law Appeals*, 28 FAM. ADVOC. 6 (2006)

Stephen M. Shapiro, *Oral Argument in the Supreme Court: The Felt Necessities of the Time*, SUPREME COURT HISTORICAL SOCIETY YEARBOOK 22 (S. Ct. Historical Socy. 1985)

Bibliography

John N. Sharifi, *Approaching the Bench: Trial Techniques for Defense Counsel in Criminal Bench Trials*, 28 Am. J. Trial Advoc. 687 (2005)
Amy Singer, *10 Common Mistakes Attorneys Make with Jurors*, 36 Trial 76 (2000)
Judge William E. Smith, *Reflections on Judicial Merit Selection, the Rhode Island Experience and Some Modest Proposals for Reform and Improvement*, 15 R. Williams U. L. Rev. 664 (2010)
Joseph B. Stulberg, Donald C. Peter, Tracy L. Allen & Judith P. Myers, *Creating and Certifying the Professional Mediator-Education and Credentialing*, 28 Am. J. Trial Advoc. 75 (2004)
Stephanie A. Vaughan, *Persuasion Is an Art But It Is Also an Invaluable Tool in Advocacy*, 61 Baylor L. Rev. 635 (2009)
Richard C. Waites, *Courtroom Psychology and Trial Advocacy*, 66 Texas B.J. 587 (2003)
Hon. Justice Thomas D. Waterman, Hon. Judge Mark W. Bennett & David C. Waterman, *A Fresh Look at Jurors Questioning Witnesses: A Review of Eighth Circuit and Iowa Appellate Precedents and an Empirical Analysis of Federal and State Trial Judges and Trial Lawyers*, 64 Drake L. Rev. 485 (2016)
Mark L.D. Wawro, *Effective Presentation of Experts*, 19 Litig. 31 (Spring 1993)
Theresa A. Webster, *The Creative Side of Law*, 80 Mich. Bar J. 38 (2001)
James Boyd White, *Law as Rhetoric, Rhetoric as Law: the Arts of Cultural and Communal Life*, 52 U. Chi. L. Rev. 684 (1985)
Hon. Penny J. White, *10 Things They Never Taught You in Law School*, 30 Tenn. B. J. 20 (1994)
Brian Wice, *Oral Argument in Criminal Cases: 10 Tips for Winning the Moot Court Round*, 69 Tex. B. J. 224 (2006)
C.J. Williams, *Advocating Altering Advocacy Academics: A Proposal to Change the Pedagogical Approach to Legal Advocacy*, 25 Suffolk J. Trial & App. Advoc. 203 (2020)
C.J. Williams & Leonard T. Strand, *Judicial Advocacy: How to Advocate to a Judge*, 43 Am. J. Trial Advoc. 281 (2020)
C.J. Williams & Dasha Ternavska, *A Series of Unfortunate Events: The Admissibility of "Other Fires" Evidence in Arson Cases*, 48 Conn. L. Rev. 685 (2016)
Karen A. Williams, *Trial Advocacy: The Use of Trial Skills in Non-Trial Experiences*, 29 Stetson L. Rev. 1229 (2000)
David M. Wilson, *Working Toward a Common Goal: Are You One of Us?*, 48 No. 3 DRI For Def. 14 (2006)
Nancy Winkelman, *Just a Brief Writer?*, 29 Litig., 50 (2003)
Ronald F. Wright, *Trial Distortion and the End of Innocence in Federal Criminal Justice*, 154 U. Pa. L. Rev. 79 (2005)
Hon. William G. Young, *Vanishing Trials, Vanishing Juries, Vanishing Constitution*, 40 Suffolk L. Rev. 67 (2006)

Index

administrative law judges 7, 23, 154
Administrative Office of U.S. Courts 12
advocacy: oral 7, 14, 20, 26, 29–33, 47, 60–61, 73–77, 89, 93–94, 99–101, 154; written 25–26, 29, 30–33, 46, 70–73, 88, 94–98, 102, 110–11, 118–19, 134
Alternative Dispute Resolution (ADR) 21
appellate advocacy 11, 15–16, 19–20, 35, 55, 57, 65, 83, 86, 90, 152–56
appellate argument *see* oral argument
appellate review 92, 130

Batson challenges 91, 136–37
bench trials, generally 13–14, 33, 34, 37–38, 42, 51, 56, 68, 78, 80, 86, 90–91, 93, 115, 118–35; closing arguments 121, 132–33, 135; criminal defendant testimony 129; evidence rules application *see* Federal Rules of Evidence; depositions, use of 120, 126–28; motions in limine 123–24; objections during 129–30; opening statements 121, 124–26, 29; post-trial briefs 133; pretrial briefs 121–23; prior testimony, use of 128; proposed findings of fact and conclusions of law 30–31, 121, 133–34; questions, by judge 80, 130; stipulations 119
briefs: appellate 20, 31, 47; drafting 71, 94–96; motions briefs, 23, 99; trial briefs 33, 118–19, 121–23, 125; page limits 46, 47, 71, 94–95; post-trial briefs 121, 133–34

closing arguments 31, 46, 47, 52, 91–92, 121, 131, 132–33, 135, 146
collateral pressures, on trial judges 26, 43–45
communication: dynamic 26, 28–29, 96; linear 26, 28–29; one-way, to jury 27–28; two-way, to judge 26, 27–28, 29, 33, 107
credibility: role in persuading judges 39, 48, 58–60, 63–66, 70, 72, 84, 104, 122, 130, 135; witnesses 56, 57, 80, 88, 107, 118, 120, 127, 144, 145

Daubert motions *see* motions
deductive reasoning 49
demonstrative exhibits 32, 79, 125–26, 132
depositions, generally 23, 71, 103, 107, 119–20; judge intervention 89; transcripts 88, 103, 120, 127, 129, 140; use in trials 119–20, 139–40; videotaped 120, 127, 139
discovery 15, 16, 23, 87–89, 103–5, 113, 122, 149, 153

education, on advocacy 17, 18–24, 40, 58, 151–56
emotions, use of in advocacy 30, 34, 35, 49–50, 55, 58–59, 61, 66, 67–70, 72, 74, 82, 100, 132, 134–35, 143–44
ethical rules 44, 48, 50, 60
evidence, generally 12, 16, 26, 29, 33, 35–38, 84, 90, 144–45; admissibility 16, 107, 111–15, 123–24; Federal Rules *see* Federal Rules of Evidence; objecting to 129–30, 141–42; presentation of 126–29; video 116

Federal Rules of Civil Procedure 45, 81, 106, 112, 148
Federal Rules of Criminal Procedure 112, 148
Federal Rules of Evidence 36–37, 80–81, 112, 148; application when judges fact-finders 35–38, 55–57, 77–81; application when jurors fact-finders 35–38, 40, 44
fonts (and typeface), use in persuading judges 30, 96

group decision-making 26, 40–43, 65, 92

185

Index

Hague Convention 91
hearings: detention 34, 36, 115; emergency 101–3; increasing number 21–22, 151; summary judgment 15, 23, 24, 34, 71, 74, 87–89. 95, 107–9, 113, 122, 154; suppression 34, 36, 87, 115

impeachment 128–29
implicit bias 49
instructions, jury *see* juries, instructions
intellectual property cases 109–11

judges: educating 111, 116, 117; knowledge of 26, 50–51, 68, 71, 84, 99; questioning of witnesses 27, 79–80, 130–31
juries: consultants 51; instructions 31, 33, 52, 91, 120, 135, 138–39, 147, 148, 153; questionnaires 51
jury trial: advocacy to judges during 46, 91–92, 135–50; decreasing number 12–13, 17, 70, 151, 156; depositions, use of 139–40; jury instructions 138–39; jury selection 136–37; objections during 140–43, 146–47; questions by judges during 130–31; questions, from jurors during deliberation 147; rights to 12, 90, 118; scheduling issues & advocacy 147–50

law school: advocacy programs generally 18–24, 151–56; moot court 18–20, 57, 152; trial advocacy 18, 20–21
legal education: apprenticeship 18–19; case method 19; Christopher Columbus Langdell 19; law schools 18–23, 25, 49, 80, 132, 152–56

magistrate judges 42, 92
moot court 18–20, 57, 152
motions: civil 15, 34; criminal 15, 34, 97, 115–18; *Daubert* 37; discovery-related 16, 23, 87–89, 103–5, 113; dismiss 15, 34; increase of 11, 15, 17, 22, 70; judgment of acquittal 92, 144–45; judgment as matter of law 107, 144–45; limine 38, 87, 111–15, 123–24, 130, 142, 144, 148, 153; mistrial 40, 91–92, 143–44; preliminary injunction 34, 72, 89, 101, 102; summary judgment 15, 23, 24, 34, 71, 74, 87–89, 95, 106–9, 113, 122, 154; suppression 15, 24, 34, 36, 49, 87, 115, 154

National Institute for Trial Advocacy (NITA) 20

objections 36, 38, 48, 80, 88, 89, 91–92, 112, 116, 129–30, 135, 139–43, 146–47
opening statements 31, 32, 47, 91, 92, 119, 121, 122, 124–25, 146–47
oral argument: appellate 4, 5, 8, 9, 11, 14–15, 17, 20–22, 41, 44, 47, 65, 83, 84, 151, 152, 155, 156; before district judge 29, 30, 31, 32, 39, 46, 52, 56, 59, 73–77, 89, 93, 96–101, 106, 107, 111, 125; requesting 96–99, 111

pedagogical aids 100, 126
pedagogy, on persuading judges 11, 18–24
power differential, role in advocacy 26, 43, 47–48, 65–66
PowerPoints, use of 75, 100
Practicing Law Institute 23

repetition, in advocacy 31, 32, 71, 82–83
rhetoric: cannons of 34, 35, 50, 58, 60, 61, 117; ethos 34, 39, 58–61, 63–66, 72, 96, 99, 101, 105, 117, 118; logos 34, 35, 50, 55, 58–61, 63, 64, 66–69, 72, 74, 118; pathos 30, 34, 35, 50, 55, 58–61, 63, 67–69, 72, 74, 118

Scalia, Justice Antonin 5, 53, 96
summary judgment 15, 23, 24, 34, 71, 74, 87, 88, 89, 95, 106, 107–9, 113, 122, 154
suppression *see* hearings or motions

trial advocacy 11, 12, 13, 17, 19, 20–22, 24, 25, 26, 27, 31, 32, 35, 36, 46, 49, 57, 79, 80, 89, 93, 129, 139, 152–55
truffles, judges' role in searching for 96
two-way communication 26, 27–28, 29, 33, 107

United States Department of Justice 4

visual aids 100, 125

186

www.ingramcontent.com/pod-product-compliance
Ingram Content Group UK Ltd.
Pitfield, Milton Keynes, MK11 3LW, UK
UKHW021843010526
5522IPUK00022B/366